PRISONERS OF THE WHITE HOUSE

ALSO BY KENNETH T. WALSH

Family of Freedom: Presidents and African Americans in the White House

From Mount Vernon to Crawford: A History of the Presidents and Their Retreats

Air Force One: A History of the Presidents and Their Planes

Ronald Reagan: Biography

Feeding the Beast: The White House versus the Press

PRISONERS OF THE WHITE HOUSE

THE ISOLATION OF AMERICA'S PRESIDENTS AND THE CRISIS OF LEADERSHIP

BY

KENNETH T. WALSH

Paradigm Publishers
Boulder • London

Copyright © 2013 Paradigm Publishers

Published in the United States by Paradigm Publishers, 5589 Arapahoe Avenue, Boulder, CO 80303 USA.

Paradigm Publishers is the trade name of Birkenkamp & Company, LLC, Dean Birkenkamp, President and Publisher.

Library of Congress Cataloging-in-Publication Data is available from the Library of Congress.

ISBN 978-1-61205-160-4 (hardcover : alk. paper)

Printed and bound in the United States of America on acid-free paper that meets the standards of the American National Standard for Permanence of Paper for Printed Library Materials.

Designed and Typeset by Straight Creek Bookmakers.

17 16 15 14 13   1 2 3 4 5

For Barclay

CONTENTS

PART III
FIVE WHO STAYED CONNECTED

PART IV
FROM WIZARDS TO CHICKEN PEDDLERS

PREFACE

This book is a work of history, but it is also the logical extension of my quarter century of covering the presidency as a journalist.

Being a White House correspondent for so long has amounted to an extended course in American leadership, politics, and government, with a special emphasis on the lives and philosophies of the five men who occupied the world's most powerful office for the past three decades—Ronald Reagan, George H.W. Bush, Bill Clinton, George W. Bush, and Barack Obama.

One lingering question is how any president, with all he has to do, all the pressures he is under, and all the security restrictions that are imposed on him, can stay in touch with our ever-changing, amazingly diverse country. Some (notably Reagan, Clinton, and Obama) have done it better than others (such as the two Bushes).

But in every case, the president has struggled to stay in touch through various means, whether by never losing sight of his roots, by having a sixth sense or intuition about what the country wants, by developing networks of family and friends, by keeping in touch with popular culture, and by utilizing polls and other forms of public-opinion research.

In preparing this book, I was given exclusive access to a remarkable array of confidential information, including internal polls, strategy memos, and reports on meetings at the highest levels of different administrations. They are most evident in the chapters on Bill Clinton and Barack Obama, known for their extraordinary efforts to avoid isolation. Such documents make this book richer, more detailed, and, I believe, more insightful. I hope many scholars will find this material useful in the future.

My contention is that the presidents who did the best job of staying in touch had the most successful presidencies.

I focus only on the modern presidents—from Franklin D. Roosevelt onward—because the country has grown and the culture has changed so much that staying in touch is a much different process today. It's also a more urgent requirement than in the past, when the job of the president was less demanding and less confining and the role of the political parties was more important. In short, presidents have more of a need today to stay in touch with the ever-changing lives of those who elected them, and they have more tools with which to do it.

It's a real challenge, but in assessing how the presidents fight isolation, one of my main conclusions is that no method is foolproof, and the main goal should be for presidents to try as hard as they can to remain connected to the lives of Americans outside Washington, D.C., using all the means at their disposal. This is vital to governing and to persuading Americans that the president is truly their advocate.

Acknowledgments

My thanks first of all go to Barclay Walsh, my wife and partner in life. Without her, this project would not have been possible, not only because of her superb research skills but also because of her understanding and unstinting support. Barclay is a very talented writer, and she improved the manuscript and frequently clarified my thinking with her suggestions, as she has done with my previous books.

Mark Penn was instrumental in shaping my first thoughts about this book and provided many insights into the era of Bill Clinton. Stan Greenberg and Doug Schoen were also generous in sharing their insights into the Clinton era, as was Joel Benenson in discussing the presidency of Barack Obama and the remarkable strides that have been made in keeping the president in touch since 2008.

I was given access to an extraordinary range of confidential materials for the Obama and Clinton polling and political operations. This allowed me to illustrate some of the major points in the book with real-time examples, ranging from the "ethnography" study conducted for Obama to polls on presidential vacations done for Clinton.

Other pollsters who were of great help included Cornell Belcher, Geoff Garin, Ed Goeas, Lou Harris, Peter Hart, Frank Luntz, and Bill McInturff. These names, along with those mentioned above, represent a who's who in American survey research, and I am deeply grateful for their assistance and their friendship.

I want to also note the invaluable contributions of two other presidential pollsters who helped me understand the themes of this book and the inner workings of the White House—the late Robert Teeter, whom

I got to know when he advised George H.W. Bush, and the late Richard Wirthlin, whom I got to know when he advised Ronald Reagan.

The Society of Presidential Pollsters at George Washington University was a valued resource, and I want to thank them for starting the development of an important archive on presidential pollsters for future historians, political scientists, and journalists.

Barbara and George Bush provided their perspectives, for which I am most grateful.

Thanks also to the many other people who helped with interviews, advice, and guidance on the themes of this book, recently and over the years, including David Axelrod, Howard Baker, Ross Baker, Doug Brinkley, Bill Burton, Jay Carney, Bob Dallek, Dave Demarest, Frank Donatelli, Matthew Dowd, Ken Duberstein, Josh Earnest, Marlin Fitzwater, Ari Fleischer, Don Foley, Bill Galston, David Gergen, Mike Gerson, Robert Gibbs, Ed Gillespie, Joe Lockhart, Ron Kaufman, Kevin Madden, Scott McClellan, Mike McCurry, Mack McLarty, Dee Dee Myers, Leon Panetta, Dana Perino, Roman Popadiuk, Reince Priebus, Larry Sabato, Jake Seiwert, the late Tony Snow, Sean Spicer, Fred Steeper, George Stephanopoulos, Debbie Wasserman Schultz, Brad Woodhouse, Julian Zelizer, and the archivists at the presidential libraries who were so helpful with their time and resources.

Several books were particularly valuable, including George Reedy's *The Twilight of the Presidency*, Diane J. Heith's *Polling to Govern*, and Robert M. Eisinger's *The Evolution of Presidential Polling*.

And a special note of thanks to Jennifer Knerr, Candace Cunningham, and the staff at Paradigm Publishers. They are true professionals, and any author would be proud to work with them. Jennifer believed in this book from the start and provided welcome encouragement throughout the research and writing process.

My quarter century covering the White House as a journalist gave me an invaluable observation post and provided many insights into presidential isolation, which I believe is one of the major challenges facing the American presidency. I hope this book shines some much-needed light on the problem.

Kenneth T. Walsh
Bethesda, Maryland, and Shady Side, Maryland

INTRODUCTION
TRAPPED IN "THE BUBBLE"

President Harry Truman famously called the White House "the great white jail," and Bill Clinton referred to it as "the crown jewel of the federal penitentiary system."[1] Barack Obama says one of the biggest mistakes he made during his first term was confining himself in the White House too much, which limited his understanding of the real America beyond official Washington.

They have a point. One can scarcely imagine an environment outside the nation's penal system that is more isolating than the presidency, which is almost guaranteed to keep America's commander in chief far removed from his fellow citizens. And it's a problem that modern presidents from Franklin D. Roosevelt onward have been acutely aware of. In fact, breaking free from the White House "bubble" of isolation is one of the fundamental challenges of the modern presidency.

How can the nation's leader solve the country's problems and help everyday people if he is distant from American life and its constant permutations? This was one of the biggest concerns of voters in the 2012 election, and it was one of the reasons that President Obama was re-elected. Voters told pollsters that Obama seemed to understand their lives much better than his opponent, Republican nominee Mitt Romney, a vastly wealthy former businessman who was a child of privilege and could never shake his image as a Brahmin. As I will discuss later in this book, Obama has taken many steps to escape the bubble of isolation throughout his time in the White House. This is greatly to his credit, but it is a constant struggle, and one that most presidents don't have the time or the inclination to pursue with as much dedication as Obama has shown.

In some ways, the history of the modern presidency—when mass media took hold and America became a rapidly changing and information-driven culture—is a history of presidents trying to stay in touch in order to best understand the American people and do what they wanted and needed. Some presidents succeeded, and some failed. All tried, whether it derived from a desire to serve or a desire to get re-elected.

*   *   *

TO BE SURE, the president deals with a particularly splendid form of isolation. A president is pampered and privileged. He lives in a mansion that has 132 rooms, 32 bathrooms, a movie theater, tennis courts, a bowling alley, and an ornate East Room that's perfect for hosting state dinners and other fancy events. He has a large household staff that does his grocery shopping, cooks and serves his meals, prepares his clothes, shines his shoes, takes his kids to school, places his phone calls, and manicures his lawn—in other words, serves his every whim. Someone is always there to run his parties, and the Marine Corps Band is available to provide the background music. Celebrities flock to the White House to entertain the president and his friends.

A president makes $400,000 a year in salary and has a $100,000 nontaxable travel account, a $50,000 annual expense account, and an additional allotment of $19,000 for entertainment. But he rarely carries money. His staff does that. He doesn't drive a car except in a few highly secure locations, such as the president's official retreat at Camp David. The Secret Service does that, as part of its assignment of protecting the president around the clock. He has a personal aide who tends to many of the routine tasks that ordinary mortals do for themselves, such as opening doors and carrying luggage; the aide even gives the president antiseptic lotion after he shakes hands with strangers to limit the spread of germs.

Of course there is *Air Force One,* the president's personal jet, always at the ready. He never has to check in at airports; his plane is always cleared first for takeoff and landing, and it is the safest, best-maintained aircraft in the world. It carries a stock of the president's favorite drinks, movies, and foods. Ronald Reagan liked jelly beans, and these were conveniently placed in jars and trays all around the aircraft. George W. Bush preferred to snack on fruit, so berries and bananas were always within reach. A massage therapist often flies with the president to soothe him when he gets tense.

The president never has to rent a car because he uses armored limousines escorted by Secret Service bodyguards and police. He doesn't rub shoulders with everyday people while food shopping or waiting for his car to be repaired. All that is done for him. He never endures the inconvenience of arranging for a plumber to fix a leaky pipe or a contractor to replace a roof or install a new refrigerator.

"There is something about a sense of entitlement and of having great power that skews people's judgment," said former defense secretary Robert Gates.[2] He was talking about the perks available to America's top generals, but his remarks apply equally to the president.

This dynamic was vividly described forty years ago by George Reedy, formerly a senior adviser to President Lyndon Johnson, in *The Twilight of the Presidency*. If anything, the problem has gotten worse since Reedy wrote, "The most important, and least examined, problem of the presidency is that of maintaining contact with reality."[3]

"There is built into the presidency a series of devices that tend to remove the occupant of the Oval Room from all of the forces which require most men to rub up against the hard facts of life on a daily basis," Reedy said. "The life of the White House is the life of a court. It is a structure designed for one purpose and one purpose only—to serve the material needs and the desires of a single man. It is felt that this man is grappling with problems of such tremendous consequence that every effort must be made to relieve him of the irritations that vex the average citizen. His mind, it is held, must be absolutely free of petty annoyances so that he can concentrate his faculties upon the 'great issues' of the day.... Even more important, however, he is treated with all of the reverence due a monarch. No one interrupts presidential contemplation for anything less than a major catastrophe somewhere on the globe. No one speaks to him unless spoken to first. No one ever invites him to 'go soak your head' when his demands become petulant and unreasonable."[4]

Since Reedy made his observations, the situation has deteriorated. The 24-hour news cycle and the social media have made public scrutiny of the chief executive ever more relentless, adding to the pressures of office. The president is captured in the lenses of innumerable cameras when he is in public, so he must always maintain appearances. Every throwaway remark and gaffe is magnified. If a president gets a cold, the media wonder if he is showing signs of weakness or if his stamina is fading. If he fails to hold regular news conferences, he is seen as snubbing the press and, indirectly, the public. If he demonstrates pique or displeasure, it sets off speculation that he has an anger-management problem. If he avoids the Washington social circuit, he is considered too much of a loner. If he takes a vacation, he is derided as an idler who wastes the taxpayers' money on transportation and security costs.

The demands on the president are heightened because of the American tradition of combining in the chief executive both policymaking and ceremonial duties. And the ceremonial part can get very tedious. One example is the custom of holding a series of holiday parties at the end of each year. The president and the first lady spend many hours in receiving lines with thousands of people, shaking hands, making small talk with strangers and folks they barely recognize, and posing for photographs. It take immense discipline and will power. But they soldier on even though there is little chance for them to have any meaningful social interactions or to learn anything interesting or important about the country.

*   *   *

IT WASN'T always this way. The founders wanted the president to be accessible and in touch, as did the early presidents themselves. George Washington, trying to avoid the trappings of monarchy, rejected grand titles for the country's leader. Among those suggested at the time he took office in 1789 were "Your Highness" and "His High Mightiness the President of the United States and Protector of Their Liberties." But Washington said "Mr. President" would be just fine, and this set a precedent.

Washington also felt it was his obligation to meet and talk seriously with his fellow citizens, who could drop in on him at the president's residence or at his home at Mount Vernon, Virginia. Thomas Jefferson felt the same way. Both Washington and Jefferson rejected plans for a presidential palace in 1792 and instead insisted upon a house of one-fifth the size. It was a mansion, true, but hardly a monarch's residence.[5]

Abraham Lincoln continued the tradition of openness, welcoming members of Congress, diplomats, lobbyists, job seekers, and regular citizens in the many public rooms of the White House. "Except for the family dining rooms, all the rooms on the first floor were open to all visitors, and anybody who wanted to could stroll in at any hour of the day and often late at night," writes historian David Herbert Donald. "A single elderly doorkeeper was supposed to prevent depredations, but often no one was on duty. On the second floor, nearly half of the rooms were also public; they were devoted to the business of the chief executive.... From early morning until dusk, these rooms were thronged with senators, congressmen, applicants for government jobs, candidates for military appointments, foreign dignitaries, and plain citizens who had favors to ask or who just wanted to shake the president's hand.... Lincoln found himself a prisoner in his own office; every time he stepped out into the corridor to go to the family quarters on the west end of the building, he was besieged with complaints and petitions."[6] Lincoln had a partition built that allowed him to walk unobserved between his office and the family's private rooms, but it wasn't enough to allow seclusion or create an atmosphere of calm and contemplation.[7]

This accessibility was one reason he chose to commute for much of his presidency between the White House and a residence he took over at the Soldiers' Home, a community for convalescing military personnel three miles from the White House in Washington, D.C.

After each presidential assassination, security was ratcheted up, starting with Lincoln's murder in 1865, then followed by James Garfield's assassination in 1881 and William McKinley's in 1901. In 1906, the Secret Service took over protecting the president and assigned 27 men to do the job. Since then, the level of protection, and the resulting isolation, has increased still further through two world wars, the murder of President John F. Kennedy in 1963, the killing of presidential candidate Robert Kennedy in 1968, and the near-assassination of President Ronald Reagan in 1981. Adding to the heightening of security were the terrorist attacks of September 11, 2001. Today the cadre of people involved in protecting the commander in chief numbers in the thousands.[8]

Security precautions have become so intense that the layers of protection are a barrier to human contact outside a president's family and inner circle. No one gets beyond the White House gates without a special pass or a special clearance or appointment. Casual visitors may gain admittance for limited access, but they are kept away from the first family under almost all conditions except for an occasional drop-by in which the president and first lady say hello to surprised tourists. But these encounters are mostly designed for public relations to show that the first couple has a common touch, not to provide them with information about what's going on beyond the gates.

*   *   *

BECAUSE OF THESE and other circumstances, truly connecting with everyday people is exceedingly difficult. And these connections are made more challenging because the trappings of history are all around, so it's easy for a president to see himself as above ordinary mortals. He walks in the footsteps of iconic leaders such as John F. Kennedy, Franklin D. Roosevelt, and Abraham Lincoln. He uses their desks, sees their portraits gazing down on him, and knows he will someday join them in the history books.

"The atmosphere of the White House is calculated to instill in any man a sense of destiny." Reedy writes. "The almost sanctified relics of a distant, semi-mythical past surround him as ordinary household objects to be used by his family. From the moment he enters the halls he is made aware that he has become enshrined in a pantheon of semi-divine mortals who have shaken the world, and that he has taken from their hands the heritage of American dreams and aspirations."[9]

President Obama acknowledges all this. "The most important lesson I've learned," he said during his successful re-election campaign in 2012, "is that you can't change Washington from the inside. You can only change it from the outside."[10] His aides said he would make it a point in a second term to get out of the capital as much as possible and talk to everyday people beyond the Washington Beltway and take their political pulse.

*   *   *

THIS DOWNSIDE of isolation became clear in what happened to the Republicans in the 2012 election. The GOP not only lost the presidency to Obama by a relatively large margin; it also lost ground in the Senate and the House to the Democrats. Exit polls indicated that many Americans thought the Republicans were out of touch and overly zealous in their conservative ideology. These losses triggered a serious round of soul-searching in the Republican party, and one strain of criticism was that GOP leaders had allowed themselves to get stuck in what *Politico,* the online political news site, called "a political-media cocoon that has become intellectually suffocating and self defeating."[11]

What happened is that the Republican cognoscenti have created their own alternative universe of news and information consisting of Fox News, the *Drudge Report,* radio commentators such as Rush Limbaugh, an array of conservative bloggers, and communities of the right on Facebook and Twitter that generate their own reality. But it is a faux reality that fails to acknowledge that most Americans aren't extremely conservative, that Latinos are surging in population and influence, that single women and young people are rising forces in the electorate. All these trends favor the Democrats.

"What Republicans did so successfully, starting with critiquing the media and then creating their own outlets, became a bubble onto itself," said Ross Douthat, a *New York Times* columnist.[12]

But the president suffers from a deeper and more personal isolation than anyone else in the Washington establishment.

*   *   *

THE EXALTED status of the president in and of itself makes it even more difficult for him to stay in touch. It encourages a strong tendency among those who meet with the president not to give him bad news and not to speak their minds candidly about what he is doing wrong. "Everybody wants to tell the president how great he is," says Frank Donatelli, former White House political director for President Ronald Reagan.[13] Adding to the problem of presidential isolation is the intimidating aura of the Oval Office, where the president works and where, as Reedy says, so much history has been made. Many White House aides have told me over the years how people promise to tell the president bluntly the error of his ways, only to melt in his presence when they step into the Oval Office. The same goes for White House staffers, who don't want to add to the boss's burdens by being negative. "It's a rare staffer or member of Congress who will say, 'You screwed up,'" says Donatelli. "The presidency does inhibit candid conversation."

*   *   *

THERE IS ANOTHER problem. "Politicians are different from you and me," says author Richard Reeves. "The business of reaching for power does something to a man: It closes him off from other men until, day by day, he reaches the point where he instinctively calculates each new situation and each other man with the simplest question: What can this do for me?"[14]

President Richard Nixon and his aides were notorious for such political calculation and arrogance. "There was no independent sense of morality there," said Hugh Sloan, who was a Nixon aide for two years. "If you worked for someone [in the White House], he was God, and whatever the orders were, you did it.... It was all so narrow, so closed." Added senior Nixon adviser John Dean, "The White House is another world. Expediency is everything." And Herbert Porter, still another aide, said, "On my first or second day in the White House, Dwight Chapin [the President's appointments secretary] said to me, 'One thing you should realize early on, we are practically an island here.' That was the way the world was viewed."[15]

*   *   *

SEPARATION FROM everyday life may not make much difference for society as a whole if one is a pampered business mogul, a movie star, or a king. They can live in splendid isolation and it won't have any larger impact. But it's an occupational hazard for a president, who is hired by the American people to understand their problems and find solutions.

"Much is made of the myth of the common man in American life," writes political scientist Thomas E. Cronin. "And this endures in part because we yearn to have everyone's situation taken into account. We want presidents, then, to understand that everyone goes through peaks and valleys, everyone is subject to risks, family adversity, and personal setbacks. We want presidents who have shared in these common experiences—who can convey a 'you are not alone' and 'I feel your pain' attitude. FDR had this, and Bill Clinton made it a central part of his campaign leadership style."[16]

This isolation is emerging as one of the most serious dilemmas facing the American presidency. In recent years, West Wing insiders have come up with the name for the syndrome. They call it the White House "bubble."

"Among the fundamental characteristics of monarchy is untouchability," Reedy says. "Contact with the king is forbidden except to an extremely few people or as a rare privilege to be exercised on great occasions. The king's body is sanctified and not subject to violation by lesser mortals unless he himself so wishes. He is not to be jostled in crowds; he is not to be clapped on the back; he is not to be placed in danger of life or limb or even put to the annoyance of petty physical discomfort. Nor can he be compelled to account for his actions upon demand."[17]

There was widespread consternation among Washington insiders and security personnel in 2012 when a pizza-restaurant owner in Florida gave President Obama a bear hug, lifting him off the ground in a display of joyful exuberance. Obama seemed surprised but delighted at this very human moment. The Secret Service was not amused.

"The 'bubble' is real, intense, hard to pierce, and hard to find your way out of," White House Press Secretary Jay Carney, a key adviser to President Obama, told me in one of several interviews for this book.[18]

Adds Princeton historian Julian Zelizer: "All presidents have that 'bubble.' Once the campaign is over, they are in a very limited circle of their advisers and themselves. They do lose touch with what's going on.... I don't think many presidents have figured it out [how to stay in touch]."[19]

Doug Brinkley, a historian at Rice University, says, "It's essential for presidents to understand the life of the middle class, to know the price of a loaf of bread and how many days children go to public school." In Washington, presidents "get distracted" and don't comprehend such details as the cost of living and the hectic pace of the school year, Brinkley told me.[20]

A related problem is that a president is surrounded by aides who live in their own world of policy, political theory, and legislative-speak that is unintelligible to most Americans and that can engulf the president. All this can make it difficult for the chief executive to understand the reaction his policies might provoke. This applies, of course, to members of Congress and their staffs, too. "People in this town [Washington, D.C.] talk to each other in language that's mutually understandable to them but not to most people," says Rutgers political scientist Ross Baker. "It's a long-standing problem—people who make policy assume the public is as deep in the weeds as they are, and they're not."[21]

Baker cited as an example the furor that erupted in February 2012 over the Obama administration's new policy to require Catholic hospitals to provide contraception services to women, including hospital employees, even though Catholic religious doctrine opposes birth control. Obama and White House aides argued that most Americans, including many Catholics, supported the new policy. But what they didn't understand was the depth of opposition that would erupt from the bishops, other members of the clergy, and devout Catholics, Baker said. Administration officials, including the president, were out of touch with Roman Catholic leaders and their many followers in that sense, according to Baker.

Brinkley argues that "the great presidents found ways to avoid the bubble." Theodore Roosevelt hopped on a train that he called "the rolling White House," and he successfully stayed in touch by talking to people in his travels around the country. Of course, this was before the velocity of life and events reached astounding proportions; it was easier to keep in touch back then at the start of the 20th century. Roosevelt also befriended reporters and got from them a sense of what was going on.

* * *

THE EXALTED AND ABNORMAL NATURE of the president's life has been driven home to me in many ways during my nearly three decades of covering the White House as a journalist. I remember a particular incident during a trip with President Bill Clinton to Latin America. At a small dinner for the staff and the traveling press, Clinton was the absolute center of attention, with everyone hanging on every word. At one point, Clinton dropped his fork to the floor, and nearly every one of his aides immediately reached for their own utensils and offered them eagerly to the boss. They needn't have worried. While a half dozen forks were waving in the air, Clinton simply took mine without a second thought, since I was sitting next to him. Clinton also felt a sense of entitlement in other ways. Throughout the first course of the meal, he would pick up my appetizers with his fingers and wolf them down as his own. Clinton may have been more self-indulgent than most. But presidents often feel entitled to things that are beyond the reach of ordinary mortals.

*   *   *

FIRST LADIES frequently become just as frustrated with the bubble as their spouses. Sometimes they resort to disguises in order to escape from the White House and move around incognito. Both Hillary Clinton and Michelle Obama left the White House secretly on occasion, wearing sunglasses, baseball caps or scarves, and casual clothes, to take a walk, go shopping, or dine at a restaurant. In October 2011, Mrs. Obama was photographed wearing sunglasses and a cap as she shopped at Target in the Washington suburbs. She has also slipped out of the White House with the family dog, Bo, to visit Petco, a shop selling products for pets. Her Secret Service bodyguards participated in the subterfuge by being more discreet than usual, staying at more of a distance from Mrs. Obama than usual, wearing unobtrusive clothing, and trying to make their security precautions invisible rather than projecting their customary intimidating presence.

And the role of first ladies in keeping their husbands informed can't be underestimated, as will be shown in later chapters of this book. As Doug Brinkley noted, Eleanor Roosevelt was particularly influential in keeping her husband Franklin informed of the massive changes going on in the country and how people were dealing with the Depression. Rosalynn Carter talked frequently with her husband Jimmy about the state of the country, and she even sat in on Cabinet meetings so she could learn first-hand how his administration was responding. Nancy Reagan sometimes felt that her husband's advisers and friends weren't telling him candidly what was on their minds, so she took it upon herself to update him.

Barbara Bush made sure to keep her husband surrounded by friends and close associates during his off-hours, including their time in the East Wing residence, the presidential retreat at Camp David, and their seaside estate in Kennebunkport, Maine. Part of the reason was simply to give her husband the warm and comfortable social atmosphere he craved. But another goal was to give him a wider view than the one offered by his official aides. Mrs. Bush told me, "Both my Georges [her husband the forty-first president and her son the forty-third] had more friends than you could imagine," and they met or talked on the phone regularly, she said. The senior President Bush agreed. They said they had an overflowing list of guests at Camp David and at Kennebunkport throughout his four-year presidency.[22]

*   *   *

UNTIL THE 20th century, presidents assessed public opinion mostly by reading newspaper stories and editorials, listening to constituents who attended town meetings, perusing constituents' letters, talking to people during travel, and interacting with friends and associates.[23]

Even making the attempt to gauge public opinion and using it to govern was frowned upon in some quarters. Many of the Founders were cynical about it. Alexander Hamilton wrote, "The voice of the people has been said to be the voice of God. And however generally the maxim has been quoted and believed, it is not true. In fact, the people are turbulent and changing; they seldom judge or determine right."[24]

For years, presidents looked to national legislators to keep them in touch. Herbert Hoover used James MacLafferty, a former member of Congress, to take soundings on Capitol Hill and report back, with an emphasis on how Hoover's policies were going over. At one point, members of Congress told MacLafferty that audience participation and media publicity were minimal at public meetings when Hoover's agenda was discussed, a warning sign that Hoover was in political trouble. But as his relations with Congress grew more hostile at the outset of the Depression, Hoover increasingly distrusted legislators as "self-interested political renegades" whose views on public attitudes were skewed to their particular ideologies and states, and were often wrong. Yet Hoover had devised few other ways to keep in touch.[25]

Hoover also tried monitoring newspaper editorials as a way to understand public opinion, directing his staff to clip and study editorials and other content of 500 newspapers. But it wasn't a satisfactory barometer partly because the editorial writers reflected the views of their corporate owners rather than everyday people.[26] When Franklin Roosevelt succeeded Hoover, he gave up on the editorial monitoring and turned to polling and the observations of his wife Eleanor, who traveled widely on fact-finding missions for her husband.

*   *   *

THERE ARE four fundamental ways in which today's presidents stay in touch, all of which will be analyzed in later chapters of this book, but in each case it requires an intense effort and commitment on the part of the president and his staff.

*   *   *

ONE IS THROUGH INTUITION, based on life experience and a "feel" for what Americans are really like, especially the vast middle class. Political scientist Bill Galston notes that the two most successful presidents of the 20th century—Franklin D. Roosevelt and Ronald Reagan—had such intuition.[27] FDR developed a keen sense of empathy and an understanding of hardship because he endured the pain of polio and the struggle (which failed) to regain the use of his paralyzed legs. His wife Eleanor said that Franklin's personal ordeal gave him an intuitive understanding of others who were struggling in their lives. For his part, Reagan had been both a Democrat and a Republican in his political life, so he understood both major parties. More important, Reagan remained forever connected to his middle-class roots in Illinois, where he grew up, and he drew on this intense middle-class immersion as president.

*   *   *

THE SECOND WAY a president stays connected is through polls and other forms of opinion research, such as focus groups. Among the presidents who have used this method to great effect were Bill Clinton and Ronald Reagan, although advisers to each of them said they didn't use the polls to make policy, only to decide how best to sell their decisions to the American people.

This has been a common claim in one White House after another. President Barack Obama made the same point in March 2010 when he told a healthcare forum in Strongsville, Ohio, that Americans have a clear preference. "They don't want us putting our finger out to the wind," Obama said. "They don't want us reading polls. They want us to look and see what is the best thing for America, and then do what's right."[28] But his aides and his party's strategists at the Democratic National Committee were intensely following the polls throughout his presidency, and often passing the results on to him.

In fact, polling has been an essential part of every modern White House, except for Harry Truman's and Dwight Eisenhower's, ever since FDR.

* * *

THE THIRD PATH to connecting with the country is to be a voracious consumer of information about American life, from television, movies, and national and regional newspapers; from friends and associates; and from many other sources. This is the approach that John F. Kennedy and Bill Clinton used, as I will describe in detail in this book.

As George Reedy says, "The significant impact of the press upon the president lies not in its critical reflections but in its capacity to tell him what he is doing as seen through other eyes. This is a service which, though little appreciated, is indispensable, as it will rarely, if ever, be performed by any other medium. Virtually all other communications that reach him will be shaped either directly or indirectly by people who wish either to conciliate or antagonize the chief executive. In either case, the contents of the message and the manner in which it is phrased will be governed as much by the sender's judgment of how best to produce a desired effect upon the recipient as by the substantive matters with which the sender deals."[29]

Unfortunately, in recent years presidents have been paying less attention to the news media. They find television, newspapers, magazines, and radio of little value in informing them about what's going on around the country. Similarly, the Internet and the blogosphere are generally not part of the president's informational diet. There are many reasons for this. Presidents get news summaries each morning and rely on their aides to update them on anything worth knowing. They are cynical about the fairness, accuracy, and seriousness of the media (as are many Americans), so they ignore media reports most of the time.

This situation is much different from when John F. Kennedy had close friends in the press corps or when Lyndon Johnson habitually watched the TV news each night and had several wire-service tickers always running in the Oval Office to update him on breaking developments.

* * *

THE FOURTH METHOD is through contact with members of Congress, friends, and associates. Says Princeton historian Julian Zelizer, "Congress can be a barometer of what's going on, a way to keep in touch."[30]

But dealing with members of Congress has become less valuable over the years. "It's harder to interact with members of Congress" in a meaningful and comprehensive way, explains Republican strategist and former White House aide Ed Gillespie. That's because when a legislator talks to a president, one on one or at congressional receptions in the Yellow Oval Room or elsewhere in the White House, it's usually "transactional in nature," as members attempt to persuade the president, pro or con, about specific pieces of legislation, Gillespie says.

* * *

PERHAPS THE BEST way for a president to avoid isolation is to always be aware of the limitations of power and be committed to testing his own ideas to guard against any sense of arrogance or omnipotence. In his natural modesty and self-deprecation, Truman had the right idea. "Well, I never thought I was God; that's one thing for sure," Truman told his biographer Merle Miller. "I grew up wanting to be as good a man as my father was and as my mother wanted me to be. I never had the notion that I was anything special at all; even when I got that job in the White House. I didn't. And I never had the notion that there weren't a lot of people who couldn't do whatever it was better than I could. [This was a notion directly opposite the feelings of John F. Kennedy, who said he didn't know of anyone who could do the job of president better than he could.]

"But that never worried me. All that ever concerned me was that I wanted to do it as best I could.... My father used to say that a man ought to leave the world a little better than it was when he came into it, and if that can be said about me, I guess you'll have to say I lived a successful life."[31]

* * *

IN THE END, the best way for a president to stay in touch is to make an intense, multifaceted effort to do so.

I

FOUR WHO LOST
THE PEOPLE

CHAPTER ONE
LYNDON B. JOHNSON

From Outreach to Isolation

Four presidents stand out as examples of leaders who became lodged so deeply in the White House bubble that it damaged their popularity and kept them from reaching their policy goals. They were Lyndon B. Johnson, Richard Nixon, Jimmy Carter, and George H.W. Bush.

* * *

LYNDON JOHNSON at the end of his presidency is a case study in isolation. Massive opposition to the Vietnam War had destroyed his once-soaring popularity. Angry protests kept him from speaking at many places, especially on college campuses, so he was in some ways a prisoner in the White House for long periods of time.

"As 1968 began, it was hard not to argue that Lyndon Johnson's presidency—like his persona—had assumed Shakespearean proportions, just as it was apparent that the press had largely taken leave of him," writes historian Mark K. Updegrove. "The barrage of scrutiny and condemnation from the media and the public added to what Johnson would call 'the nightmare year,' in which he faced a series of crises that amounted to greater anguish than any he had faced earlier in his term—or that had been faced by nearly any other man who had held the office."[1]

At 59 and not in the best of health, he appeared exhausted and beaten down during that final year in office, the lines in his face deepening and dark circles appearing under his eyes. He felt that "exposing himself to the torrent of dissent would be to diminish the presidency itself," so he stayed in his special cloister, an observer said.[2] His staff stopped announcing many of his appearances in advance rather than tip off demonstrators on his where-abouts, and he preferred to give speeches at military bases, where the crowds of uniformed troops would be controlled and polite to their commander in chief. But the White House was still flooded with letters of protest and disdain, and the media continued to ridicule him for being so insular.

He had tried everything he could think of to extract America from Vietnam with what he considered a sense of honor and without leaving a disaster behind, and he had come up short. He couldn't rely on his advisers for sage counsel because they had run out of new ideas, too. Polls showed that Johnson was likely headed for defeat in 1968, when he would be up for re-election, and that Robert Kennedy, the slain president's brother, was increasing in popularity and might defeat him in the Democratic primaries.

In early 1967, a survey by pollster Lou Harris found that only 43 per cent of Americans gave Johnson a positive overall job-approval rating, "exactly where it was in December ... the low point in his standing." Public approval of his handling of the Vietnam War hit 40 per cent, its lowest point up to then.[3]

On January 30–31, 1968, Viet Cong and North Vietnamese forces launched surprise attacks all across South Vietnam during the Tet religious holiday. This offensive was beaten back over a period of weeks, but it was a costly "victory." Above all, it showed Americans that the enemy remained fierce and determined, and that the war would require even more sacrifice, spending, and lives for an undetermined number of years. It broke America's will.[4]

After a relatively brief rally-around-the-president period, public support for Johnson's war policies plummeted. CBS anchor Walter Cronkite told viewers on his February 27 news show that he had concluded the war was a stalemate that neither side could win. Johnson confided to a friend, "If I've lost Cronkite, I've lost Middle America."[5]

Within weeks, LBJ's ratings hit new lows. In March, only 26 per cent of Americans approved of his handling of Vietnam and 63 per cent disapproved. Only 36 per cent approved of his overall job performance, and 52 per cent disapproved.[6]

On Sunday evening, March 31, a weary and demoralized Johnson gave a speech on Vietnam and stunned the nation when he announced that he would not run for another term. "I shall not seek, and I will not accept, the nomination of my party for another term as your president," he said.

An aide recalled that he "bounded from his chair in the Oval Office to join his family in watching the television reviews. His shoulders temporarily lost their stoop. His air was that of a prisoner let free."[7]

*   *   *

JOHNSON WAS a case study in losing touch. As his former aide George Reedy says,

> From the president's standpoint the greatest staff problem is that of maintaining his contact with the world's reality that lies outside the White House walls. Very few have succeeded in doing so. They start their administration fresh from the political wars, which have a tendency to keep men closely tied to the facts of life, but it is only a matter of time until the White House assistants close in like a Praetorian Guard. Since they are the only people a president sees on a day-to-day basis, they become to him the voice of the people. They represent the closest approximation that he has of outside contact, and it is inevitable that he comes to regard them as humanity itself.
>
> Even the vision of so earthy a politician as Lyndon B. Johnson became blurred as the years went by. He mistook the alert, taut, well-groomed young men around him for "American youth" and could never comprehend the origins of the long-haired, slovenly attired youngsters who hooted at him so savagely when he traveled (and eventually made most travel impossible) and who raged and stormed outside the White House gates. To him, they appeared to be extraterrestrial invaders—not only non-American but unearthly. Certainly, they did not fit the pattern of young men and young women whom he had assembled so painstakingly and who were so obviously, in his eyes, the embodiment of the nation's dream.[8]

As his political plight worsened, Johnson dug himself ever deeper into his bunker. "White House aides repeatedly ignored the objective conditions in Vietnam and worried more about the president's image," writes historian Gil Troy.[9] One senior aide concluded in March 1968 that "television in particular is stimulating a national mob psychology working to the disadvantage of the president."[10] In response, White House advisers looked for PR techniques rather than policy changes in a futile effort to lift LBJ's popularity. This echoed a memo written in February 1965 by aide Jack Valenti advocating a campaign to show "a strong and compassionate President involved in the hopes of people and their dreams, and thereby diminishing some public concern about Vietnam."[11] But this approach missed the point. No amount of public relations could alter the public's deep dissatisfaction with the state of the nation, including inflation, student rebellions, urban decay, and especially the Vietnam War, and Johnson and his aides couldn't seem to understand this. Hubert Humphrey, Johnson's peripatetic vice president, confirmed after leaving office how out of touch he had become about Vietnam. He conceded that Americans were "sick to the teeth" over the war, and he added, "Now that I'm out and among the people, I can feel it as I never did."[12]

*   *   *

IT WAS NOT always so. At the start of his presidency, Johnson was as aggressive and engaging a leader as America has ever had. He was often described as a force of nature, tirelessly pursuing his goals and determined to stay in touch. He had telephones installed in many rooms at the White House and at his Texas ranch, including the bathrooms and under his dinner table, so he would always be only a few steps from making or receiving a call. He rang people up, and sometimes asked them to come to the White House, at all hours in a constant effort to get things done, to assert his will, or to get information. He had two wire-service tickers installed near his Oval Office desk so he could check the news at a moment's notice. He often had more than one television running in a three-screen console so he wouldn't miss reports that interested him on the evening news shows of ABC, CBS, and NBC.[13]

He began with a good understanding of what the country wanted and how he could deliver it. He felt that John F. Kennedy's assassination had generated enormous shock across America and he needed to demonstrate continuity and show that he would pursue JFK's legacy in as many ways as he could, including following through on Kennedy's commitment to civil rights. This conformed neatly to LBJ's own ambitions because he knew it would increase his popularity if he came across as the keeper of Kennedy's legacy. He also took the opportunity to cast himself as Franklin Roosevelt's heir in terms of delivering as much assistance to Americans from the federal government as possible.

Historian Updegrove writes that the experiences of Johnson's childhood and young-adult life "made their mark on him: the effects of growing up poor without basics such as electricity or indoor plumbing, in Johnson City, a place his father described, 'where folks care when you're sick, and go to your funeral when you die.' Neighbors feel a certain responsibility toward each other and help out when they can, and Johnson took to heart the struggles they endured as a daily fact of life. And, of course, there were those poor Mexican American schoolchildren of Cotulla [a rural Texas community where Johnson had taught fifth, sixth, and seventh grades as a young man in 1928 and 1929], who were seared into Johnson's consciousness, plus the experiences he had in the National Youth Administration, where he first came into close contact with African Americans."[14]

Johnson won the 1964 election against the zealous conservative Barry Goldwater. "But even at his most popular, Johnson never bathed in the popular affection that Kennedy, Eisenhower, or Johnson's mentor Franklin Roosevelt had enjoyed," says historian Troy. "And Johnson's mismanagement of the Vietnam War not only ruined his presidency, it helped destroy the Cold War consensus and aura of reverence that Harry Truman, Dwight Eisenhower, and John Kennedy had built."[15]

* * *

FROM THE START of his presidency, Lyndon Johnson had grand ambitions for himself as a social engineer. "Some men want power simply to strut around the world and to hear the tune of 'Hail to the Chief,'" he said after leaving office. "Others want it simply to build prestige, to collect antiques, and to buy pretty things. Well, I wanted power to give things to people—all sorts of things to all sorts of people, especially the poor and the blacks."[16]

Johnson, propelled by polling that showed most Americans favored his expansion of government programs, succeeded in pushing through more social legislation than at any time since Franklin Roosevelt's New Deal, including civil-rights and voting-rights bills and a vast array of social-welfare bills, including measures creating Medicare and waging a "war on poverty."

He named Thurgood Marshall as the first black justice on the Supreme Court, and fought with Southern conservative legislators over his liberal agenda. At one point early in his presidency, he met at the White House with Democratic governors of Southern states who berated him for going too far on civil rights, which they felt was damaging the Democratic party in their regions. Afterward, Johnson complained to an adviser, "Nigger, nigger, nigger. That's all they said to me all day. Hell, there's one thing they better know. If I don't achieve anything else while I'm president, I intend to wipe that word out of the English language and make it impossible for people to come here and shout, 'nigger, nigger, nigger' to me and the American people."[17] One problem was that Johnson himself would use that term occasionally, a reflection of his living in segregated Texas during his younger days.

But Johnson lost touch with urban African Americans, who believed he wasn't moving fast enough on civil rights.

Johnson was personally offended by a series of riots that started in August 1965. Five days after he signed the Voting Rights Act to clear obstacles to African American voting, Watts, a poor black area of Los Angeles, erupted in a riot that killed 34 people, injured 856, and resulted in 3,000 arrests and $35 million in property damage.[18] The violence erupted amid long-standing tensions between police and the black community and a 30 per cent adult unemployment rate. The situation indicated that America's race problem was far worse than LBJ had imagined. Riots also had occurred in the summer of 1964 in New York City, Rochester, and Philadelphia, and they would continue over the next three summers in Cleveland, Chicago, Detroit, Newark, Jacksonville, and elsewhere.

But it was the Watts riot that shocked LBJ the most because of its extent, the deaths and damage caused, and the anger that was displayed.[19] LBJ "just wouldn't accept it," said Johnson adviser Joseph Califano. "He refused to look at the cables from Los Angeles.... He refused to take calls from the generals who were requesting government planes to fly in the National Guard."[20]

During the summer of 1967 alone, there were riots in 125 American cities, including Newark, New Jersey, where 26 people died and, even worse, Detroit, Michigan, where 40 people died, hundreds were injured, 7,000 were arrested, and $50 million in property damage was sustained.

Johnson was hurt, a wound that lasted for the rest of his life. "How is it possible that all these people could be so ungrateful to me after I had given them so much," he complained to a friend after he left office. "Take the Negroes. I fought for them from the first day I came into office. I tried to make it possible for every child of every color to grow up in a nice house, to eat a solid breakfast, to attend a decent school, and to get a good and lasting job. I asked so little in return. Just a little thanks. Just a little appreciation. But look what I got instead. Riots.... Looting. Burning. Shooting. It ruined everything."[21]

And Johnson continued to avoid or misunderstand such unpleasant realities, including the morass in Vietnam.

*   *   *

HE WAS AGGRESSIVE on foreign policy but didn't seem to realize that he was wearing out the patience and resolve of the country, such as when he sent U.S. Marines into the Dominican Republic with the stated objective of protecting American lives amid what his advisers considered a likely leftist coup in April 1965. The operation succeeded in saving lives and forestalling a leftist takeover, and it was at first popular with Americans, which pleased the president.[22]

"Johnson also took satisfaction," historian Robert Dallek writes, "from a poll in August showing that 69 per cent of the American people approved his decision to send in the Marines. But Oliver Quayle, Johnson's pollster, advised the White House to 'tell the President that while this is highly favorable, he should not kid himself into thinking it was overwhelming. The truth is that one in five disapprove of sending Marines to the Dominican Republic. The main reason is that we're butting into another people's affairs.'"[23]

More important, Johnson's decisions on what to do in Vietnam were immensely complicated at the start of his administration—when he made crucial decisions to escalate the fighting—by the conflicting advice he got from the Pentagon and Capitol Hill, and by polls indicating the public was divided on a future course of action. This showed that presidents can't rely on polls to determine foreign policy; public opinion is too fickle.

"In the winter of 1964–65, Johnson felt pressured much more by hawks than doves," Dallek writes. "He complained to some liberals 'that all the [military] chiefs did was come in every morning and tell him, "Bomb, bomb, bomb," and then come back in the afternoon and tell him again. "Bomb, bomb, bomb."'"[24] His principal advisers also favored using force to resist a Communist takeover in South Vietnam. To be sure, they argued about the means and timing of attacks on the North Vietnamese and Viet Cong, but they believed it had to be done. Moreover, though polls revealed no well-defined majority in favor of escalation, a substantial plurality supported military action against the Communists, with only between 26 per cent and 30 per cent opposed.

Johnson decided to escalate, but as time wore on he didn't adjust his thinking to the realities on the ground, where the United States was losing the war, and to the new reality at home, where increasing numbers of Americans were turning vehemently and sometimes violently against it.

At the end of 1964, Johnson had told advisers, "I've tried this to get out of Vietnam; I've tried that; I've tried everything I can think of. What can I do next?"[25] He could never find a satisfactory answer.

As Dallek observes, "With still no clear answers to his question, Johnson followed his political instincts. When confronted by sharp divisions of opinion throughout his career, he had almost always adopted a moderate position, identifying himself as an accommodationist who reflected the national desire for compromise rather than ideological rigidity. Since abandoning Vietnam seemed unthinkable and since public opinion and congressional support for a full-scale conflict seemed unlikely to outlast substantial human and material costs, he chose measured increases in U.S. military action with continuing efforts to negotiate a settlement."[26]

* * *

AS PRESIDENT, Johnson thought that one way in which he could keep track of public opinion was to talk to as many members of Congress and other members of the Washington establishment as he could. He had, after all, served many years on Capitol Hill, rising to Senate majority leader, one of the nation's most powerful legislators, and had a huge personal network.

He cut a wide swath through Washington as he attempted to constantly expand his seemingly endless network of friends, associates, and acquaintances. He regularly phoned the leaders of the House and Senate, such as House Speaker John McCormack, a Democrat from Massachusetts; Senate Majority Leader Mike Mansfield, a Democrat from Montana; Senate Minority Leader Everett Dirksen, a Republican from Illinois; and Sen. Richard Russell, a Democrat from Georgia. Outside Capitol Hill, John Connally, then the Democratic governor of Texas, was a regular phone pal and confidant.

Johnson kept very close track of his media coverage and his public standing. In a phone call to aide Reedy at 12:49 a.m. on March 17, 1964, he said, "This son of a bitch [columnist] Stew Alsop has got a mean article—'The Texas Mafia Moves In'—and shows that all the intellectuals are gone, and all of Johnson's guys are in, but the only thing they know is Texas."[27]

In a phone call to Edwin Weisl, Sr., a friend and New York lawyer, at 8:09 a.m. on March 18, 1964, he again complained about Alsop's charge that Johnson was driving President Kennedy's aides out of government and replacing them with men from his home state of Texas. "Stewart Alsop—he's kind of a supercilious intellectual that thinks he's real smart," Johnson said. He also showed how closely he was following the polls, asking Weisl if he had seen the Gallup poll that morning, which gave him 68 per cent of the vote in a hypothetical 1964 matchup with Richard Nixon, who had 27 per cent. Nixon was widely considered a possible contender for the Republican nomination to challenge LBJ in the 1964 election. Johnson gloated that Robert Kennedy, the slain president's brother and LBJ's political nemesis, was doing much worse against Nixon than Johnson was in a hypothetical matchup. Robert Kennedy was only ahead of Nixon 53–47.[28]

* * *

UNLIKE MORE-RECENT presidents, LBJ cultivated the media relentlessly and in personal ways that seem extraordinary today, when there is such a distance between the president and the press corps.

At 9:54 p.m. on Monday, December 23, 1963, Johnson called Frances Lewine, White House correspondent for United Press International. He was apparently worried that Jacqueline Kennedy, the former president's widow, was angry that he had revealed parts of a private conversation they had. Lewine had written a story about it, but she denied that she had disclosed anything except that Johnson wished Mrs. Kennedy a merry Christmas and that he promised to try calling Mrs. Kennedy every day or two to make sure she was all right. After Lewine's explanation, Johnson said, "Thank you, darling, I appreciate it. And I knew it was true but I got a call from the news office and they were upset. . . . I'm gonna do some things once in a while. So you help protect me." Lewine replied, "Well, we certainly appreciate it and I certainly will protect you."[29]

Two days later, at 8:12 on Christmas night, he called James Reston, the influential columnist and Washington bureau chief for the *New York Times* and, armed with flattery, said, "I just called you to tell you that I was thinking of you and hope you had a merry Christmas, appreciate your friendship and want your advice and counsel in the days ahead because, God A-mighty, I've got so much to do. I don't know how I'll ever do it. And I've got to have some friends who will speak with candor."[30]

After some chitchat, he invited Reston to spend some time with him at his Texas ranch. Reston agreed, and Reston and his wife and son Richard stayed overnight at the LBJ ranch. The next day, January 5, 1964, they flew back to Washington with LBJ and his wife on *Air Force One*. Johnson, it turned out, was on a political intelligence mission of sorts.

Reston had been in Arizona to interview Barry Goldwater, who had just announced his candidacy for the Republican presidential nomination. Reston wrote later in his memoirs that President Johnson "didn't particularly want to see me, but he wanted to know how the press had reacted to Goldwater's announcement. When we got there, he was worried, not only about Goldwater, but also about all the appointments he would have to make and the first budget he would have to present to the Congress in a few days."[31]

But as his policies such as the Vietnam War and his civil-rights agenda lost favor on Capitol Hill or generated increasing hostility, Johnson came to rely much less on the Washington insiders he once counted on, and his outreach to the media slowed dramatically. Everyone, he told aides, seemed to be turning against him.

*　*　*

ONE ALSO wonders how much candid advice and insight Johnson got from members of Congress and his own staff because of his overbearing presence. He had a need to dominate every situation and every person. "I think he used to see if he could intimidate people from their positions just to see how strong their positions were," said adviser Larry Temple. "He would say such things as, 'That is the dumbest thing I ever heard. Any sixth grader would know better than so-and-so.' The president, I think, frequently would do that just to try to test people. I think all of us had the experience where somebody would tell him something and he'd say, 'Oh, everybody knows better than that,' and then within 24 hours he'd be repeating that same position as his own."[32]

On one occasion, he embarrassed his spokesman George Reedy by mocking the way he dressed and his being overweight. "I want you to do better than anybody else does and look nicer, and take your shirt and bring it down and change it at lunch so that you've on a clean shirt and a big enough suit for you," Johnson instructed. "Try to leave a good impression on 'em. . . . I want to try to build you up, build you up gradually. . . . You're entitled to prestige. You've worked for it harder than anybody else. . . . But you've got to help yourself. You don't help yourself. You come in those damned old wrinkled suits and you come in with a dirty shirt and you come in with your tie screwed up. I want you to look real nice. Get you a corset, if you have to." Reedy managed, "Okay, sir." Johnson added, "But look like a top-flight businessman. You look like a goddamned reporter and I want you to look better."[33]

On another occasion, he scolded Reedy for not being accessible to him at all times. "Why don't you leave word where you're going to be?" an irritated Johnson said. "I couldn't get you at the Press Office. Couldn't get you at your office.... You just tell your girl, your secretary, where you are and where you're going to eat or drink or screw or whatever it is you're doing and let me get in touch with you. I don't need to know the number. You just leave word."[34]

*   *   *

AS THE VIETNAMESE quagmire deepened, LBJ retreated further into his White House bunker. At one point, he shouted to an aide, "They all just follow the communist line—liberals, intellectuals, communists—I can't trust anybody any more.... I'm going to get rid of everybody who doesn't agree with my policies."[35] This approach just made matters worse by driving another wedge between him and his critics, and discouraging dissent within the White House.

Everything about Vietnam became personal, and his ego and his macho attitudes were so wrapped up in the war that he couldn't see how distant he was getting from the country. Johnson friend Arthur Goldberg told the remarkable story of how reporters once pushed LBJ to explain why the United States was in Vietnam, and "LBJ unzipped his fly, drew out his substantial organ, and declared 'This is why!'"[36]

Despite his arrogance and self-importance, he tried to gather information from as many sources as he could, sometimes in personal ways that directly affected his policymaking. At the end of 1965, his adviser Joe Califano's son accidentally ate too many aspirin and had his stomach pumped. Johnson took the matter to heart and demanded that Congress pass a Child Safety Act that included mandatory child-safety caps and warning labels on many products.[37]

But there were some things that Lyndon Johnson had trouble fathoming. One was the diversity of societies around the world. "LBJ had no particular grasp of foreign cultures," observed National Security Council staffer Robert Komer. "He felt no particular need to delve into what made Vietnamese Vietnamese—as opposed to Americans or Greeks or Chinese. He was a people man, and he thought people everywhere were the same. He saw the Vietnamese farmer as being like the Texas farmer or the Oklahoma farmer. 'We're going to provide them with rural electricity. We're going to provide them with roads and water, and we're going to improve the rice crop.'"[38]

Journalist Hugh Sidey of *Time* said, "His weakness was that he did not know the world, because he was not a creature of it in any way. Dwight Eisenhower had spent his adult life in contact with Churchill and Roosevelt and Marshall and people like that. John Kennedy read ten books a week while he was in the White House. He read about foreign affairs; he liked it. Lyndon Johnson was probably the best president we've ever had: as a legislator; as a man who understood Washington, who could persuade people, who could understand the workings of men. But he missed a lot of the world outside the United States. He was never interested in it. He never studied it that much. He wasn't exposed to it as much. I'll always remember, on *Air Force One,* flying back from one of those Asian trips after meeting with [South Vietnamese leaders] Thieu and Ky, and he turned to us and said, 'Boys, I don't understand foreigners. They're different from us.'"[39]

* * *

EVEN THOUGH LBJ and his staff downplayed their use of polls, privately they relied on them heavily. Johnson even hired Albert Cantril, the son of Hadley Cantril, who was FDR's pollster, as the resident interpreter of polls on the White House staff. Albert Cantril's role was unusual, but Johnson found it useful to have an expert on hand to balance out the official opinion-takers, suggesting, as political scientist Robert M. Eisinger points out, that "the president was not only concerned about the attitudes of the public, but he was also informed about misinterpretations of poll results."[40]

"Questions about Vietnam saturated [these White House] polls during 1965 and 1966," reports Eisinger, mainly to clarify voters' views on the war.[41] Among the questions asked by White House pollster Oliver Quayle was this:

> Which statement do you most agree with?
> We should go all out (short of using nuclear weapons) and either win or force negotiations.
> We should do as we are: Keep on fighting a limited war, but increase military operations as necessary while seeking negotiations.
> We should stay in Viet Nam, but reduce military operations.
> We should get out of Viet Nam now.
> Not sure.[42]

Quayle, a former assistant of Lou Harris whose work was funded by the Democratic party, also asked about public attitudes on "a temporary cease fire in Viet Nam," "all out bombing if pause and cease fire fail," "use of napalm," "not [using] atomic weapons," "allowing Viet Cong [pro–North Vietnamese guerrillas] represented in Government of South Viet Nam as a means to end war," and "increasing taxes to help pay for war, or decreasing domestic programs."[43]

"Like Harris' polls for JFK, President Johnson's polls were frequently comprised of local samples (that is, residents of a particular state, county or congressional district, as compared to a national sample)," writes Eisinger. "In keeping with his predecessors Cantril and Harris, Quayle secretly sent his poll reports to senior White House officials, who attentively interpreted public opinion both about the president's popularity and about particular policies. Johnson was an avid pollreader; and when he knew that surveys were in the field, Johnson eagerly awaited poll analyses."[44]

"Johnson frequently sought to assess citizens' views by conducting and interpreting local polls as national snapshots of the public's mood," says Eisinger.[45]

As the 1968 election approached, Quayle was active in gaming out Johnson's re-election prospects and his potential opponents, and in suggesting tactics, the most effective words to use in the campaign, and topics for television ads. Quayle took extensive surveys in New Hampshire, site of the first Democratic primary, to determine how to combat the rising threat from Senator Eugene McCarthy of Minnesota, who was considering a campaign based on his opposition to the Vietnam war. Quayle considered McCarthy a serous threat and suggested ways to undermine him. "If McCarthy goes, a major effort must be made to have him come through as 'the extreme candidate,' 'the appeasement candidate,' or 'the surrender candidate,'" Quayle wrote in a memo to LBJ advisers. "And if the preceding phrases seem a little extreme themselves, then we suggest consideration of such alternatives as 'the knuckle under candidate,' or 'the back down candidate.' ... McCarthy has always been more interested in dissension than anything else, and here he is at it again. It would make a good TV spot.... This is more evidence that McCarthy can be hurt if the issue becomes give in versus stand firm on Viet Nam."[46]

There is considerable evidence that Quayle's polls were often misinterpreted by Johnson and his advisers, showing that just because a poll is taken, there is no guarantee that it will be understood.

"Johnson's pollsters, misled by the numbers, declared that only '3 to 5 %' disliked the president 'solely on personality,'" historian Gil Troy writes. "They suggested a 'job oriented' communications strategy. If Eisenhower had 'the Father Image' and JFK was 'Prince Charming,' Lyndon Johnson could be 'The Professional.' This focus on accomplishments only perpetuated Johnson's delusions and made him introduce more legislation while still failing to charm the American public. Successful statesmanship requires more than listing achievements; effective leaders have to cast a spell."[47]

Troy adds, "Unlike Franklin Roosevelt, who so carefully nudged the nation toward war and succeeded in gaining their support, Johnson surreptitiously plunged into war and failed to win the country's approval. He soft-pedaled the costs of both the Great Society and the Vietnam conflict. As the public soured on the war, Johnson refused to budge. In avoiding debate, escalating the U.S. presence secretly, and lying, Johnson demanded a lack of faith in the people, breeding a culture of distrust."[48]

Another indication of the skewed view of polling inside the LBJ White House came when Chief of Staff James Jones decided in March 1968 to conduct a poll from the White House as a supplement to what the professional pollsters were doing. Instead of using sophisticated survey researchers, he had his secretaries ask the questions. In a memo from Jones to another Johnson aide on March 11, 1968, Jones said, "My two secretaries will use a Watts line and they have phone books from small and large cities in every section of the country. They will make a sample poll too."[49] It isn't known what the secretaries, whom he identified as "Sally and Donna," learned, but the fact that they were used in this inappropriate way shows that sometimes even the most sophisticated White House staffers can badly misunderstand polling.

Earlier in his regime, Johnson and his team seemed more savvy about polls. "In April [1964]," writes historian Robert Dallek, "when Oliver Quayle, LBJ's pollster, assessed the President's strength in six states in the West, Middle West, and East, he pitted Johnson against three moderates and one conservative, Rockefeller, Nixon, Michigan Governor George Romney, and Goldwater. Johnson decisively beat all of them. And though some voters were suspicious of him as a 'Southern conservative, and some find his less sophisticated appearance and personality lacking,' Quayle saw 'no serious weaknesses' in his candidacy."[50]

"Partly responding to opinion surveys by . . . Quayle of the most important election-year issues, Johnson publicly made Medicare a high legislative priority in the 1965 congressional term. In November, on the eve of the [1964] election when asked by a reporter whether Medicare would be a 'must' bill next year, Johnson answered: 'Just top of the list.' Two weeks later, the President told HEW Assistant Secretary Wilbur J. Cohen, who was the administration's principal advocate of Medicare, that he would make it our 'number one priority.' He asked Cohen to 'touch base with everyone concerned,' keep Cabinet members abreast of developments, and put his 'full energies' behind the bill."[51] Congress passed Medicare in July.

*   *   *

PERHAPS THE BEST summary of Johnson's isolation came from his former aide George Reedy. "I think [Johnson's] downfall was basically a kind of separation from reality," Reedy said. "He'd reached a point where he didn't know what was real and what wasn't. I know he was terribly bewildered by the student demonstrators ... [b]ecause nobody, nobody, had done more financially for college students [and for civil rights] than Lyndon Johnson.... And he didn't realize a number of things. When he was a young man, a college education was a tremendous prize. Just tremendous. It meant the keys to the kingdom. Well, it doesn't mean the keys to the kingdom today. Today, a lot of college is a babysitting proposition. And I doubt whether students value it that much. And it didn't mean a thing to them that this was the man who had gotten all those scholarships and educational funds. What do they care? They were more interested in Vietnam.

"Second, their life style was totally different from his life style as a young man. When he was a young man, as soon as you graduated from college you were very careful to comb your hair right and tie your tie right, get a pressed shirt, pressed suit, and you'd start making the rounds looking for a job which you'd get pretty quick. The long hair bothered him, the careless, sloppy clothing, the blue jeans, and he'd look around in the White House and he'd see a lot of young people that looked exactly like his ideal—what a young person should look like. And so to him that was the real American youth. I don't know where he thought those people outside came from, probably Mars or Neptune, or something like that. But he did, he got separated from reality."[52]

As the Vietnam war dragged on, the president's popularity declined to disastrous levels. "He stuck to his policy, however, as CIA assessments depicted a battle-weary North Vietnam," writes historian Gerald Astor. "He attributed the rising fever of the antiwar movement to communist instigators." Asked a hostile question by a reporter, he responded, "What kind of chicken-shit question is that to ask the leader of the free world!"[53]

His approval for handling Vietnam sank to near 30 per cent, but he stayed the course. "I'm not going to be the first American president to lose a war," he told TV interviewer David Brinkley at one point.[54] But his delusion, his isolation, and his obstinacy caused him to lose both the war and his presidency.

In the end, Johnson pushed too far and too fast for conservatives, and he didn't go far enough to satisfy the dissidents on the left, notably liberal college students and African Americans impatient for their full civil rights. His ego and intimidating personality also caused him problems, and his escalation of the Vietnam war far outran public acceptance.

*   *   *

JOHNSON started off with the best of intentions and the highest level of political savvy. He was more interested in leading public opinion than following it on controversial issues such as the Vietnam War and the civil-rights movement. And Johnson monitored public opinion in many ways, using polls, watching television, reading newspapers and magazines, talking to as many Washington leaders as he could, and trying to stay true to his roots in the hardscrabble towns of central Texas. His problem was that while he understood public opinion, he wouldn't heed it, especially in Vietnam. He was unable to push the country where he wanted it to go, resulting in vast unpopularity for himself and his presidency.

CHAPTER TWO
RICHARD NIXON

IN THE BUNKER

In his second term, Richard Nixon was perhaps the most isolated and solitary president of the modern era. He became obsessed with the Watergate scandal, and this intensified his worst qualities, such as his penchant for seeing himself as a victim and his willingness to lash out at his perceived enemies.

The Vietnam war also brought out the worst in Nixon, as it had done with Lyndon Johnson. He considered the antiwar movement, coupled with the student rebellion against authority, "the greatest national crisis since the Civil War."[1] He told an aide, "A President must come through as very strong, bold and even ruthless when the problems of the country are involved."[2] He felt that the United States was embroiled in a titanic struggle between the left versus the "great silent majority" that shared his conservative views.

To further their objectives, Nixon and his advisers conducted a campaign against the news media, which they believed were infested with liberals. Nixon told an adviser that reporters would always pursue "a story which will be harmful to the administration." He warned his aides to always "be on guard" with reporters, and Nixon spent much of his time scheming on how to outfox the media, how to isolate critical journalists, and how to punish media outlets for their bias.[3] Far from learning from the media, Nixon declared war on the Fourth Estate.

In June 1970, the United States invaded and bombed Cambodia to curtail Viet Cong attacks on neighboring South Vietnam, but the administration denied it to the media. When the truth came out, the lies made the war and Nixon even more unpopular, and his war with the Fourth Estate intensified.[4]

*   *   *

NIXON WAS never as committed to personal outreach as most other presidents of the modern era. He was cerebral and in some ways shy, and didn't cultivate a wide range of contacts, either in Congress or among friends and associates across the country, to keep him in touch. An aide once described him, aptly, as "a very interior guy."[5] And he didn't have the intuition to understand human nature from his life experiences, as Truman and Reagan did.

Instead, Nixon relied on polls to shape his views and the views of his senior advisers.

Adviser John Maddox provided opinion research during Nixon's successful 1968 presidential campaign, when Maddox made a habit of giving extensive presentations to the staff explaining his results. At one of his briefings, he displayed a chart projected onto a screen that showed the qualities that Americans had told him they wanted in their ideal president, including strength, firmness, sense of humor, and generosity. The negative traits that people didn't want included weakness and being "wishy-washy," "a stuffed shirt," and stingy. All this was part of what Maddox called the "Ideal President Curve." In a separate report, Maddox said, "It is of substantial significance, we believe, that the widest gap of all is the 'cold-warm.' We believe it highly probable that if the real personal warmth of Mr. Nixon could be more adequately exposed, it would release a flood of other inhibitions about him—and make him more tangible as a person to large numbers of Humphrey leaners [a reference to Democratic candidate Hubert Humphrey]."[6]

Even if Nixon couldn't act more warmly, the goal was to produce TV commercials that made him seem genial and approachable. This turned out to be only partially successful, as what media pundits called "the new Nixon," supposedly an updated, warm, and engaging version of "Tricky Dick," only managed to win by the narrowest of margins in 1968.

The problem for Nixon's image-makers was that voters knew him all too well and they had many negative perceptions about him. He had been vice president under President Dwight Eisenhower for eight years, and didn't have an extensive record of achievement to show for it. He lost the 1960 race for the White House to John F. Kennedy when he came across to many as aloof and unlikable. He went down to defeat in his bid for the governorship of California in 1962, when he showed himself to be a sore loser. After his California defeat, he told reporters at what he billed as his last news conference that they would no longer have Nixon to "kick around."

In 1968 Nixon committed himself to a makeover, but he also focused on demographics and specific issues that he thought would get him votes, even if they divided the country in the process.

He counted on the man that his campaign team called the "ethnic specialist"—Kevin Phillips, then 27 and a brilliant intellectual, later to become a nationally known conservative theoretician. His job was to study America's ethnic groups, such as Germans and Scandinavians in Wisconsin, and figure out how to make them vote for Nixon.

Phillips believed that a conservative revolution was gaining steam.[7] But he realized that Nixon needed to identify potential supporters and work aggressively to reach them in order to hasten the revolution. Among his insights was that patriotism sold best in the South and adjacent border states. Giving advice to his bosses on the content of TV ads, Phillips said, "We need a red-hot military music, land of pride and glory special for the South and Border. I think that this is very important. Secondarily, we need a more concern for the countryside, its values and farmers welfare spot, complete with threshing threshers, silos, Aberdeen Angus herds, et al. Look, I have no interest in how many voters can fit on the head of a pin. All I care about is how many we can get there by hook or by crook who will vote for us."[8]

Another key 1968 adviser was Len Garment, a conservative strategist. In a November 16, 1967, memo to Nixon about voters in New Hampshire, site of the first presidential primary in 1968, Garment said, "The early intimations from the group interviews indicate that foreign policy (Vietnam) is by far the major preoccupation among Republicans. The state may well be atypical; it seems that they are only remotely concerned about such things as riots, cities, the young people, even cost-of-living. They appear mainly concerned about the incomprehensible drift of foreign policy, the lack of comprehensible communication (or persuasion) about the war, the lack of defined goals ... the feeling that they were mousetrapped, the lack of credibility. The need for leadership dominates the talk so far."[9]

All this survey research into voter attributes was part of Nixon's policy-formulation process, and he chose to adopt a divide-and-conquer strategy.

Still, his flaws had to be addressed and his staff delved deeply into polling data to find answers. A memo from Nixon strategist Patrick Buchanan, who would later run unsuccessfully for president himself and become a television commentator, showed the importance of survey research to Nixon. Based on polls and reports from GOP political operatives, Buchanan told Nixon just prior to the 1968 New Hampshire primary that the Nixon coalition in that state consisted of 40 per cent "Republican regulars," 40 per cent "conservative Republicans," and 20 per cent "moderates and liberals." Buchanan went on that those in the Nixon coalition believed "RN is the best qualified man to be President, most capable in foreign policy, most capable on the issues. There is widespread concern through this coalition that a) RN is a loser, and b) he cannot generate sufficient enthusiasm and excitement."[10]

This led Buchanan and other Nixon advisers to urge him to give speeches to reinforce his stature and statesmanlike qualities, but also, in dealing with the negatives, to project confidence and amiability. "Then, to hammer the loser thing (at the same time we dispel the myths of RN being tough and mean and political and intense)," Buchanan wrote, "we use the tv to show everyone in New Hampshire that RN is enjoying the hell out of this campaign. He is smiling, confident, easy-going (no cornball stuff), comes off well in 'feature' settings, with kids, with folks, etc. In short, while RN talks like the President-in-Exile, he is a good democrat (with a small d) who believes that communicating with the people is one of the great joys of seeking the Presidency."[11]

The campaign adopted this advice, even though the cerebral Nixon was not really comfortable as a gregarious back-slapper and did not find great joy in communicating with the people.

*   *   *

AT THE OUTSET of his presidency, Nixon made the same claim as most modern-day presidents have made—that the purpose of using polls "will not be to help us work out our policy but let us know what obstacles we confront in attempting to sell a policy."[12] But over time, his interest in polls became an obsession fed by a deep-seated animosity toward his critics, whom he desperately wanted to conquer.

Nixon came into office with a series of grievances against his perceived enemies, including the Democrats and federal bureaucrats. "Most bothersome of all, however, were the press and the news system," historian Theodore H. White wrote. "Nixon's anger at the press had been building ever since 1952 [when as the Republican candidate for vice president he first realized the power of the media, especially the insiders who ran TV news, and how little he could control them] ... but now that he was President, it intensified. The news system was the carrier of ideas, the manager of the stage, the molder of images; and it was, simply, an element completely out of his control. No other leader in any country lives with such a press as America's, for it is the only absolutely free and uncontrolled press in the world, cramped only by loose libel laws and the dictates of making a profit. No President can tamper with it, except at his peril."[13]

After Nixon left office in disgrace, a member of his personal staff offered an explanation of what went wrong, and his analysis offered a window on the White House's persecution complex: "We were operating in a totally hostile environment," the former aide said. "Press. Congress. Bureaucracy. And our people were young and inexperienced. If we made any mistakes at all, they would get us, even the same mistakes previous administrations had gotten away with. They were out to get us. And we made a lot of mistakes."[14]

Nixon assigned his White House chief of staff H.R. "Bob" Haldeman to "get in touch" with the average American, and be the point man for measuring public opinion.[15] This was partly because the Democrat-controlled Congress was hostile to the new Republican administration and couldn't be trusted to keep White House officials informed about what was going on around the country. Nixon also didn't trust fellow Republicans to provide him with their candid assessments of public opinion. So, at Nixon's behest, Haldeman developed an unlimited appetite for polls.

Despite his penchant for seeing the world in Manichaean terms, and a certain pleasure in confronting his opponents, there were signs that Nixon was deeply troubled by the venom directed at him, especially by young protesters of the Vietnam war. "Even Richard Nixon left the insular confines of the White House in the wee hours of a restless night during the Vietnam War to reach out to student protesters who had congregated there [at the Lincoln Memorial]—though he ended up talking to them awkwardly about football," writes historian Mark K. Updegrove.[16]

* * *

BUT MOSTLY, Nixon controlled his emotions, curbed his efforts at outreach, and used polls not only to stay in touch but also as political ammunition. He authorized his staff to give the results of favorable polls to outsiders if he thought this would advance his agenda. Haldeman wanted to control the polls tightly, fearing that White House strategy might be revealed.[17] He didn't want any members of Congress demanding access to the polls if there was a congressional appropriation for them, so he had the surveys financed through the Republican National Committee and sometimes wealthy individuals who backed Nixon.

"President Nixon recognized more than his predecessors how polls could be used to advance his agenda," writes political scientist Robert M. Eisinger. "Haldeman's power as it related to gauging public opinion was unparalleled; he streamlined presidential polling operations in irreversible ways."[18]

"The Nixon administration was quite hard on the pollster who offered information that was not up to its exacting standards," writes political scientist Diane J. Heith.[19] Haldeman, as the gatekeeper, kept tight control of access to polling data and was very strict about what he wanted. He scrawled at the top of one memo, "Useless—I can read the statistics myself—what we need is analysis, not highlights."

As the Nixon administration progressed, Nixon and Haldeman classified the American public in ever greater detail, slicing and dicing the electorate in new ways—a process known today as micro-targeting. They were impressed with the analyses of former Bureau of the Census director Richard Scammon, who was informally advising White House officials, and presciently told them that in the 1970s "political power will shift to the suburbs.... The constituency is relatively affluent, essentially middle aged.... These people are less committed to parties as an electorate. They are drawing their knowledge from television and can be reached much more so than 25 years ago."[20]

Scammon's advice and other information led to Nixon's conclusion, cited earlier, that a "silent majority" existed in America. He felt that it was in large part suburban and conservative, a massive group of nonprotesters who believed in traditional values such as the work ethic and patriotism, and he decided to rest his presidency upon it.

To that end, Nixon and Haldeman began to survey the silent majority as much as possible, directing pollsters to make an ongoing study of this group and learn as much about it as they could. Their inquiries included questions of lifestyle, such as television-watching habits; probing the silent majority's support of the Vietnam war, at least during Nixon's first term; and attitudes about anti-war protesters and government programs.

Looking at what he considered a central lifestyle issue, Nixon wrote to senior adviser John Ehrlichman that his analysis of poll results had convinced him that "people who live in homes that they own tend to take a much more conservative view on public issues than people who rent. I think this has significant consequences as far as our own programs are concerned.... I would like you to follow through in any way that you think would be appropriate to reach our homeowner constituency."[21]

His pollsters from the start delved into the "positive themes that have come through in the first year" and the "positive themes that have not come through."[22] The pollsters provided him with regular data on how his environmental programs were going over: the popularity of his policies on the economy, welfare, fighting crime, and many other topics. Nixon personally designed some poll questions, including one on whether the public favored "a guaranteed income" for every American.[23] (Most didn't.)

Nixon also authorized polls on the Vietnam war, whether J. Edgar Hoover should retire as director of the FBI, and, later, whether Nixon was being held responsible by the public for the Watergate break-in.[24]

Political scientist Robert M. Eisinger observed, after studying the Nixon polling operation, that "it is hard to imagine a topic about which ORC [Opinion Research Corporation, one of Nixon's favored research firms] did not poll."[25]

Among the questions that were asked:

> President Nixon participated in a televised interview last week with the commentators of the three networks. Did you see that television program?
> Do you approve or disapprove of President Nixon's decision to send a rescue mission to Son Tay, North Vietnam to free American POW's?
> In 1972 there will be another presidential election. Suppose this election were being held today and the candidates were Richard Nixon and Edmund Muskie, which one would you vote for?
> The United States is on the verge of a nervous breakdown (strongly agree, somewhat agree, somewhat disagree, strongly disagree, no opinion).[26]

*   *   *

AS TIME WENT ON, Nixon and his chief aides became even more embittered, concluding that the administration was being savaged by Nixon's enemies in politics, government, and the media. "Because they thought of the media as sabotaging them," Eisinger writes, "President Nixon and his advisers attempted to manipulate public opinion by disseminating poll data showing the president in a positive light and by discrediting polls and pollsters when the president's polls were less than flattering."[27]

White House officials began to stew about what they considered the inaccurate and biased polling of Lou Harris, who had been such a close adviser and pollster for Kennedy, Nixon's nemesis. White House aide Dwight L. Chapin wrote a memo dated June 22, 1970, suggesting to Haldeman that members of Congress be encouraged to investigate Harris and other pollsters who were considered anti-Nixon. "There is a good case to be made on the fraud of publishing inaccurate polls and attempts to mislead the public," Chapin wrote. "Do you think this is a good idea? Can we assign [Lyn] Nofziger the project of seeing that the Congressional group is pulled together and they launch their investigation?"[28]

The plan proceeded, with Haldeman insisting that the White House role be kept secret. Meanwhile, White House officials disingenuously invited Harris to social functions at the White House and even hired him to poll for the Domestic Policy Council as a way of cultivating and co-opting him. But privately, Haldeman considered Harris a liberal and a Nixon enemy.

The congressional investigation apparently went nowhere. But Haldeman wouldn't give up his campaign against pollsters he considered anti-Nixon. A month after the get-Harris memo, Haldeman suggested that Harris could be discredited if he were criticized by another pollster, the respected Elmo Roper. Haldeman wrote, "Can we start a fight here between Roper and Harris and get Roper to take Harris on, on the basis of how far off he is? If Roper won't do it directly, can we get someone else to do it?"[29]

That fight never happened as the White House intended. But on June 7, 1972, Haldeman took aim at another pollster he considered unfair, Mervin Field and his Field Poll organization in California. In a memo summarizing a telephone conversation that day, Haldeman wrote to adviser Charles Colson, "We should launch an all-out attack on the Field Poll in California and try now to totally destroy their credibility. We have the golden opportunity. We should make the point that they were wrong in 1968 (you will have to check the facts on this); they were wrong on McGovern in 1972; they were wrong on Proposition 9 (where they said it would carry 3 to 1 and it lost 2 to 1); in other words, Field has an unblemished record of wrong predictions. We also should build from this that the media and the pollsters have combined in a conspiracy to get McGovern the nomination, which is obviously the case...."[30]

Nixon became "disturbed" by the Gallup poll, too, Haldeman wrote in his diary, because the president felt it was greatly underestimating his public support. "He's suggesting that we should probably build our own established poll, such as ORC [Opinion Research Corporation], on a continuing basis, so that we have a third poll that's taken regularly to counteract Gallup and Harris," Haldeman wrote. "He makes the point that the results of the polls directly affect our ability to govern, because [of] their influence on Congressmen, foreign leaders, etc., and that it's important that we keep the published polls honest, and that we know ourselves exactly what the actual poll status is."[31]

On some occasions, positive results from the White House polling operation were hand-delivered by 3:30 p.m. in order to make the deadlines of journalists at powerful media outlets, including ABC, CBS, NBC, UPI, AP, Reuters, the *Washington Post,* the *New York Times, Time, Newsweek,* and *U.S. News & World Report.*[32]

The Nixon White House also used polls to help determine the kinds of events that Nixon did in order to get positive publicity. A premium was placed on events that illustrated Nixon's domestic accomplishments, with the goal of getting him on the television news shows with at last one event per week on "the economy, drugs/crime, or pollution."[33] Republican pollster Robert Teeter wanted Nixon to arrange his official schedule according to the polls. Teeter wrote to another aide that a survey "used in conjunction with the ticket-splitting maps we went over this morning should be of assistance to you in scheduling the President and the First Family."[34]

Haldeman agreed that polling should be a determinant of Nixon's schedule. He favored "More emphasis on basing all scheduling and other decisions on political grounds. Especially emphasize Italians, Poles, Elks, and Rotarians, eliminate Jews, blacks, youth."[35]

What this meant is that Nixon's advisers were placing a very heavy bet on the polls, considering them the basis for projecting a favorable image of the president, determining his legislative strategy, and running his re-election campaign. "Polls determined which constituencies needed wooing and which ones could be ignored," Eisinger writes.[36]

*   *   *

STARTING IN August 1972, the Nixon team began asking polling questions about the Watergate burglary and related matters.[37] By January 1973, the questions were very pointed, such as, "Do you believe this whole break-in and bugging attempt at the Democratic National Committee headquarters is just more politics, or is it something serious?" Other examples from January 1973: "Have you seen, read, or heard about the so-called 'Watergate' incident last June when five men were arrested while trying to break in and bug the Democratic National Committee headquarters at the Watergate Hotel?" "Who do you think put these men up to the break-in and bugging attempt at the Democratic National Committee headquarters—President Nixon, President Nixon's campaign committee, the Republican Party, or Cuban exiles?" "Do you think President Nixon was responsible for the break-in and bugging attempt at the Democratic National Committee headquarters or not?" [38]

Nixon's pollsters also tested words and phrases. Nixon wanted to be known as being tough on crime but not racist, so his administration asked questions to better assess public perceptions of his rhetoric. One question asked of voters was whether the phrase "law and order" was actually a code for racism, but 70.5 per cent of those polled disagreed and only 20 per cent agreed. The administration was thereby assured that the president and other senior officials could use the phrase "law and order" in speeches without fear of seeming racist.[39]

Nixon's pollsters tested other phrases and themes that worked, including "identify with Middle America," "orderliness and calm restored," and "ending the [Vietnam] war honorably." The themes that were not successful, according to polls, included "dealing with the problems of the poor," "the new federalism," and "the streamlining of government decision-making."[40]

Haldeman argued that polls showing high presidential approval would help deter candidates from running against the president, so they leaked such results to the media.[41] In 1970, with his eye on the 1972 re-election campaign, Haldeman told an aide that such polls should be made public "to show the desire of the people throughout the country for the President's support in the election.... This will help to build the idea that running against the President is dangerous [politically]."[42]

And polling results on policy issues were passed along to members of Congress in order to solicit their votes if the polls showed support for Nixon's positions. Kennedy had done the same thing.

*   *   *

THE WATERGATE SCANDAL was Nixon's worst crisis, and he tried to use polling to survive as he fought for his political life. At first his polling found that few Americans knew about or cared about Watergate. In March 1973 Nixon asked specifically for more Watergate-related polling and Haldeman obliged. Haldeman later told Nixon that, "[pollster] Oliver Quayle says nobody gives a damn about the Watergate. Sindlinger [another pollster] says where it used to be ... only about ten per cent was the highest it ever got that said Watergate was a big issue, now it's two or three per cent. He said we just can't find anybody who is interested."[43]

Over time that changed again, as the scandal intensified and evidence of White House involvement began to accumulate. Political scientist Diane J. Heith says that "as the Watergate scandal grew in significance, public opinion increasingly entered the decision-making process. On April 25, 1973, Haldeman writes [in his diary], 'Because of the weight of public opinion, a voluntary departure is necessary,'" so he and senior adviser John Ehrlichman resigned.[44]

Nixon hung on the polls to bolster his spirits and persuade himself that he was going to survive, even though the political establishment in Washington and the news media were moving against him. He clung to the idea that many Americans who had been supportive of Nixon weren't paying much attention to the details of the scandal yet. On May 8, 1973, Nixon told his new chief of staff Alexander Haig to look at the polls. "By a vote of 59 to 31," Nixon said, "they thought the President should be given the benefit of the doubt on this matter and should be allowed to finish his term. You know, the next three and a half years. But the other interesting thing is by a vote of 77 to 13 they opposed suggestions that the President resign."[45] It's important to note that Nixon unwisely describes the polls as "a vote" rather than a highly changeable snapshot of public opinion at the moment.

And opinion did change. There were more revelations, including tape recordings of Oval Office conversations showing that Nixon and Haldeman had discussed using the CIA to block an FBI investigation into the Watergate break-in. Public approval of Nixon declined to 20 per cent and he resigned in August 1974.[46]

His obsession with public opinion was intense, but he drew the wrong conclusions—that he could manipulate public opinion to his advantage and outmaneuver his adversaries. The effort failed.

*   *   *

NIXON, in sum, isolated himself in the White House, perceiving an alternative universe populated only by friends and enemies, a black-and-white, Manichaean world. He cut himself off from the media; he trusted few people, and he saw the polls as tools to win victories and crush his opponents rather than to learn about the country and how it was changing. He lost touch with the middle-class world of his youth and was driven by his insecurities and resentments. As a result, Nixon had no reliable way to stay in contact with the country that he was trying to lead.

CHAPTER THREE
JIMMY CARTER

GOOD INTENTIONS, BAD OUTCOMES

Jimmy Carter was so sure of himself that, on many issues, he didn't think he could learn from anybody else. Even friends considered him sanctimonious and arrogant.

Patrick Caddell, Carter's pollster, managed to become part of Carter's inner circle during the 1976 campaign and he remained a very influential figure in the White House after his patron became president. In fact, Caddell's influence over polling and assessing the public mood was unparalleled. No one had the power or the credibility within the White House to argue with him or balance out his views. This was a dangerous situation for Carter because it concentrated the power over polling information—and assessments of issues and the mood of the country—in one person's hands. And that person, Caddell, was far off the mark in suggesting solutions on some fundamental issues.

In the end, Carter's problem was that while he understood public opinion, including widespread opposition to his ideas, he stubbornly adhered to unpopular views and was unable to change people's minds about his agenda.

*   *   *

AFTER CARTER'S ELECTION in November 1976, he commissioned polls on a variety of topics, particularly what he called the energy crisis, which he felt would be one of his biggest challenges. But surveys taken that December found that the public did not share Carter's view that the energy situation required major changes in lifestyle, much less sacrifice. This put the incoming president at odds with the country he hoped to lead.[1]

In a 56-page strategy memo sent to Carter in December, the month before he was inaugurated, Caddell argued that the new president should continue campaigning for his ideas without letup and use fireside chats, town-hall meetings, and other techniques to dramatize his agenda and stay close to the public.[2]

Carter had a big chore on his hands to convince Americans to accept his energy agenda, especially his argument that the energy crisis required drastic action, and in the end he failed. But not for want of trying. "The Carter administration undertook every public opportunity imaginable to explain, educate, and manipulate the American people toward a new way of thinking about energy," writes political scientist Diane J. Heith. "However, no amount of urging, cajoling, or berating from the president altered public opinion. As the polls continually demonstrated, Americans did not want to own smaller cars, conserve energy, or otherwise change their consumptive lifestyle."[3]

Carter "spent his tenure futilely advising Americans to accept a world of limited resources, power, and horizons as Iranians kidnapped American diplomats, the Soviets invaded Afghanistan, and Americans sat in their cars in endless gas lines watching prices soar," writes historian Gil Troy.[4]

Carter understood the problems he faced and the resistance of the public to his solutions, but to a large extent he stubbornly refused to back away from his perceptions and his prescriptions, and this undermined his leadership.

* * *

DURING HIS FIRST few days in office during January 1977, Carter served notice that he would be a people's president, and he went about it in a typically methodical fashion that was unprecedented in scope and symbolism. He told his staff, "I am determined to stay in touch with the people," and he asked his Cabinet officers to send him memos explaining how they would do the same.[5] He tried to set a tone of informality and to do away with trappings of what he considered the imperial presidency, such as the playing of "Ruffles and Flourishes" and "Hail to the Chief" whenever he entered a room. On February 2 he held a "fireside chat," as

Franklin Roosevelt had done, to explain his agenda. He wore a sweater, both to emphasize his disdain for formality and to show that he was committed to conservation of energy and keeping the thermostats at the White House at low levels to conserve fuel.

During that fireside chat, the new president promised to impose austerity on the government, including his own staff at the White House, which he would reduce by one-third. "We have eliminated expensive and unnecessary luxuries, such as door-to-door limousine service for many top officials, including all members of the White House staff," Carter said. "Government officials can't be sensitive to your problems if we are living like royalty here in Washington."[6]

He made a serious attempt to remove the barriers separating him from the people. In late February, he announced his intention to ensure that 5 to 10 per cent of the guests at state dinners would be regular Americans, a remarkable gesture of populism and outreach. As with many of his initiatives, he tried this for a while but it eventually fell by the wayside.[7] He found that too many Washington insiders and his campaign workers wanted to be included at these events, and he didn't want to alienate them.

On March 5, he hosted a televised call-in show in which he was available for two hours to any American who could get through the White House switchboard, with screening by CBS anchorman Walter Cronkite. More than nine million people tried to reach him, and he answered the questions of 42 of them. They were all respectful and serious, sharing Carter's tone. In a dig at the news media, Carter told Cronkite that Americans were telling him "what they were concerned about" and asking questions that had not been "asked of me and reported through the media."[8]

He held town meetings to speak directly to voters. The first was in mid-March in Clinton, Massachusetts, and the second was a bit later in Yazoo, Mississippi. He also visited the homes of what his aides called "average people." And sometimes he spent the night there. The Secret Service must have been apoplectic at the security and communications challenges involved, but Carter seemed serious about bonding with everyday America. Eventually, though, he spent these overnights with Democratic Party workers or volunteers from his campaign, bowing to the demands of politics in an effort to reward loyalists.

He would stop at local schools and make unexpected phone calls to people who had written the White House about their problems. He sent 450,000 letters to Americans asking for their suggestions about the energy problem. As his popularity eroded and the nation's problems worsened, especially the economy, he would spend hours each night talking to 20 to 40 political activists and supporters in key states such as Iowa, New Hampshire, and Maine, soliciting their ideas and stroking their egos. He met with members of Congress, governors, civil leaders, business executives, students, and others.[9]

Carter tried to reach out to experts outside his staff to figure out what to do. On May 30, 1979, he hosted what he called a "strange private dinner" at the White House with opinion leaders "to assess the depth of despair, hopelessness, discouragement and what I as president should both know and do." In his diary, he characterized the dinner, which included professors David Bell and Christopher Lasch, the Reverend Jesse Jackson, and journalists Haynes Johnson and Charlie Peters, as "remarkably nonproductive."[10]

Carter added, "The whole session ended in confusion, but there was a general belief that I should be not so involved in details, be more inspirational, be frank about analyses of problems, assume the role of the American people as much as possible, emphasize the strength of our country and our ability to resolve problems if we work together." Years later, Carter wrote, "My administration was searching for a better understanding of how to address the disturbing public opinion poll results that Pat [Caddell] was finding. That evening's discussion did not provide much illumination."[11]

His concern that he was losing his connection to the American people deepened over time, fueled by a series of negative assessments and polls by Caddell. Carter blamed the country for many of his own shortcomings as a leader, and he felt that forces beyond his control were at work.

In July 1979, prompted by Caddell's gloomy poll-derived analysis of the nation's mood, he canceled both a vacation and what was billed as a major speech on the issue of energy and gasoline shortages that were crippling the nation. Instead, he closeted himself for ten days with senior advisers at the presidential retreat at Camp David. His goal during this "domestic summit" was far-reaching—to reassess his entire administration—and it seemed to get more profound with each passing day. "I feel I have lost control of the government and the leadership of the people," he told his advisers during the retreat.[12]

His re-evaluation didn't stop with government officials. "With his administration in disarray, his influence evaporating, and the course of the nation uncertain, he invited some 130 ministers, friends, intellectuals, reporters, business and labor leaders, civil rights activists, and government officials to critique his administration and recommend changes in it," notes sociologist Kenneth E. Morris. "He also made impromptu visits to 'ordinary' families in Pennsylvania and West Virginia—as he so often had during his 1976 campaign—in order to find out whether the citizens agreed with the experts. Through these and other means he hoped to understand the conundrum of American despair that seemed to be thwarting his every effort to confront the nation's huge but solvable problems and he also hoped to prepare a rhetorical response equal to the challenge of that despair."[13]

On July 15 "Carter discussed his retreat in a televised speech analyzing America's 'crisis of confidence' as reflected in Americans' search for individual meaning and loss of national purpose. He detailed the materialism, cynicism, pessimism, skepticism, apathy, alienation, and defeatism threatening America's social and political fabric. Carter's speech was searing, thought-provoking, and self-critical. It was also ill-advised and self-destructive. Americans did not want a president preaching a gospel of doubt and negativity."[14]

This speech turned out to be one of the most damaging moments of the Carter presidency. He seemed to be blaming the country for his own shortcomings as a leader. He said there was a "crisis of the American spirit" and that none of the country's immediate problems—including energy shortages, inflation, and recession—would be solved until Americans "faced the truth."[15]

"All the legislation in the world can't fix what's wrong with America," he declared. What was needed was a rebirth of "faith in each other, faith in our ability to govern ourselves, and faith in the future of this nation."

Far from rebirth, what he got was a loss of faith in his leadership.

*   *   *

ON NOVEMBER 4, 1979, he spent several hours on the phone "talking to political leaders around the nation" to assess his standing in view of the looming challenge for the Democratic nomination from Senator Ted Kennedy of Massachusetts.[16]

It was early that morning that he learned that Iranian students had taken over the U.S. Embassy in Tehran and captured about 60 Americans—all with the approval of the Tehran government. This proved to be the worst crisis of Carter's final year in office. The Iranian radicals held the Americans captive for 444 days. This reinforced Carter's weakness. He did himself no favors by refusing to conduct many of his normal activities, such as traveling frequently around the country, until the hostages were freed. This made him, literally, a prisoner of the White House, by his own choosing. He made matters worse by ordering a military rescue mission that failed. Within two months of the start of the hostage crisis, the Soviet Union invaded Afghanistan, making Carter look even more inept and powerless.[17]

That same night in November, a Sunday, he watched a CBS special about Ted Kennedy, showing how closely he was following news of the campaign and his challenger. Carter wrote in his diary that he thought the CBS interview with Kennedy "was devastating to him. It showed him not able to answer a simple question about what he would do if elected or why he should be president."[18]

Carter kept reading the news, even though he was often annoyed by how he was treated (a common feeling among presidents over the years). In an August 17, 1980, entry in his diary, Carter wrote from Camp David, "Fished again until about 3:00. In reading the Sunday *Washington Post,* I couldn't believe the obvious hatred and vituperation leveled against me. It was as though I was a combination of Adolf Hitler and Goofy. I was incompetent and untrustworthy. They ignored the fact that we had beaten Kennedy, won the rules fight, had the nomination, prevailed well on the platform, and that Kennedy had endorsed. Really unbelievable."[19]

*   *   *

FOR CARTER, everything seemed to come back to Caddell, who had emerged as Carter's designated thinker, in-house philosopher, and interpreter of social trends, as well as the White House pollster, and who was sending the president a stream of troubling memos. On July 4, 1979, Carter read an analysis from Caddell, which the president wrote in his diary was "one of the most brilliant analyses of sociological and political interrelationships I have ever seen. The more I read it along with Rosalynn, the more I became excited. I think we two are the only ones that are reasonably sold on his premises. It will take a lot of courage."[20]

This analysis became the basis for Carter's conclusion that Americans had descended into a malaise and he needed to shake them out of it, illustrating how extensively a pollster could influence a president. (See Chapter Eleven.) It led to Carter's "malaise speech" making those points on July 15, 1979.[21]

Despite low job approval, Carter saw hope. On January 1, 1980, the first day of the election year, Carter was pleased that he was outdistancing Kennedy in voter preference. "A new public opinion poll showed we were leading Kennedy 58–38," he crowed in the first entry of his diary.[22]

On January 3, he gloated that CBS and the *Chicago Sun-Times* reported that a poll in the key state of Illinois had him with 69 per cent of the Democratic vote, and Kennedy with 18. "It's difficult for us to maintain the posture of an underdog!" Carter wrote happily.[23]

On January 9, he met with "about forty-five of the top-ranked political advisers in our country," including W. Averell Harriman, George Ball, and James Schlesinger, and wrote in his diary that they "were highly supportive of our action in Iran and Afghanistan and thought we should, if anything, be even more forceful. Ham [Hamilton Jordan, a key Carter adviser] reported a good situation in Iowa, although Kennedy's focusing his nationwide effort there, whereas we have strong programs going in Maine, New Hampshire, Florida, Alabama, Illinois, et cetera."[24]

In the end, Carter overwhelmingly defeated Kennedy for the Democratic nomination.

* * *

RONALD REAGAN was another story. Carter and his advisers, along with many Democratic strategists, thought Reagan as the Republican nominee would be a relatively weak candidate in the general election because he seemed too conservative and unfamiliar with many policy details.

But in an August 1980 memo designed to prepare Carter for the campaign against Reagan that fall, Caddell told Carter, "You suffer because you are held to have no vision." Caddell argued that "the greatest argument against you is the idea that the next four years will be like the last four," and he urged Carter to come up with an agenda for "where you would take the country"—and offered that these moves would enable Carter to win in a landslide.[25]

As the days wore on, and basing his assessments largely on Caddell's polls, Carter became more upbeat in late summer, with less than three months until election day. On August 24 the polls were the centerpiece of a political meeting of Carter and his inner circle. Carter was at this time six points behind Reagan in internal polling, and Carter wrote in his diary that he was pleased that he seemed to be closing the gap. "The [Democratic National] convention and my speech had a tremendous impact on the American people and their opinion. Every issue I emphasized had a dramatic change in voter reaction.... The campaign looks a lot better than it seemed to be prior to the convention. My main problem is still the opinion of the American people that I am not a strong leader and have inadequate vision for the future."[26]

The lone debate with Reagan, held on October 28, a week before the election, was pivotal, but Carter didn't realize how poorly he had done until later. "In the debate itself it was hard to judge the general demeanor that was projected to the viewers," Carter wrote. "Reagan was 'Aw, shucks' ... this and that.... 'I'm a grandfather, and I would never get this nation in a war' ... and 'I love peace....' He had his memorized tapes. He pushes a button, and they come out. He apparently made a better impression on the TV audience than I did, but I made all our points to the constituency groups—which we believe will become preeminent in the public's mind as they approach the point a week from now of actually going to the polls. Both sides felt good after the debate. We'll see whose basic strategy is best when the returns come in next Tuesday."[27]

Carter lost ground in the polls after the debate, but the race remained tight, according to Caddell's polls. In the final days before the balloting, there was a huge shift to the challenger. "Our people felt good," Carter wrote. "But Pat was getting some very disturbing poll results, showing a massive slippage as people realized the hostages [in Iran] were not coming home. The anniversary date of them having been captured absolutely filled the news media. *Time* and *Newsweek, U.S. News,* all had front-cover stories on the hostages. By Monday, only a tiny portion—19 per cent—thought the hostages were going to be coming home anytime soon. Almost all the undecideds moved to Reagan. Strangely enough, my favorable [ratings] went up—both the way I handled the Iran situation and the percentage that thought it was used for political purposes. There was a general sense of rejection of incumbents."[28] Reagan's landslide win was a colossal rejection of Carter's leadership.

* * *

CARTER was a rarity—a president who took great pains not only to understand public opinion in every way possible, but to live a life in the White House that kept him close to regular Americans. It wasn't a matter of publicity stunts. He was seriously trying to show his "everyman" qualities when he ended some of the more egregious perks of office, such as widespread limousine service, or when he carried his own bags aboard *Air Force One.* Carter was very serious about ending many of the trappings of elitism that he found when he took over. The problem was that he stubbornly kept to his goals and his initiatives long after it became clear that the country didn't agree with him and never would.

CHAPTER FOUR
GEORGE H.W. BUSH

MISSING THE OBVIOUS

George H.W. Bush impressed many as a man of decency and generosity. But he also was an American aristocrat who didn't understand the depth of the economic problems that regular Americans were going through while he was in office.

Although the effort often failed, he did try to get a clear picture of what was going on around him. Bush, who had been vice president for eight years, knew that many times White House advisers would hold back in expressing their opinions until the president gave his own views; they wanted to avoid disagreeing with their boss. So Bush often withheld his views at staff meetings. "He wanted to get a wide range of opinions so he rarely said what he was thinking," says Roman Popadiuk, a former spokesman for the National Security Council during the Bush era (and later U.S. ambassador to Ukraine). "He wanted points of view that were unfiltered and he didn't want people to just fall into line."[1]

Popadiuk says it was a "bum rap," though widely held at the time, that Bush was disengaged and didn't seek outside advice. Unknown to most Americans, Bush talked regularly to many friends outside the White House, including members of Congress past and present, including former Representative Thomas "Lud" Ashley of Ohio, and commentator and former Bush adviser Vic Gold. Bush also relied on Lee Atwater, his chief political adviser and chairman of the Republican National Committee, for advice and updates on what was going on outside the Washington Beltway.

Atwater's illness and untimely death at age 40 from a brain tumor in March 1991 deprived Bush of this important lifeline to everyday Americans.

But First Lady Barbara Bush, speaking of both her husband and son, told me, "My two Georges have more friends than you can imagine."[2] They often entertained and talked politics and policy not only at the White House but at the presidential retreat at Camp David in Maryland's Catoctin Mountains, and at the Bush family's seaside estate in Kennebunkport, Maine. In addition, the children of George and Barbara were adults and "out in the world," Mrs. Bush said, and this gave their father another line to life outside the White House.

Bush sought the advice of a wide range of experts on many issues, especially in foreign policy, and he was particularly interested in the politics of the Soviet Union, China, and the Middle East. Sometimes he would gather these experts at Camp David, and sometimes he consulted with them on the phone.[3]

*   *   *

THE QUICK and overwhelming U.S.-led victory in the Persian Gulf War against Iraq in early 1991 made Bush overconfident about his re-election prospects in 1992. "The stunning victory had come more quickly than anyone expected," write historians Peter and Rochelle Schweizer. "On March 6, George spoke before a joint session of Congress. It was the high point of his political career. His approval ratings put his popularity at 90 per cent. One poll of white males in the South gave him an approval rating of 100 per cent. George W. Bush, his eldest son, believed that things looked fine for 1992. 'Do you think the American people are going to turn to a Democrat now?' he asked the media."[4]

But Americans were losing faith in Bush as an economic steward. "Even with the Gulf War victory, the economy was in recession," the Schweizers point out. "And with attacks coming from three directions [conservative challenger Pat Buchanan, independent Ross Perot, and Democrat Bill Clinton], it was no surprise that George's poll ratings were way down. The campaign tried everything. They even brought in Professor Robert Wellstein of the University of Michigan, an expert in setting up statistical models, to determine how people would respond to different messages. He had been doing it for years for the automobile industry, telling Detroit what kind of cars people might buy. If it worked for General Motors, why not try it on voters?"[5]

Bush couldn't find a message that worked when tested with voters. Yet neither he nor his senior advisers could believe that he would actually lose, a fundamental misreading of the recession-battered electorate. This blind spot was acknowledged by the president's sister, Nancy Bush Ellis, who said after the election, "He never thought that the American people would elect someone like Bill Clinton," with his lack of national and international experience and his character flaws.[6]

But Americans came to believe that their president didn't understand their problems, that he was a good foreign-policy president but lacked a domestic agenda that would strengthen the economy and improve their lives. His out-of-touch image was reinforced when Bush visited the National Grocers Association in Orlando, Florida, and was shown a grocery-scanner display arranged by the National Cash Register Company (NCR).

"This is the scanner, the new scanner?" Bush asked.

Bob Graham, the NCR official who escorted Bush, replied, "Of course, it looks like the typical scanner you'd see in the grocery store. But there's one big difference." Graham gave Bush a card torn into pieces but the scanner could still read the bar code.

Bush, like any consumer, was impressed. "Isn't that something," he exclaimed, and pronounced the technology "amazing."

But the White House reporter on the scene saw things differently. In his pool report to the rest of the press corps, which couldn't attend because of space limitations, the reporter made it seem that any grocery scanner was news to the president. Based on this report, he appeared to be hopelessly out of touch with a basic reality of middle-class life. The pool report was used as the basis of a *New York Times* story headlined "Bush Encounters the Supermarket, Amazed."

Bush was angry, and he wrote a letter complaining to Arthur Ochs Sulzberger, chairman of the board at the *Times*, that the story was distorted. Sulzberger admitted in a letter, "There was no question that Andrew Rosenthal's article on the supermarket electronic checkout system was 'just a teeny-weeny bit naughty.' Little did any of us expect that the story would be picked up by others, including some not too subtle political cartoonists." But the *Times* declined to run a correction or clarification.[7]

Bush had a legitimate cause for complaint, but his image as an out-of-touch rich man couldn't be explained away by one embarrassing story. Bush never would acknowledge that he even had a problem seeming out of touch, and he didn't do much to counteract it.

* * *

INSIDE THE WHITE HOUSE, some Bush aides did recognize that he was too removed and did their best to correct the situation. One was chief speechwriter and communications adviser Tony Snow, who later became the White House press secretary under George W. Bush. Snow knew that his boss had a problem understanding key elements of American society, especially the lives of African Americans and their relationship to the police.

Snow was one of the few advisers who tried to break out of the happy-talk mentality within the West Wing that gave Bush too much positive spin on what was going on. Some of Snow's internal memos were startlingly blunt and contrarian. If Bush had taken them to heart, he might have minimized his isolation.

In an April 5, 1992, memo to six other senior staffers, including chief of staff Sam Skinner, communications director David Demarest, and chief campaign strategist Robert Teeter, Snow offered a plan for dealing with Bush's upcoming trip to California that week. The president was going to meet with state and local officials and inspect the damage caused by a race riot in Los Angeles earlier that spring. Snow wrote,

> Here's the key: We must get the President to talk from the heart. We must draw links between the policies and the things George Bush loves most: family, friends and country. So far, we have put him before audiences and asked him to read lists: Five Fundamentals; Six National Education Goals; Seven Basic Reforms in the State of the Union; Four Tracks of America 2000—and so on. We sound like a bunch of Gringo Maoists. Worse, we have precious little to show for these things. Most of our State of the Union initiatives remain moribund. We haven't followed up on our March 20 rescissions. We look like people searching for phrases, and not for solutions—and that won't do.
>
> If we don't put the President's heart and soul into these things, he will look like a bemused marionette.... In crass political terms, we must understand that we will squander a great opportunity if we confine our comments to law and order or to safe, traditional Republican issues. The American people don't trust Bill Clinton and they want George Bush to lead. He should do so by relying on his incredible personal decency and his fierce commitment to doing what is right. His personal virtues should serve as the springboard for what should amount to a revolution in domestic politics.[8]

On another occasion, also in April 1992, Snow conducted his own informal survey of police officers and what he called "average" residents of Los Angeles after the rioting there that followed the acquittal of police officers who beat a black motorist named Rodney King.

In an unusually blunt memo to President Bush dated June 1, 1992, and entitled "Los Angeles," Snow wrote, "The cops are hopping mad at you, although for reasons that have more to do with their treatment by L.A. politicians and media than by anything we have done. They took our original comments about the King verdict personally, and read a snub into the Challenger Boys and Girls Club event (police and military forces) during the first trip when they thought you deliberately refused to shake the hand of a police representative. When pressed, they admit that they don't really believe that you would snub them, even for a minute. They just feel that they have been hung out to dry and they're quick to find insults in any small gesture, oversight or piece of false gossip."[9]

Snow seemed to grasp public opinion about his boss more than most of the president's other advisers, and he tried to sound the alarm. Looking ahead, Snow said Bush's acceptance speech at the Republican nominating convention in late August should be bold. "When the President steps off the stage in Houston, every listener should be able to answer the question: If we re-elect George Bush, what will our lives be like four years from now? If they cannot answer that question, we're in deep trouble.... The President must tackle the key personal claims against him: That he broke his word with the budget agreement; that he lacks any real convictions; and that he really wants to manage the status quo, rather than to lead America toward a defined destiny."[10]

Snow wrote grandly that "people don't know George Bush, and that bugs them. Frankly, they have no desire to know the 'inner' George Bush, and they don't want the encounter-group goopiness we get from Al Gore and to a lesser extent, Bill Clinton. They want a mensch, driven by defining passions and principles; determined to achieve clear and worthy goals. They also want someone who combines the humility of Mother Teresa and the daring of Sergeant York. They want, in other words, George Bush."[11]

But most of Snow's advice was ignored, as the president and his more senior advisers didn't think he was in as much political trouble as Snow did.

* * *

OTHER INTERNAL memos showed how closely President Bush and his senior advisers were keeping track of opinion polls, but they were interpreting them too optimistically. A February 20, 1991, memo from pollster Fred Steeper to Ed Rogers, a top aide to White House Chief of

Staff John Sununu, was entitled "Highlights of RNC and Public Poll Results." It concerned public perceptions of the war in Iraq, which was then in a bombing phase. Steeper wrote that 49 per cent of Americans favored "continuing the war to remove Hussein from power even if he agreed to withdraw from Kuwait. This attitude is especially found among our voters. The public polls over the last few days have also shown that the public places a high importance on [Iraqi ruler Saddam] Hussein's removal. However, our additional questioning has found there would not necessarily be a backlash if Hussein remained in power." This was an important distinction, and in the end President Bush decided that it was enough for U.S. and allied forces to push Iraq out of Kuwait rather than invade Iraq with ground troops to drive Hussein out of office.[12]

"The public does believe that the U.S. is carrying more than its fair share of the financial costs of the war," Steeper wrote. "This could be a problem for the Administration in the aftermath of the War.... Their perceptions of the U.S. military's performance is very positive. They believe they are receiving enough information about the war and that the restrictions on the media are justified. The public thinks the military is doing a very good job avoiding civilian casualties and that military targets should be hit even if there are civilians located there. The public believes that the country is largely united behind the war. The anti-war protestors have not created a sense of national strife. The public does not expect a quick end to the war."[13]

*   *   *

BUSH ALSO showed a personal interest in polls by political strategist and veteran survey researcher Robert Teeter. Bush aides say he didn't use Teeter's surveys to determine his policies, but instead to decide how to best explain them to get maximum support. A former adviser told me, "He saw polls as what happened in the past and not what's happening at the moment. And he felt the polls couldn't tell you what was going to happen."

But that wasn't the full story. Polls were important to Bush, and he and his senior aides used them extensively. Teeter, a calm and scrupulously polite Midwesterner, was not flashy or overbearing, but was smart and perseverant, as was Bush, and the president trusted him. In 1990, looking ahead to the 1992 re-election campaign, Teeter defined Bush's constituency as "the expected Republican coalition: putting together large majorities of Northern white Protestants and Southern whites with a smaller majority of Catholics and over 40 per cent of union families. Blacks, Jews, and Hispanics went overwhelmingly Democratic [in 1988]."[14]

Political scientist Diane J. Heith reports, "The Bush White House took identifying information using the poll apparatus to an entirely new level.... The Bush administration devoted 54 per cent of its poll apparatus to informational activities, more than twice the 21 per cent average by the other four administrations [prior to it—those of Nixon, Ford, Carter, and Reagan]. The bulk of the exchanged public opinion information stemmed from memos beginning with 'FYI.' These information memos did cover Bush agenda items such as education, the environment, and the budget. However, the variety of public opinion referenced ranged across some topics few would have imagined residing in the White House archives." One memo from Environmental Protect Agency administrator William Reilly in August 1991 identified things that Americans thought were "in." Reilly said 85 per cent of Americans felt that environmentalism was "in," prompting Bush to scrawl the comment "Good." Eighty-three per cent listed "safe sex" as "in" and Bush said, "For it." The animated TV show *The Simpsons* was listed as "in" by 74 per cent and Bush said, "Don't care." Also "in" were "short skirts for women" (72 per cent) and Bush wrote, "For it," and "having children" (66 per cent) and Bush wrote, "Too late."[15]

In June 1990, White House aide Ed Rogers sent his boss, Chief of Staff John Sununu, detailed polling information about the political climate. One of the findings, Rogers said, was "58% believe Congress has the responsibility to make the first concrete proposal to reduce the deficit. 37% believe the President has this responsibility. By 69% to 24% the public prefers that Congress and the President reach a deficit reduction plan that increases taxes and cuts spending vs. reaching no agreement at all."[16]

There's no doubt that it was wise for Bush's inner circle to know these findings. The problem was that the research didn't go far enough. Bush and his advisers didn't realize how deeply a segment of the electorate—Republican conservatives—would be angry and upset if Bush did what the more generalized polling seemed to suggest. When he did agree to a congressional plan to raise taxes, he was vehemently attacked for it, and many conservatives pointed out he had broken his 1988 campaign pledge not to raise rates.

The acute sensitivity of the pollsters to issues that could hurt Bush was clear in an August 31, 1991, memo to Teeter from his deputy Fred Steeper entitled "The Spotted Owl Issue." Steeper wrote, "The spotted owl issue in Washington and Oregon gives the President an excellent opportunity to carry these two states in 1992." Timber interests were fighting environmentalists over protection of the birds, and most voters in those states, by a two-to-one margin, backed the timber industry on the grounds that protecting the owls within their "entire range" would destroy too many jobs in the timber industry. Steeper put the choice starkly: "If the President is perceived as stepping in to save timber jobs, he could put together a coalition of the traditional Republicans with non-Republican blue collar voters which would carry these two states. If he allows the U.S. Fish and Wildlife proposal to protect an additional 12 million acres to stand or to be modified only a little he can kiss Washington and Oregon good-bye."[17]

The Fish and Wildlife Service sided with timber interests over environmentalists, but a federal judge blocked the government's plan to allow more timber sales in the owl's habitat. Even though Bush portrayed himself as taking the side of workers over owls, as Steeper advised, he still lost Washington and Oregon to Democratic challenger Bill Clinton.

* * *

NEARLY A YEAR LATER, with Bush clearly in trouble in the polls because of the sour economy, a few administration officials saw the looming problem for Bush's re-election. But their bosses, and Bush, didn't agree that it needed dramatic and urgent attention. With Clinton showing signs of national strength, Bill Kristol, the chief of staff for Vice President Dan Quayle, tried to alert his superiors to the gathering political storm. In a memo on July 22, 1992, Kristol wrote to Chief of Staff Sam Skinner, Teeter, and three other top aides,

> After reflecting on yesterday's legislative strategy meeting I can't help but be struck by the air of unreality that pervaded it. We're not (apparently) going to aggressively push our economic growth agenda in the Senate because 1) it won't pass and 2) we're scared of the "fairness" issue. But we are at the same time going to complain to the country that Congress has failed to pass our growth agenda, thereby getting the best of the PR war on the economy without the danger of a real legislative fight.
>
> This strikes me as both cynical and fanciful. The American people won't be impressed by talk about our growth agenda when it's not backed up by fighting for it. As for the "fairness" issue, is fairness the reason we're down almost 30 points? I suspect the poor economic record of the last three years, and our perceived passivity and failure of leadership, have far more to do

with our problems. Aren't we now missing a huge chance for the President to show boldness and conviction and leadership on the key issue of the election?

But our discussion proceeded as if we were 20 points ahead and the economy were doing fine. We're not, and it isn't, and conflict avoidance doesn't strike me as the way to go.[18]

No matter how much he tried to stay in touch, Bush failed to see the political freight train bearing down on him in the form of public opposition to his economic policies in 1991 and 1992. When conservative insurgent Patrick Buchanan got 48 per cent of the vote in the New Hampshire primary in February 1992, to Bush's 52 per cent, Bush was stunned. And when the news media made that close margin seem like a defeat, Bush was nonplussed. "Since when is 52 per cent losing?" he asked an aide. Several of Bush's advisers told me he had a "tin ear" for public opinion, especially in his final year in office, when he was running for re-election. He simply could not believe that Democratic nominee Bill Clinton would defeat him. Clinton, in Bush's mind, was little more than a former draft dodger during the Vietnam War who had no foreign policy experience and couldn't compare to the incumbent who had won the Persian Gulf War against Saddam Hussein's Iraq and who had presided over a smooth transition to the end of the Cold War with the Soviet Union.

"Bush thought the war would carry him to re-election," says Republican pollster Frank Luntz, who was doing polling for congressional Republicans at the time.[19] He also thought a recession that hit during Bush's single term was not as serious as it really was. Bush and his advisers spent most of the 1992 campaign ignorant of the hostility swirling around them. "They didn't engage with working people," Luntz recalled. "They were completely unaware of the anger."

The nation was tuning out its past national-security concerns and was single-mindedly focused on the troubled economy. When Clinton won handily in November 1992, Bush was shocked. It showed how out of touch he had become.

*   *   *

BUSH was one of the most qualified people ever to serve as president, as a former businessman, congressman from Texas, director of central intelligence, chairman of the Republican National Committee, U.S. envoy to China, and vice president for eight years. But he was a man of privilege who lacked an intuitive sense of how most of America lived or what most people wanted from the president in terms of improving the economy and empathizing with them during a recession. Bush was also locked in the White House bubble and couldn't quite believe that an upstart like Bill Clinton could topple him. He was, of course, wrong about that.

II

TWO DEFIANT PRINCES

CHAPTER FIVE
JOHN F. KENNEDY AND GEORGE W. BUSH

STRANGE BEDFELLOWS

Two presidents stand out as men who not only declared their independence from public-opinion polls but flaunted their disdain—the unlikely duo of John F. Kennedy and George W. Bush. Each was the product of a privileged background, but the similarity ended there. Kennedy was urbane, articulate, and glamorous. Bush was rough-hewn, often inarticulate, and down-home. Kennedy ran a successful presidency because he had a good intuitive sense of what the public would accept, and Bush's presidency failed in many ways because he lacked that sense.

* * *

KENNEDY WAS a transition figure when it came to keeping in touch. He started out as another rich striver whose father financed a big part of his presidential campaign. But he understood the country's desire for generational change, and he capitalized on that spirit by billing himself as the leader of a new, youth-oriented Camelot to succeed the stolid and unexciting Dwight Eisenhower.

Still, Kennedy won by only a razor-thin margin over Richard Nixon in 1960, and he started out underestimating the profound changes that the country was going through, especially on civil rights. He had known very few African Americans in his life, and it was only in 1963 that he began to side with the civil-rights movement in an intense way, prodded by his admiration for the protesters' physical courage that he saw in news coverage of their demonstrations and arrests.

"Kennedy would welcome debate about his presidency," writes political scientist Thomas E. Cronin. "He liked spirited discussion about leaders and their use of power, and he often celebrated poets and artists who were skeptical about the use of power. Only the artist and writer can, from a disinterested perspective, determine whether we use power or power uses us, he once said, sounding much like Alexander Solzhenitsyn."[1]

While a senator from Massachusetts, Kennedy wrote *Profiles in Courage,* in which he outlined his views on leadership and the extent to which politicians should follow the wishes of voters. He defended independent thinking rather than following the crowd:

> Those who would deny the obligation of the representative to be bound by every impulse of the electorate—regardless of the conclusions his own deliberations direct—do trust in the wisdom of the people. They have faith in their ultimate sense of justice, faith in their ability to honor courage and respect judgment, and faith that in the long run they will act unselfishly for the good of the nation. It is that kind of faith on which democracy is based, not simply the often frustrated hope that public opinion will at times under all circumstances promptly identify itself with the public interest.
>
> The voters selected us, in short, because they had confidence in our judgment and our ability to exercise that judgment from a position where we could determine what were their own best interests, as part of the nation's interests. This may mean that we must on occasion lead, inform, correct and sometimes even ignore constituent opinion if we are to exercise fully that judgment for which we were elected. But acting without selfish motive or private bias, those who follow the dictates of an intelligent conscience are not aristocrats, demagogues, eccentrics or callous politicians insensitive to the feelings of the public. They expect—and not without considerable trepidation—their constituents to be the final judges of the wisdom of their course; but they have faith that those constituents—today, tomorrow or even in another generation—will at least respect the principles that motivated their independent stand.[2]

Kennedy quoted with approval the comments of John C. Calhoun, who served in Congress from South Carolina and as vice president before the Civil War: "I never know what South Carolina thinks of a measure. I never consult her. I act to the best of my judgment and according to my conscience. If she approves, well and good. If she does not and wishes anyone to take my place, I am ready to vacate. We are even."[3]

"Kennedy enjoyed the kind of public-approval ratings that any other postwar president would envy," writes historian David G. Coleman. "They waxed and waned, but his average Gallup poll approval rating of 70 per cent measured across his whole presidency was historically high, almost 20 points above Ronald Reagan's and 25 points above that of the previous Democratic president, Harry Truman. When only first terms are considered, only Lyndon Johnson fared better in his abbreviated first term, with numbers swelled by Kennedy's assassination and before the Vietnam escalation that would drag his public approval ratings, and his presidency, down precipitously."[4]

Kennedy showed a savvy and skepticism about public opinion that eluded some of his successors. When the Cuban Missile Crisis pushed his approval ratings upward, Kennedy wouldn't make too much of it; he said such ratings were only a snapshot of public opinion, shaped by media coverage, while he was confident that the country's long-term assessment of him would be based on more solid and enduring assessments. "These things go up and down so fast," he told a reporter, arguing against giving too much credence to the fluctuations in the polls. He added, "I don't think the people are as mercurial out there as they are in Washington. . . . Impressions are longer lasting out there. In Washington there is a terrific change of temperature with each issue. That is all they do here. Out there, there are other things that are important."[5]

*   *   *

HE CAME into office in 1961 as a World War II hero who was the nation's first celebrity president, known more for his TV-cultivated image of excitement and sophistication than his policies or his achievements. He used TV and the print media to create magnificent myths and perceptions of his administration as a new Camelot; used photos, interviews, and stories about his wife and kids to portray himself as a devoted family man (despite his private adulteries); and associated with Hollywood types such as Frank Sinatra and Peter Lawford to make his White House seem fashionable and cool.

His initial months were precarious because of his own faulty judgment. He took the advice of the military and authorized a disastrous attempt by 1,400 Cuban exiles to invade their island homeland after they were trained, equipped, and directed by Americans. The resulting landing at the Bay of

Pigs on April 17, 1961, only a few weeks after Kennedy's inauguration, was an utter failure. To some, Kennedy looked immature, rash, and foolish. But he turned to his public-relations skills and his understanding that, at that moment in time, Americans wanted to rally around their commander in chief, and he actually scored a political victory at home.

He took responsibility for the debacle and apologized, telling a news conference, "There's an old saying that victory has a hundred fathers and defeat is an orphan. I am the responsible officer of this government." Polls indicated that public support for Kennedy soared to 82 per cent after the Bay of Pigs, and Kennedy remarked, "Jesus, it's just like Eisenhower. The worse I do, the more popular I get."[6] But Kennedy learned valuable lessons that he applied for the rest of his presidency—trust your instincts and don't rely too much on the "experts," whether they be generals or pollsters. He used these lessons to successfully manage the Cuban Missile Crisis in October 1962, in which he confronted the Soviets for placing their missiles in Cuba, imposed a blockade on the island, and forced the Kremlin to withdraw the missiles.

*　*　*

ONE OF KENNEDY'S prime traits was his adaptability. As president, Kennedy's staff periodically gave him a file of friends and associates around the country that he should call, and he tried to contact four or five people a day to keep in touch. He would ask, "What do you hear out there? How'm I doing?"[7]

Kennedy had other means to stay in touch. He was a voracious reader of the newspapers and magazines and he "never missed what any of them said about him or his administration," says political scientist M.L. Stein. "He also ranked high among presidents who became steamed up over criticism, sometimes personally berating newsmen for stories he didn't like. The chastised reporter might be on the White House's untouchable list for two or three weeks." He was particularly upset on a long-term basis with the Republican-leaning *New York Herald Tribune,* and he briefly cancelled the White House subscription to the paper in a fit of pique, but it was eventually restored.[8] Kennedy was so sensitive about his image that it's unclear whether he learned much from critical stories.

He also tried to stay in touch by talking with members of Congress and checking tabulations of White House mail to see what was generating the most correspondence and to assess the mood of Americans. He used meetings with citizens' groups to take the same soundings.[9]

The Reverend Martin Luther King, Jr. once said of Kennedy, "The basic thing about him—he had the ability to respond to creative pressure. I never wanted—and I told him this—to be in the position that I couldn't criticize him if I thought he was wrong and he said, 'It often helps me to be pushed.'" King added that Kennedy learned how important the civil-rights movement was. "He had the vision and the wisdom to see the problem in all of its rich dimensions. And he had the courage to do something about it. He grew until the day of his assassination. Historians will record that he vacillated like Lincoln but he lifted the cause far above the political level."[10]

Kennedy had learned about poverty during his campaign in 1960, and these lessons never left him. The Democratic primary in West Virginia was particularly illuminating as he competed with Senator Hubert Humphrey for the Democratic nomination. Presidential chronicler Theodore H. White wrote, "Humphrey, who had known hunger in boyhood, was the natural workingman's candidate—but Kennedy's shock at the suffering he saw in West Virginia was so fresh that it communicated itself with the emotion of original discovery. Kennedy, from boyhood to manhood, had never known hunger. Now, arriving in West Virginia from a brief rest in the sun in the luxury of Montego Bay, he could scarcely bring himself to believe that human beings were forced to eat and live on these cans of dry relief rations, which he fingered like artifacts of another civilization. 'Imagine,' he said to one of his assistants one night. 'Just imagine kids who never drink milk.' Of all the emotional experiences of his pre-convention campaign, Kennedy's exposure to the misery of the mining fields probably changed him most as a man; and as he gave tongue to his indignation, one could sense him winning friends."[11]

*   *   *

AFTER HE TOOK office in January 1961, Kennedy made use of polls more than any president before him, mostly to help determine how to effectively market his policies, not to formulate them. He followed the same pattern he had established in the campaign's nominating phase by sharing positive poll results from newspapers and other public sources such as Gallup with "those we hoped to sway," including reporters and members of Congress, according to Theodore C. Sorensen, one of his top aides.[12]

"Equally important, however, were the results of polls privately financed and conducted, polls which were primarily taken for the Senator's information though given to friendly politicians and columnists at his discretion. More than any previous candidate in history, Kennedy sought help from the science of opinion polling—not because he felt he must slavishly adhere to the whims of public opinion but because he sought modern tools of instruction about new and unfamiliar battlegrounds. Tens of dozens of private polls were commissioned at great expense to probe areas of weakness and strength, to evaluate opponents and issues, and to help decide on schedules and tactics. Showings of strength in a particular state were often shared with the leaders of that state. States with Presidential primaries were polled more than once before he would decide on his entry, usually many times once he entered."[13]

*   *   *

KENNEDY HAD HIRED Lou Harris as his chief presidential pollster after Sorensen met him in New York on December 19, 1958, exchanged memos with him, and guaranteed him at least $100,000 in fees.[14] Lou Harris was 38 when he started advising Kennedy's presidential campaign in 1959 and was described by a Kennedy intimate as "young, shrewd, vibrant, a man who found subtleties in statistics, a student of depth tides in American thinking."[15] As the owner of a successful market-research firm, he had gotten to know John F. Kennedy when he was Senator Kennedy, and Harris eventually played a crucial role as an adviser in both Kennedy's presidential campaign and presidency. Harris had first worked for Kennedy as a public-opinion analyst when JFK successfully sought re-election to the Senate from Massachusetts in 1958. Over time he had become so entranced with JFK that presidential chronicler Theodore H. White called him "a Kennedy zealot and a member of the inner circle."

Harris "was to poll [during 1960] more people across the country than had ever been done by any other political analyst in American history; upon his reports, upon his description of the profile of the country's thinking and prejudices as he found them, were to turn many of John F. Kennedy's major decisions," White reported.

His behind-the-scenes impact was described this way: "A Lou Harris survey early in the campaign had come up with the oddly interesting fact that while fewer than 30 per cent of American families now send their children to college or junior college, no less than 80 per cent hope in the future to send children to college. In the suburbs, early and late, Kennedy hammered at educational themes within the broader theme of We Must Move, and the 'young marrieds,' worried about their children, must have hearkened. In the suburbs of the top fourteen Northeastern metropolitan areas, Kennedy was able to increase the Democratic percentage in these naturally Republican girdles from the 38 per cent netted by Adlai Stevenson in 1956 to 49 per cent in 1960. On the East Coast, his gains in the Protestant suburbs of Baltimore and Buffalo were of the same order as his gains in the heavily Catholic suburbs of New York and Boston."[16]

Harris became such an important adviser that on election night in November 1960, he was at the communications control center at presidential brother Robert Kennedy's home across the lawn from JFK's home at the family compound at Hyannis Port, Massachusetts.

Harris was stationed in a data-analysis section on the second floor in what was usually a children's bedroom, decorated brightly in pink and white. The pollster spent the long night analyzing reports coming in from Kennedy operatives around the country and from four teletypes, set up in an adjacent bedroom, over which the wire services were sending their own election updates.[17]

From 4 p.m. onward, Harris had been growing more discouraged. Nixon was doing much better than the Kennedy brain trust had expected in many areas, including Kansas and other sections of the Midwestern farm belt. Using a slide rule, he saw that it was going to be a very close election.[18] It was, but Kennedy won.

Throughout his presidency, Kennedy relied on Harris for soundings on public opinion. One of Harris's contributions was to encourage Kennedy to bill himself as the tribune of a new generation. Kennedy, whose birthday was May 29, 1917, was the first president born in the 20th century, and he tried to use this generational distinction for all it was worth.[19]

Harris also conducted a secret poll early in the administration indicating that "the public is judging the President for his style, manner and approach rather than on the specifics he is proposing or acting upon." This encouraged the Kennedy White House to pay increasing attention to image. For example, to impress black voters, Kennedy invited prominent African Americans to the White House, including heavyweight boxing champion Floyd Patterson. Kennedy integrated the White House day-care facility by inviting a black aide's five-year old son to join his children Caroline and John as playmates. The resulting photos were widely used in the African American press.[20]

In the end, he made it more acceptable to be tolerant, and more unfashionable to be racist.[21]

*   *   *

BEYOND THIS, political scientist Robert M. Eisinger writes, "Candidate and President Kennedy employed polls as a means to assess citizens' attitudes about character, personality, religion, and image. Kennedy's secretly funded polls served as indispensable tools to learn about what would sway the electorate, especially when other candidates did not have the financial resources to conduct polls."[22]

Kennedy used polls to help him campaign and govern, but his skepticism also grew and he came to recognize their limits. Sorensen says he blamed his loss of a Wisconsin primary district in 1960 on a last-minute Harris poll that showed the district solid for Kennedy. Harris persuaded the candidate to spend more time in another part of Wisconsin where his chances seemed shakier. Kennedy and his aides took it as a learning experience on the limits of polling.[23]

He was also "disgusted with his own folly" in believing Harris polls prior to the Wisconsin vote, showing him ahead of Humphrey in West Virginia by a margin of 70 per cent to 30 per cent. This led him to enter the West Virginia primary. But after Wisconsin highlighted the issue of his Roman Catholicism, Harris found a 60-40 majority for Humphrey in 95 per cent Protestant West Virginia.[24] After a spell of hard campaigning, Kennedy ended up winning West Virginia by 61-39, so he felt Harris was partially vindicated.[25]

Overall, Kennedy used polls extensively, but he always preferred his own interpretation to the analysis of his pollster. Once, early in their relationship, Harris gave Kennedy a report on the latest survey research and began to tell him what they meant. Kennedy brought him up short. "Just give me the numbers," the future president said. "I'll figure out what they mean."[26]

Before entering the Maryland presidential primary in 1960, he relied on Harris surveys to shape his message for that particular state, which he also did elsewhere. His Maryland platform emphasized achieving "a world of peace and freedom in place of the fantastically dangerous and expensive arms race"; spurring economic growth; ensuring civil rights; spreading the American food surplus to feed the hungry at home and abroad; and promoting public education.[27]

He used Harris polls to test the potential popularity of vice presidential running mates. "Harris Polls showed [Texas senator Lyndon] Johnson and [Minnesota senator Hubert] Humphrey helping in some areas and hurting in others, while most other prospects made little difference," Sorensen writes.[28] Of course he ended up picking Johnson largely because of his potential to help Kennedy carry his home state of Texas and other parts of the South and because as vice president, Johnson was thought to have great potential to help Kennedy deal with Congress in passing his legislation.

Throughout the 1960 campaign, Harris showed no reluctance to offer strategic advice in addition to summarizing the polls. He repeatedly urged Kennedy to go on television to demonstrate his wit, intelligence, independence, and charm.[29]

Harris was also preoccupied with the issue of Kennedy's Roman Catholic religion, which was a concern for many Protestant voters. He tried to devise a way to measure what he called "degrees of bigotry" state by state, and at one point wrote a memo to campaign leaders of his concern about religious bigotry in Minnesota and Maine and in the South.[30] Harris urged Kennedy to "hit the religious issue on television," especially in Minnesota, and that "in Maine, the Senator must bluntly and directly once again state his unequivocal belief in the complete separation of church and state."

* * *

DURING HIS BRIEF PRESIDENCY, cut short by his assassination, Kennedy used Harris polls to formulate his strategy on many issues. In 1961, Harris polls in Florida, West Virginia, and Illinois found that Kennedy's plans for trade expansion fell short of majority approval because voters wanted their home states' products protected.[31] Kennedy won approval of his trade legislation by emphasizing that trade was "no longer a matter of local economic interest but of high national policy" and would enable the United States to "strike a bargain with the Common Market" and "strike a blow for freedom" against the Communists.[32]

In December 1961, near the end of Kennedy's first year in office, Harris polled on the political climate in the key swing state of Florida, including questions about whether Floridians favored a U.S. invasion of Cuba, whether trade with Cuba under dictator Fidel Castro should be cut off or continued, and voters' reactions to the influx of Cuban refugees. In January 1962, Harris polled West Virginians on a variety of policy initiatives, including whether citizens favored or opposed liquor by the drink.[33]

Harris sometimes piggy-backed questions for the Kennedy administration on polls designed for other clients, to save the Kennedy team money because others were then billed for most of the survey. His relations with Kennedy and his team were close, a key development in the history of presidential polling that gave Harris increased influence.

Looking ahead to JFK's re-election campaign in 1964, Harris wrote in an October 4, 1962, memo, apparently to Kennedy himself, "It is my belief that you are more in control of this election than ever before." In a December 12, 1962, memo, Harris urged Kennedy, "commit your administration to a three point reduction in the corporate tax over a five year period (from 52 to 49 per cent)."[34]

*   *   *

KENNEDY NAVIGATED the issue of civil rights—probably the most challenging of all the issues he faced domestically—by staying just ahead of public opinion, but not too far ahead. In fact, it was more his own intuition than polls that guided him. "Great leadership requires good judgment," historian Gil Troy observes. "Shrewd leaders know that if they are half-a-step ahead of their constituents, and are headed in the right direction, they will be perceived as geniuses; if they are three giant steps ahead they are scorned as fools. Moreover, success earns credibility and followers' indulgence, whereas failure is not forgiven."[35]

Kennedy was impressed not by polls but by the bravery of the black and white protesters who were being beaten, subjected to attacks by police dogs, and harassed with fire hoses in the South—images that were seared into his consciousness by news coverage. He was moving ahead of public opinion and beyond his own limited commitment to civil rights when he first became president.

During the integration crisis in the spring of 1963 at the University of Alabama, in which local authorities led by Governor George Wallace tried to block the admission of black students, Kennedy met with leaders from Americans for Democratic Action, a liberal group. He told them that he had seen that morning a photograph on the front page of the *New York Times* of a Birmingham police dog attacking a black protester, and it made him "sick."[36] However, he said he had little power under the Constitution to intervene.

But on June 11, the governor stepped away from the doorway of the university's registration building and ended his symbolic opposition after Deputy Attorney General Nicholas Katzenbach insisted that two black students be allowed to register. Katzenbach was backed by the newly federalized Alabama National Guard. This ended the immediate crisis.

But Kennedy decided that, given the national TV and newspaper coverage that the event has drawn, it was time to act. He went on the air at 8 p.m. that night, June 11, 1963, and delivered one of the most important speeches of his presidency. For the first time, he framed the civil-rights issue as a moral choice. Kennedy pledged to work with Congress to pass laws "to make a commitment it has not fully made in this century to the proposition that race has no place in American life or law."

He added, "We are confronted primarily with a moral issue. It is as old as the Scriptures and is as clear as the American Constitution. The heart of the question is whether all Americans are to be afforded equal rights and opportunities, whether we are going to treat our fellow Americans as we want to be treated."[37]

Later, he told Commerce Secretary Luther Hodges, "There comes a time when a man has to take a stand and history will record that he has to meet these rough situations and ultimately make a decision."[38]

Over two and a half years in the White House, Kennedy had come a long way. He had gone the distance on civil rights not because polls told him the time was right but because he sensed the nation was ready to be educated about the issue and it was the right thing to do. It was one of his best moments.

*　*　*

SHORTLY AFTER George W. Bush became president in January 2001, he took a stroll on the South Lawn with an aide one evening, with the White House illuminated gloriously in the background. Bush looked at the lovely scene but shook his head. "It's like living in a museum," he said. "You can't really go out."[39] He noted that the grounds were heavily guarded, and people were constantly peering through the wrought-iron fences hoping to catch a glimpse of the president or the first lady. Inside, armed guards were in nearly every corridor. Bush complained that a president can't go out for dinner or a movie or visit a hardware store without bringing along a cavalcade of Secret Service agents, military aides, reporters, and photographers.

Matthew Dowd, pollster and senior strategist for George W. Bush's winning campaigns in 2000 and 2004 called presidential isolation "a huge issue" because it's so difficult for presidents to get diverse opinions outside of their inner circles.[40] Dowd says presidents including Bush easily fall into a "confirmation" syndrome in which they only seek information from those who confirm their views or attitudes. President George W. Bush, for example, liked to read *The Wall Street Journal* and *The Dallas Morning News* from his home state because he felt they mostly agreed with what he was doing and saw the world as he did. He mostly got reinforcement from these news sources, not fresh information or insights into the views of those who disagreed with him.

*   *   *

IN 2000, Bush lost the popular vote by 500,000 votes nationwide to sitting vice president Al Gore, the Democratic nominee. But Bush won the electoral vote narrowly when a dispute erupted over Florida's count, and the Supreme Court voted 5-4 to award Florida to Bush, giving him the White House.

Bush turned to Karl Rove, a consultant who had run Bush's presidential campaign and his two successful gubernatorial campaigns in Texas, to take charge of his political operation at the White House as deputy chief of staff. Bush considered day-to-day monitoring of the polls beneath him. But Rove loved polls, and he became Bush's main conduit to public opinion.

As a policy-maker and what he called "the decider," Bush forged ahead aggressively even though many Americans suspected that he was moving too far, too fast on a number of fronts. One of his most consequential acts was to take aim at the terrorist group Al Qaeda, which was responsible for the terrorist attacks of September 11, 2001. He declared a global "war on terror" and escalated U.S. military operations in Afghanistan, considered a haven for the terrorists.[41]

His dismissal of public opinion was clear when Bush met with Italian prime minister Silvio Berlusconi in the Oval Office two days after his State of the Union address in January 2003. Bush said he hadn't made up his mind whether to invade Iraq at that point. But he added, "I have made up my mind that one way or another [Iraqi leader] Saddam Hussein will be disarmed." He brought up the idea of public opinion, which was running against an invasion. "This is going to change," he told Berlusconi. "You watch. Public opinion will change. We must lead our publics. We cannot follow our publics."[42]

He ordered the invasion of Iraq in March 2003. "Rarely in this age of poll-driven politics had an American leader defied so much of the conventional wisdom, dismissing so many experts so boldly and calmly," Troy writes. "Bush did not falter during the tense buildup to the war. He also did not adjust, learn, mollify, or compromise. Even Franklin Roosevelt in 1940 and 1941 was less bold than Bush was in 2003. Roosevelt eased America toward entering World War II through half-steps such as the Lend-Lease program, and only achieved clarity after Pearl Harbor, when the Japanese attacked. Americans were not prepared for the Bush doctrine of preemption, with its necessary ambiguities."[43]

*   *   *

BUSH'S ISOLATION caused particular problems while he was vacationing at his Texas ranch during the summer of 2005, when Hurricane Katrina hit. He wasn't paying attention to the news—he rarely did—and was relying on aides to update him on any important developments. But his staff wanted to fulfill his wish to get away from the burdens of office, so they tried to leave him alone. As a result, in the case of Katrina, the aides didn't immediately alert him to the growing disaster in New Orleans and along the Gulf Coast until it had reached catastrophic proportions. It was only when senior White House aide Dan Bartlett put a video together and showed Bush scenes from hurricane-ravaged communities that the disaster finally made an impression on the president. He belatedly cut his vacation a few days short and flew over the wreckage on his way back to Washington. The White House released a photo of him looking out an *Air Force One* window at the scene below, which reinforced the idea that he was too far removed from the human toll that Katrina had taken.

More attention paid to the news might have led to more understanding by Bush of what was going on, including public-opinion polls that showed Bush dropping in public esteem as he seemed more and more isolated. But Bush was adamant that he wasn't going to be controlled by the polls. "I believe great decisions are made with care, made with conviction, not made with polls," Bush had said at the 2000 Republican National Convention in his speech accepting the nomination. "I do not need to take your pulse before I know my own mind." But this attitude led to more isolation.

Another insight into Bush's desire to set himself apart as a leader came as he prepared to deliver a much-anticipated speech to a joint session of Congress on September 20, 2001, just days after the terrorist attacks of 9/11 in New York and Washington, D.C. At a meeting with senior adviser Karen Hughes and his speechwriters, it was suggested that Bush include in his speech a Franklin Roosevelt quote, "We defend and we build a way of life, not for America alone, but for all mankind." Bush cut off the discussion, "I don't want to quote anyone," he snapped. "I want to lead! I want to be the guy they quote!" And he said that he wouldn't close his speech on a note of introspection but would emphasize action. "This is what my presidency is about," he said.[44]

In the end, his speech contained two signature lines that summarized Bush's no-nonsense, unilateralist approach that had nothing to do with polls. "We will not tire, we will not falter, and we will not fail," he declared. He also said, "Whether we bring our enemies to justice or bring justice to our enemies, justice will be done."[45]

*　*　*

BUT BUSH'S ISOLATION was troubling to some in his orbit. Dowd cited as an example a meeting in May 2004 to discuss the upcoming re-election campaign. Among the dozen people attending were the president, First Lady Laura Bush, senior advisers Karl Rove, Karen Hughes, and Dan Bartlett, and political advisers Ken Mehlman and Ed Gillespie. Bush said he thought things were going well, that the administration was doing a good job, and that the country appreciated it. He expressed confidence that he would win re-election with a landslide margin like the one Ronald Reagan amassed in 1984.

Dowd was appalled. He knew from his polling that Bush wasn't nearly as popular as the president thought he was, and that he was headed for a very difficult campaign that he could easily lose. Dowd, who generally sported a boyish grin and seemed inexorably affable, looked shocked and he fell silent, and the president noticed the change. Bush asked why Dowd seemed to be in disagreement, and Dowd explained his concerns about how badly Bush was doing in public perceptions and how his job-approval rating with the voters was dangerously low. Bush turned to Rove, the chief campaign architect, and asked, "What is he talking about? Karl? Karl? You told me everything was fine."

Rove said Dowd was exaggerating the problem, and the discussion ended there. But Dowd told me that there was never another such campaign meeting. The inner circle led by Rove apparently decided that they needed to tighten their control over information and keep dissenters such as Dowd from expressing their views in front of the president.

Bush ended up narrowly winning re-election in 2004 against Democratic candidate John Kerry, a senator from Massachusetts who was savaged by the GOP for being an elitist and a liberal zealot. But it was a competitive race and showed that Dowd was correct about the extent of dissatisfaction with his boss.

Bush was "a conviction politician," Troy writes. "His critics find him far too imprisoned by these convictions, which they abhor. 'You may not agree with me, but you know where I stand,' Bush often said, defiantly. . . . Popular politics requires compromise; democracy needs a broad, inviting center with maximum public investment. Conviction politicians risk being imprisoned by ideology, handcuffed to the world they wish to see rather than adjusting to the world that is."

*   *   *

NOT THAT BUSH completely disregarded public opinion. But he did keep his knowledge of the polls, conveyed through Rove, under wraps.

Most of his polling was conducted by Jan van Lohuizen, a low-key practitioner from Washington who avoided publicity. Focus groups were run by Fred Steeper, a long-time Republican pollster from Michigan who also avoided the media, and the same analyst who had worked closely with Robert Teeter during the elder Bush's administration. Both of them funneled their findings through Rove. They also gave much of their data to Dowd, Bush's informal director of polling under the Republican National Committee until he broke with Bush in his second term over the Iraq War and left Bush's orbit.[46]

Beyond polling and focus groups, Bush tried to keep up with public opinion in different ways. "In President Bush's case," says Ed Gillespie, one of his senior White House advisers, "he had a lot of friends who were not in politics and who he would stay in touch with, by phone and by having them over [to the White House]."[47]

Bush, aware that many visitors to the White House were reluctant to speak candidly to the president or raise uncomfortable subjects, would try to loosen them up and make them feel at ease. He would joke with them, ask about their families, their hometowns, and their jobs, and tell anecdotes. Then he would often say, simply, "Just tell me what's on your mind."

Once, Bush was informed by a member of Congress that a bank in the legislator's home state had felt it necessary to hire more compliance officers to make sure the institution was complying with federal law than loan officers to actually make loans. At Bush's request, a White House staffer phoned the bank in question and learned that the story was true. This reinforced Bush's belief that federal regulations on banks should be trimmed.

Gillespie, the son of middle-class parents in New Jersey who saw his extended family frequently, took it upon himself to keep Bush informed about what his family members were saying about their lives and their assessments of the president. Gillespie said he did it because he concluded that every bit of information about everyday Americans would be useful to his boss. "You're in a bubble," he told me. "You have to be."

Overall, Bush had a weak second term, featuring increased hostility with congressional Democrats. Legislative and public opposition was growing to his attempt to partially privatize Social Security, which died in Congress; his administration's weak response to Hurricane Katrina in late August and early September 2005; and the wars in Iraq and Afghanistan. A meltdown of the economy in 2008 made Bush seem dangerously ineffectual. "Amid it all," Troy writes, "Bush remained insulated from bad news, dismissed critics, resisted change, and never admitted making mistakes. This 'conviction politician' appeared imprisoned by his rhetoric and earlier decisions."[48]

*   *   *

HOW TO EVALUATE THESE TWO DEFIANT PRINCES? Kennedy was a prisoner of his sheltered past for the first part of his presidency. He was a spoiled rich kid who was smart and self-indulgent and had showed little interest in regular Americans and their problems. But as president he matured and began to learn about the country. At the time of his assassination in November 1963, his empathy was clearer than ever. No one will know if a second term would have led to greatness or disappointment, but he seemed to be headed in the right direction

Bush was also a prisoner of his past, another child of privilege and the son of a famous father, a former president, who wanted to achieve great things on his own. But unlike Kennedy, Bush didn't learn humility or empathy. His second term led to overreaching in the Iraq and Afghanistan wars and a massive recession that turned many voters against him. Through it all, Bush said he was elected to make decisions and that's what he was going to do, based on his own judgment and not the polls or public opinion of the moment.

PRESIDENTS WHO STAYED IN TOUCH

Among those who overcame the isolation of the White House, at least to some degree, were Franklin D. Roosevelt, Ronald Reagan, Bill Clinton, and Barack Obama.

FDR relied on his wife Eleanor for much of his information about the state of the country and how his New Deal programs were working. Mrs. Roosevelt took very seriously her role as her husband's "eyes and ears." She penned voluminous notes during her many trips about the country and abroad, and briefed her husband exhaustively on her findings. Here she is pictured in 1935 wearing a lighted miner's cap before descending into the depths of a coal mine near Bellaire, Ohio. (AP Photo)

Harry Truman disdained public-opinion polls, but he reached out to regular folks as much as he could. In contrast to the urbane John F. Kennedy, Truman considered himself Everyman. His train trips, during which he addressed crowds large and small, helped him win the 1948 election. This photo shows him shaking hands with a boy during a whistlestop tour of Ohio. (AP Photo)

John F. Kennedy was, like Roosevelt, an American aristocrat, but also like Roosevelt, he tried to stay in touch with middle-class people and the poor. His visits to destitute families during his 1960 campaign seared him with the realities of poverty, which he never forgot. He gained a strong admiration for civil-rights demonstrators when he saw news coverage of their bravery while under attack. Here JFK meets with Dr. Martin Luther King, Jr. and fellow civil-rights leaders from the March on Washington. (AP Photo)

Ronald Reagan was derided by his critics for favoring the rich and big corporations in his policies, but he never forgot his roots in Middle America. A gifted communicator, especially on television (having been a TV and movie star before entering politics), Reagan was able to talk to the country in ways that connected him with everyday people. Here he is shown in both aspects: eating a hamburger with a supporter and shaking hands before addressing a crowd of 10,000 people. (Bettmann/Corbis/AP Images)

Bill Clinton was energized by talking to people from all walks of life, and he was a good listener. His pollsters gave him their assessments of public opinion on an endless stream of issues and events, including welfare reform, Social Security, and the Monica Lewinsky sex-and-lies scandal. Here Clinton is pictured in 1998 with Ohio senior citizens wearing T-shirts asking to "Save Social Security." (AP Photo/J. Scott Applewhite)

Barack Obama is perhaps more sensitive to the isolation of the White House than any of his predecessors, and is more eager than most to break out of what he calls "the bubble." His friends and family, especially his wife Michelle and daughters Malia and Sasha, serve as sounding boards. Because of his strong family ties, he has always been especially attuned to the needs of children, particularly in the wake of shooting tragedies in 2012. Here President Obama is pictured in the White House play-acting in response to a child dressed as Spider-Man, and posing with faculty and students at a school in Florida during the 2012 campaign. (Top: Rex Features via AP Images; Bottom: AP Photo/Pablo Martinez Monsivais)

PRESIDENTS WHO LOST TOUCH

Those who were too aloof or who didn't pay enough attention
to public opinion included Lyndon Johnson, Richard Nixon,
Jimmy Carter, George H.W. Bush, and George W. Bush.

Jimmy Carter often understood public opinion, even when it was running against him, but he overestimated his ability to change American attitudes and was excessively influenced by his pollster. He tried to end Nixon's "imperial presidency" in a number of ways, such as by carrying his own garment bags when traveling and spending occasional nights in the homes of everyday people. Here he is shown at a 1976 campaign stop in Philadelphia, where a child is tapping him on the back to try to get his attention. (Bettmann/Corbis/AP Images)

Richard Nixon promised to bring Americans together, but he turned out to be one of the most divisive presidents in history. He tried to maintain the veneer of Everyman, bowling at the White House and emphasizing his nonglamorous side, to appeal to what he called the "great silent majority." But Nixon let his hostility toward his adversaries get the best of him, and he ended up resigning in disgrace amid the Watergate scandal. (AP Photo)

Lyndon Johnson seemed in tune with America when he succeeded to the presidency after the assassination of John F. Kennedy in November 1963. He pledged to continue the Kennedy legacy, which is just what the country wanted. But Johnson lost touch with America after he won the 1964 election. He didn't understand the massive social changes underway, especially the deep and angry opposition to the Vietnam War. One of the most vivid images of his presidency is this 1968 photograph of him agonizing over a tape recording from his son-in-law who was fighting in Vietnam. (LBJ Library photo by Jack Kightlinger)

George H. W. Bush, a vice president with vast experience in foreign affairs, was considered the right man for the job when he was elected president. But during his single term, the country shifted its focus from foreign policy to domestic issues, mainly the economy. And by the time he ran for re-election, Bush was widely considered to be out of touch, caricatured as a wealthy man who didn't understand economic hardship and didn't even seem familiar with a supermarket scanner, as pictured here. (AP Photo/Barry Thumma)

George W. Bush came into office by virtue of a divisive and hotly contested election decided ultimately by the Supreme Court in Bush v. Gore 2000. *From that moment forward, he operated like the lone cowboy he was. In one of the most damaging photos of his tenure, Bush is shown here surveying the Hurricane Katrina disaster scene from the remove of* Air Force One. *(AP Photo/Susan Walsh)*

III

FIVE WHO STAYED CONNECTED

CHAPTER SIX
FRANKLIN D. ROOSEVELT

READING THE NATION'S PULSE WITH ELEANOR

In the modern era of mass communication, global politics, and immense presidential power, five chief executives made special efforts to stay in touch and largely succeeded—Franklin D. Roosevelt, Harry Truman, Ronald Reagan, Bill Clinton, and Barack Obama.

FDR had a special method. He relied on his wife Eleanor to conduct "listening tours" of the country and report back to him on what she learned. He encouraged her to "gather the grassroots knowledge he needed to understand the people he governed," writes historian Doris Kearns Goodwin.[1] Partly because she was so successful as his personal reporter, Roosevelt had an unparalleled grasp of the conditions and attitudes in the country, and he became one of America's most iconic and empathetic leaders.

As historian Conrad Black has written, "Remote and unrepresentative of the country though he was in his tastes and manner, he was an intuitive and tactical political genius and an electrifying political personality.... Roosevelt was a master of every aspect of American politics. He knew how to maneuver with the congressional leaders, how to mobilize public opinion, how to frame and time legislation, how to take care of the machine captains and war heelers. He had an uncanny intuition of where public opinion was and where and how fast it could be led."[2] Black observes that "his record of four consecutive presidential election victories, his seven consecutive congressional election victories, the huge crowds that always came out to see and cheer him throughout his long reign, attest incontrovertibly to this genius at operating every lever of the vast and intricate political machinery of the United States. His insight into common men was all the more remarkable because he was certainly not one of them, and never pretended for an instant that he was."[3]

In 1936, as he campaigned for re-election, he roamed widely, including visits to flooded areas of New England and drought-plagued regions of the Midwest.[4] But his limitations, due to his legs being paralyzed by polio, became very clear that year as he prepared to speak to 100,000 persons at Franklin Field in Philadelphia. "When the President moved to greet the eighty-four-year-old poet Edwin Markham, one of his leg braces buckled and the President was sent sprawling to the floor," according to one account. "Surrounded by his entourage, this was not visible to the crowds and he told his aides to 'clean me up.' He was quickly back on his feet with a refastened brace. Jimmy Roosevelt [his son] retrieved the speech text but had not completed putting the pages in order when his father was introduced (after completing the task of greeting Mr. Markham, who was visibly moved by the President's attention and his courage). The President, ever the unflappable master of the multi-task problem, arranged the pages himself as he warmed up the crowd, and he then delivered one of the greatest speeches of his life."[5]

The address may have been wonderful but the incident also showed that FDR did have serious limits in what he could do physically that only got worse as he aged and as the pressures of his job took their toll on his stamina and health.

*   *   *

IT WAS Eleanor who provided Franklin with the details, the overview, and the texture of life around the country.

From her husband's inauguration in 1933 until the U.S. entry into World War II in 1941, when her domestic schedule became somewhat curtailed, Eleanor traveled an average of 40,000 miles per year in the United States acting as what FDR called his "eyes and ears."[6] During her first seven years as first lady, Eleanor visited every state except South Dakota. "She could be found virtually anywhere at anytime: in impoverished Appalachia, a derelict urban slum, or a small farm town ravaged by Dust Bowl winds," writes historian Mark K. Updegrove. "A cartoon in the *New Yorker* showed two miners deep in a quarry looking toward its opening, as one exclaims, 'For gosh sakes, here comes Mrs. Roosevelt!' ... She became a powerful advocate for the poor and disenfranchised, and a champion of civil rights ... Here, though, Eleanor Roosevelt's 'spurring' of her husband did not amount to much, at least legislatively. No major New Deal initiative addressed the ongoing plight or the inferior treatment of blacks throughout the country, due in part to FDR's conscious decision not [to] rock the boat among Southern Democrats by pushing for civil rights measures."[7]

President Roosevelt wanted his wife to collect information from average people in as many walks of life as possible and tell him how their lives were going, what problems they had, what they wanted from their president and their government, and how his policies were affecting them.

This arrangement was not new for the Roosevelts. Unable to travel easily because of polio, Franklin had taught Eleanor how to inspect state institutions for the blind, the elderly, and the mentally ill during his first term as governor of New York.[8] Mrs. Roosevelt also visited prisons and reform schools. She would return and report back to her husband, and he would coach her on how to improve her techniques to get as much information as possible.

After her first inspection tour, which took her to an insane asylum, FDR took a look at a printed copy of a day's menu his wife brought him and asked whether she checked to see if the patients were actually getting the food listed, such as by looking into pots on the stove to see if the contents corresponded to the menu.[9] She said she had not checked. After a few such omissions and oversights, she got the point. "I put my best efforts after that into missing nothing and remembering everything," she said,[10] and over time she improved her investigative and observational skills. She made a habit to do the unexpected, to look into closets and behind doors.

"She saw many things the President could never see," said labor secretary Frances Perkins. "Much of what she learned and what she understood about the life of the people of this country rubbed off onto FDR. It could not have helped to do so because she had a poignant understanding.... Her mere reporting of the facts was full of a sensitive quality and could never be escaped.... Much of his seemingly intuitive understanding—about labor situations ... about girls who worked in sweatshops—came from his recollections of what she had told him."[11]

During the first summer of her husband's presidency, Eleanor visited Appalachia and found the conditions appalling. She wore a hard hat and miner's overalls and descended into a deep mine shaft to learn about mining operations and the difficult conditions experienced by workers. She noticed the ragged clothes on the wash lines, and talked to the residents in their backyards and shanties. At Scott's Run near Morgantown, West Virginia, Eleanor found a boy in a shack sadly hugging his pet rabbit. His sister had just told him it was the only thing left to eat.[12] After Eleanor reported her findings to the president, he immediately created a program to resettle as many Appalachian residents as possible in areas with better economies.

"The following year," Goodwin says, "Franklin had sent Eleanor to Puerto Rico to investigate reports that a great portion of the fancy embroidered linens that were coming to the United States from Puerto Rico were being made under terrible conditions. To the fury of the rich American colony in San Juan, Eleanor took reporters and photographers through muddy alleys and swamps to hundreds of foul-smelling hovels with no plumbing and no electricity, where women sat in the midst of filth embroidering cloth for minimal wages. Publicizing these findings, Eleanor called for American women to stop purchasing Puerto Rico's embroidered goods."[13]

Eleanor told a radio interviewer, "I realized that if I remained in the White House all the time I would lose touch with the rest of the world.... I might have had a less crowded life, but I would begin to think that my life in Washington was representative of the rest of the country and that is a dangerous point of view."[14]

She became famous because of her travels. When she visited migrant-labor camps in California's San Joaquin Valley, she saw some shacks built of boards, tar paper, and tin cans pounded flat as she was being driven through the area by car. She ordered the driver to stop, got out, and walked across a field toward some migrant workers. One of them wrinkled his face as he strained to see who was coming and he recognized the first lady immediately. "Oh, Mrs. Roosevelt, you've come to see us," he said matter-of-factly, so familiar was he with her trips to similar places.[15]

Over the years, a tradition developed. Eleanor would return from one of her trips and on her first night back in the White House, FDR would make sure to arrange for the two of them to sit alone at dinner and talk about her experiences and what she had absorbed about the state of the Union. These dinners became essential to both of them, partly because, since their relationship was strained, they were the main bond between husband and wife.[16]

*   *   *

ELEANOR LEARNED much from the letters she received from everyday people, and she publicly encouraged them to write her. In August 1933, she made this request in an article she penned for *Woman's Home Companion* under the headline "I Want You to Write to Me." Mrs. Roosevelt said, "Whatever happens to us in our lives, we find questions constantly recurring that we would gladly discuss with some friend. Yet it is hard to find just the friend we should like to talk to. Often it is easer to write to someone whom we do not expect ever to see."[17]

This caused a flood of mail, a pattern that continued for years. Mrs. Roosevelt received 300,000 pieces of mail in 1933; 90,000 in 1937; and 150,000 in 1940. She clearly had persuaded millions of Americans— through the many interviews and speeches she gave, the radio shows on which she appeared, and the trips she made—that she cared about them and wanted to know the details of their problems. Many believed that Mrs. Roosevelt could help by telling her husband, referring their cases to appropriate agencies of the federal government, or intervening herself.

Citizens' letters addressed many aspects of life at the time, reflecting the widespread desperation and anxiety caused by the Depression among unemployed workers, farmers who were losing their land through foreclosure, people who needed medical care, and others in dire straits. "I think I have been asked to do something about everything in the world except change the weather!" Mrs. Roosevelt wrote in 1940.[18]

She cited a vivid example. "A woman wrote and asked me to find a baby for her to adopt. Her second letter explained that if I found the baby, she would need a cow, and if she had the cow, she would need an electric icebox in which to keep the milk for the baby!"[19]

Many of the letter-writers were embarrassed by their situations and their need of help. "It is very humiliating for me to have to write you," wrote one woman who was down on her luck. A young mother with children wrote "*Please* Mrs. Roosevelt, I do not want charity, only a chance somehow we will manage but without charity." The mother sent Mrs. Roosevelt two rings, which she described as "my dearest possessions," to keep as security. "If you will consider buying the baby clothes, please keep them until I send you the money you spent."[20]

Eleanor was appalled by the stories she heard about discrimination against African Americans, especially black soldiers upon their return home from the war. In one letter, a black Army private encountered prejudice when he traveled to Washington, D.C., in January 1943. He said he requested a drink at a Peoples Drug Store and after initially being refused service at the counter, he was served his beverage in a paper cup while a white man next to him received his drink in a glass. The soldier added that he had four brothers in the military and said, "But, as to what they are fighting for God only knows. I'm going to feel fine, fighting in a Jim Crow Army, for a Jim Crow Government and when I might see a white boy dying on a battlefield, I hope to God I won't remember Peoples Drug Store on January 11." He attached the paper cup to his letter. [21]

Mrs. Roosevelt replied, "I can quite understand how what happened to you made you feel as bitterly as you do feel. There are many things of that kind which many of us in this country deeply regret. The only thing I can say to you is that under the Germans or the Japanese you would have very little freedom and you certainly would not have the freedom to write to me as you have. You are free to go on working as a people for the betterment of your people and you are gradually gathering behind you a larger and larger group of white people who are conscious of the wrongs and who are helping to correct them." [22]

Eleanor was moved to action by such letters. She also learned about national and world problems through her aides or the newspapers, and from female reporters that she got to know as first lady. She encouraged these women to convey to her their impressions of who and what they saw, in the United States and abroad, said one observer. What she got in return, the observer said, were valuable "exchanges from Lorena Hickok on politics and relief activities across the country in the 1930s, correspondence from Ruby Black describing economic conditions and politics of Puerto Rico, letters from Martha Gellhorn Hemingway on the Spanish Civil War and the plight of refugees, reports from Anna Louise Strong during and after her visits to Russia and China, and material from war correspondent Doris Fleeson concerning Mrs. Roosevelt's wartime trips to Australia and the Pacific." [23]

Mrs. Roosevelt once wrote, "My interest or sympathy or indignation is not aroused by an abstract cause but by the plight of a single person. Out of my response to an individual develops an awareness of a problem to the community, then to the country, and finally to the world. In each case my feeling of obligation to do something stemmed from one individual and then widened and became applied to a broader area." [24]

*   *   *

FOR HIS PART, President Roosevelt received thousands of letters, too, especially after each of his "fireside chats" in which he addressed the country on the radio. Many of the letters contained poignant words of praise for Roosevelt in his fight against polio, which had lasted for many years. Some of the letter-writers found a need to explain how they were faring in their own battles against the disease. They must have driven home for FDR the mettle of his fellow citizens and brought out what Eleanor called his sense of empathy. Eleanor once remarked that polio had made Franklin much more appreciative of character and perseverance, and deepened his admiration for people who shared those traits. Franklin appeared to have a special affinity for children with the disease, which becomes clear in a review of his correspondence.

In a handwritten letter dated November 27, 1937, William Neely of Fort Madison, Iowa, wrote,

> I am a boy 10 years old and I have been sick 4 months with Infantile Paralysis. I can't walk, I crawl. My Mother has to carry or lift me to put me on a chair, I am going to Iowa City Hospital in about 3 weeks. I gess [sic] I will be in the Hospital when Santa Claus comes. I sure hope that I can walk some day. I am writing this letter to you in hopes of receiving a personal letter from you for my keep sakes. Thanking you, I am. William Neely. P.S. I wish you a Merry Xmas.[25]

The president replied in a typewritten letter on December 8:

> My dear William: I have received your letter and am very sorry to hear of your illness. I do hope your stay in the hospital will be very helpful and that you will soon be well on the way to complete recovery. Best wishes to you.

In a letter scrawled in large, uneven letters, Jimmy Stone of Fillmore, New York, wrote on March 23, 1934,

> I am 6 years old. My birthday is Jan. 30, too. When I was little I had infantile paralysis. My right arm is in a brace. My left foot is better since my operation. I like to see your picture. I like to hear stories about you. Jimmy Stone.[26]

Roosevelt replied in a typed note on April 9:

> My dear James, I have received your letter telling me that you celebrated your birthday on the same day that I celebrated mine. I hope you had a perfectly grand time.
>
> I am sorry that you have been suffering from infantile paralysis and do hope that you will keep up your courage and that you will soon be much better.

President Roosevelt appeared to have been especially moved by a letter from the mother of a child stricken by polio. On November 2, 1933, Bertha C. Huse of Lowell, Massachusetts, wrote in a neat, clear hand,

> May I tell you what your high courage is doing for me?
>
> I am the mother of a little boy facing life on crutches and in two long braces and I need courage pretty badly sometimes.
>
> Every time I hear your voice on the radio and read about your attitudes toward physical handicaps—that they don't amount to a 'hill of beans'—I am strengthened and my courage is renewed.
>
> I pray for the kind of strength and courage you have—that I may help my son as he faces life. Now he is cheerful and happy—he is only eight—but when he says to me "Mummie, will I be a Scout and will I be able to play in the High School Band?" and talks about playing football in college my heart stops and I don't know what to say, and I've got to know what to say when the time comes. I've got to help him then.
>
> So I pray for courage and guidance to help him—and your life is, in a way, an answer to my prayers. It is a daily inspiration and source of help and strength.
>
> Sincerely, Bertha C. Huse[27]

On November 25, FDR replied from his retreat in Warm Springs, Georgia, where he took therapy in the thermal waters for his own paralysis:

> I am deeply touched by your letter of November second appealing to me for advice in your son's case. I realize that this is a mother's appeal for her child, and I do wish I could offer some helpful advice which would bring about a speedy recovery. But in cases of this kind, much depends upon the patient's attitude of mind and his willingness to follow instructions as to exercises. A strong will and a determination to win the fight are very helpful and I feel that with this attitude of mind, in connection with such exercises as his physician may prescribe, it is bound to produce results.
>
> With an expression of my deepest sympathy and best wishes for your boy's recovery, I am
>
> Very sincerely yours

* * *

AS WORLD WAR II advanced, President Roosevelt didn't have as much time for Eleanor and her domestic intelligence reports, which hurt her feelings, but she kept at it. She called her husband's attention to the need for a larger food allowance for unemployed mothers; more focus on preventing illiteracy; the need for better housing and more pensions for the elderly, and more attention to guaranteeing civil liberties.[28]

Harry Hopkins, a key FDR aide and friend who was in charge of a vast work-relief program, was a strong ally of Eleanor's in advocating more government help for those in need. Hopkins and Mrs. Roosevelt shared a deep conviction that the unemployed were worthy and decent people who had no jobs through no fault of their own and were fully deserving of government assistance.

They told Franklin how desperate people were, and how much folks needed help, serving as the most committed and sensitive opinion analysts possible. "Both Harry Hopkins and Mrs. Roosevelt were driven during the depression by a sense of urgency," said Works Progress Administration administrator Elizabeth Wickenden. "They never forgot there were these millions of people who had absolutely nothing, who had once held a steady job and had a sense of self-respect. From their wide travels across the country they kept in their minds a vivid picture of the lives of these people, and that image drove them to push the government to create as many jobs for as many people as it possibly could."[29]

Realizing how much American life was changing for women during World War II, Eleanor successfully advocated government funding for day-care centers and after-school programs for children while their mothers worked and their fathers were fighting the war. She successfully promoted Frances Perkins for secretary of labor, the first time a woman had held a Cabinet position.

Mrs. Roosevelt and Hopkins were weather vanes for Franklin on civil rights. Eleanor learned during her travels that African Americans were increasingly impatient, and many were angry, over the pervasive racial discrimination, segregation, and oppression. Gradually during the '30s, she became one of the strongest civil-rights advocates in the country and befriended many in the civil-rights movement, including educator Mary McLeod Bethune and activist Walter White.

In 1939, she resigned from the Daughters of the American Revolution when they prohibited American opera singer Marian Anderson from performing at Washington's Constitution Hall because she was black. Eleanor persuaded her husband and Interior Secretary Harold Ickes to let Anderson sing at the Lincoln Memorial instead.

Historian Goodwin writes, "More than anyone else in the White House, Eleanor was responsible, through her relentless pressure of War

Department officials, for the issuance of the two directives that forbade the designation of recreational areas by race and made government-owned and -operated buses available to every soldier, regardless of race. (In 1948, President Harry S. Truman would issue Executive Order 9981, lifting the final barrier for full equality when he ended segregation in the armed forces.)"[30] She eventually had many outside allies in her campaign to improve social conditions and promote equality, such as civil-rights and labor leaders, but inside the White House she was also influential even if many times her views did not prevail because FDR felt she was pushing too hard and trying to move too fast.

Amid a rash of racial disturbances across the country in 1943, including ugly incidents between white and black welders in Mobile, Alabama, and a vicious race riot in Detroit, Michigan, Eleanor's sense of urgency increased.

She sent the president a stream of memos warning about the horrendous living conditions of blacks in many areas and she said rising racial tension was a problem he needed to address. She called for a national interracial conference of black and white leaders, but her husband declined to put his imprimatur on the idea. FDR also refused to make a national statement or speech about race because he felt it would anger Southern members of Congress whose votes he needed for war bills and social programs.[31]

Eleanor also traveled abroad many times, trying to gather information about how American troops were doing and serving as a goodwill ambassador for her husband. On Saturday, August 28, 1943, after a secret trip from Washington, she turned up in Wellington, New Zealand, and visited the camps of U.S. soldiers, inspected facilities of the American Red Cross, and talked with sick and wounded troops at Silverstream Hospital. She later addressed several hundred women at a local theater and they treated her to a song, "For She's a Jolly Good Fellow."

*   *   *

FRANKLIN ROOSEVELT WAS the first president to take an active interest in polls as a way to keep track of public attitudes.[32]

"Throughout his long political career, Roosevelt had worked hard to fathom the unfathomable force of public opinion," observes historian Goodwin. "From long experience, he had learned that in a democracy one man alone cannot guide tens of millions of people without following (and shaping, as far as one could) that intangible force called the spirit of the country. He had seen at first hand President Woodrow Wilson's failure to reinforce his foreign policy with public and congressional backing. He had, in effect, made what historian Eric Larrabee has called 'a compact with the electorate which he had every reason for wishing to keep.' Yet so confused and so volatile was public opinion in the spring of 1941 that Roosevelt was like a man staring into a fog."[33] But he felt that he could eventually swing public opinion his way.[34]

He kept track of polls more than any of his predecessors. Surveys by Emil Hurja were financed by the Democratic National Committee, and Hadley Cantril did polls directly for FDR, signaling the start of presidential polling. "Polling penetrated the executive branch as the Department of Agriculture, the Works Progress Administration, and the Social Security Administration all sought public attitudes," political scientist Diane J. Heith says. "In addition to forging connections between pollsters, the party, and the president, Roosevelt also established a secret polling operation" conducted by Cantril, so he could "receive politically valuable information independent of his party" and make his own decisions about how best to use the information.[35]

Cantril became an important voice in the administration. A Princeton University psychology professor and early specialist in polling, Cantril secretly worked as an unofficial public opinion adviser for FDR and his White House.[36]

"The polls that FDR received differ from the private polls of modern presidents in that FDR never hired Cantril or another public opinion expert as a private White House pollster," writes political scientist Robert M. Eisinger. "FDR welcomed the public opinion information offered by Cantril and expressed interest in receiving more. By utilizing private poll data, FDR did not abandon other forms of gauging public opinion, such as tabulating incoming White House mail, but Cantril's surveys for and advice to the FDR administration legitimized polls as viable political instruments for presidents to gauge public opinion."[37]

Eisinger observes that "polls educated the Roosevelt administration as to where public opinion was located, thereby enabling them to market policies to specific constituencies," such as selling agricultural policy to farmers and marketing elements of U.S. policy toward Italy to Catholics.[38]

*   *   *

ROOSEVELT ALSO UNDERSTOOD that he could be isolated by his staff, and he took pains to avoid it. "He understood thoroughly the weaknesses of the staff system in the White House," wrote George Reedy, a former White House adviser for Lyndon Johnson. "He saw to it that under no circumstances could the people in his immediate vicinity control his access to information. Every staff assistant from the New Deal days recalls the experience of bringing a report to FDR and discovering, in the course of the conversation, that the president had gained from some mysterious, outside source knowledge of aspects of the project of which the assistant himself was not aware. No assistant, with the possible exception of Harry Hopkins, ever felt that his position was secure. And none of them would have dared to withhold any information. The penalties were too swift and too sure to permit what would anyway have been a futile exercise."[39]

"It is difficult, however, for a president to maintain sources of information outside his immediate staff. It requires a positive effort of will," Reedy observed.[40]

One of Roosevelt's information-gathering techniques was to hold news conferences—998 of them over a bit more than 12 years, an extraordinarily high number.[41] He used the sessions not only to explain his ideas to the country and demonstrate mastery of his office, but to learn. He felt, author M.L. Stein said, that "the questions from newsmen often gave him a clue to what the country was thinking. And Roosevelt's open door for the press created similar hospitality in other administration departments where cabinet members and other officials held regular conferences of their own."[42]

FDR knew that he would be the issue in his first re-election campaign, in 1936. But he was confident that most Americans liked him, and that he would win. He had tended his political garden well. "The Roosevelt administration's largesse at combating drought and flood and collapsed farm prices had resonated with farmers," wrote historian Conrad Black. "The fact that African Americans, under the order of both [key advisers Harry] Hopkins and [Harold] Ickes, with Roosevelt's firm approval, were receiving relief employment at the same rates as whites, albeit most of them in segregated (but not greatly inferior) camps, as well as the recovery program generally, was attracting the black votes away from the party of Lincoln, where it had been for seventy-five years. It now represented about five percent of the total vote (even though the black percentage of the population was double that, reflecting the disenfranchisement of most African Americans in the southern states)." Organized labor also was happy with Roosevelt.[43]

He knew that the American people believed he was on their side and that at least the economy wasn't getting worse. He played off these assessments of public opinion, which were accurately gleaned from Eleanor's travels, his polling, and his own sense of the country, including a train trip he took in early October 1936. He set forth a theme—which he would use time and again over the years—of how awful things had been when he took office. He said that "starvation was averted, that homes and farms were saved, that banks were reopened, that industry revived, and that the dangerous forces subversive of our form of government were turned aside." He said the New Deal's deficit spending was really an "investment' in the country on which there would eventually be a return—the same argument that Democrats have been making on behalf of government programs ever since.[44]

That November, FDR won a smashing victory, with 523 electoral votes and 46 states, while his Republican opponent Alf Landon won only 8 electoral votes and 2 states. Roosevelt got 27.48 million votes or 61 per cent to Landon's 16.68 million or 37 per cent.

It was the second of his four presidential victories.

* * *

FDR WAS MORE careful in dealing with public opinion on foreign affairs, which he felt was less firmly on his side as he tried to move the nation toward support of America's allies in Europe and Asia against the threats from Germany and Japan. "He had begun the delicate and implacable process of moving ahead of opinion on foreign affairs, then retreating slightly and pulling opinion in behind him before moving ahead of it again," writes Conrad Black. "He was at the same time trying to encourage greater boldness by the front-line states, without inciting them to impetuosity on false hopes of what the United States was really prepared to do."[45]

After a Chicago speech in 1937 in which he warned ominously that America couldn't be a complete bystander when the forces of violence and "lawlessness" were running rampant, he told a friend, "It's a terrible thing to look over your shoulder when you're trying to lead—and find no one there."[46] Americans were opposed to moving toward actions that could lead to war, according to polls.[47]

FDR kept to his policy of incremental moves toward helping the allies and isolating Germany as public opinion slowly hardened against the Nazis. Propelled by German aggressiveness and abuse of Jewish citizens, 94 per cent of Americans disapproved of Nazi treatment of Jews; 97 per cent disapproved of Nazi treatment of Roman Catholics, and 57 per cent approved of Roosevelt's withdrawal of the U.S. ambassador to Germany, according to the Gallup poll in November 1938. Ninety-two per cent of Americans that autumn disbelieved that Hitler had no more territorial ambitions; 77 per cent thought that the German demand for annexation of the Sudetenland was unjustified. In November, 61 per cent of Americans approved a boycott of German goods. In August 1939, 86 per cent opposed Hitler's claim to a section of Poland, and in October 1939, 78 per cent of Americans rejected Hitler's argument that the "Polish question" had been settled after the Nazi and Soviet partition of Poland.[48]

In May 1941, 55 per cent of Americans supported convoys to help Great Britain in its conflict with Germany, an increase from 41 per cent, even though three-quarters of Americans believed that those convoys would eventually tug the country into war. But 79 per cent of Americans said they wanted to stay out of the conflict in Europe and 70 per cent said the president had gone too far or was already doing enough to help Britain. "Roosevelt recognized that with education he could command a national majority on convoys and even on direct involvement in the war," Goodwin writes, "but he feared that his consensus would quickly vanish if a substantial portion of the people felt that he, rather than a recognized threat to national security, had compelled involvement."[49] For many weeks, he waited for outside developments to force his hand. Then came the Japanese attack on Pearl Harbor in December, which settled the matter and brought the United States fully into World War II.

* * *

NO PRESIDENT was more beloved in his own time than Franklin Roosevelt. His background as the son of a wealthy, privileged family from upstate New York provided little indication that he would be so popular with regular people. But he had an intuitive sense of what the country wanted—strong leadership, a sunny disposition, and an optimistic attitude—and provided it. He kept in touch through his network of friends and associates, by paying attention to the media, through the then-fledgling enterprise of polling, and, most of all, through the influence of his wife Eleanor. She traveled the country and the world and then reported back to her husband in great and insightful detail. Eleanor's reports deepened Franklin's resolve to expand the New Deal, his use of the federal government to help people and right society's wrongs, partly because he knew this was the direction in which the country wanted him to go.

CHAPTER SEVEN
HARRY TRUMAN

CONNECTED TO EVERYMAN

Harry Truman was the most down-to-earth and old-fashioned of all the modern presidents as he attempted to avoid isolation through persistent effort and a humble approach to his job.

He always felt that life in the White House was artificial. In a letter to his daughter Margaret in early September 1946, he wrote, "This old place cracks and pops all night long and you can very well imagine that old Jackson or Andy Johnson or some other ghost is walking. Why they'd want to come back here I could never understand. It's a nice prison but a prison nevertheless. No man in his right mind would want to come here of his own accord."[1] Truman was once asked about the observation by Alonzo Fields, a longtime butler at the White House, that Truman was the only president he served who took the trouble to understand Fields as a person. The other chief executives that Fields worked for were Herbert Hoover and Franklin D. Roosevelt.[2]

Truman said this shouldn't be surprising: "I've never understood how to do anything else except try to understand the other fellow and most of the time I've succeeded to some degree, I believe." Truman said that whenever he traveled to Boston, where Fields retired, the former butler would visit the president at his hotel and they would have a lengthy chat.

"You see the thing you have to remember when you get to be President," Truman continued, "there are all those things, the honors, the twenty-one gun salutes, all those things, you have to remember it isn't for you. It's for the Presidency, and you've got to keep yourself separate from that in your mind. If you can't keep the two separate, yourself and the Presidency, you're in all kinds of trouble."[3]

An interviewer told Truman the story of a boy who was very upset to learn that President Calvin Coolidge had to go to the bathroom just like everybody else. "That's right," Truman said. "We've had a few presidents who've not remembered a thing like that, and the minute it happens, you can't possibly do the job."[4]

Truman didn't believe in polls, but to avoid isolation he tried hard to connect with the people around him, including members of the household staff, such as Alonzo Fields. He mostly kept his ego in check, so he could generally see himself in realistic terms.

Daughter Margaret said that he was indeed Everyman. "He hated to use the buzzers on his desk to summon a man peremptorily," she wrote in a biography of her father. "Nine times out of ten he preferred to go to the aide's office. When he did summon a man, he would usually greet him at the door of the Oval Room office. More often than not the purpose of the call was to get his opinion on one of the many problems confronting the nation. This constant consideration for others, the total lack of egotism with which Dad conducted the day-to-day affairs of the White House was the real source of the enormous loyalty he generated in those around him.

"To really understand Harry S. Truman, you must grasp the importance of humility in his thinking. To him humility meant never blowing your own horn, never claiming credit in public for what you did or said, above all never claiming that you were better, smarter, tougher than other people. But his *practice* of humility never meant that Dad downgraded his worth, his accomplishments, in his own mind."[5]

* * *

WHEN HE SUCCEEDED to the presidency after Franklin Roosevelt's death in 1945, Truman faced many formidable challenges. In fact, it was one of the most turbulent and dangerous times in American history. Although he realized how unprepared he was for the job (even though he was vice president, FDR had not included him in many decisions, such as the development of the atomic bomb), Truman proceeded to follow his instincts and his judgment.

In the process, he far outran public opinion, offering a prime example of how even a president who tried to stay in touch could get into deep political trouble because he was unable to muster popular support. He said he was crafting an admittedly controversial foreign policy, based in part on containing the Soviet Union and supporting freedom around the world, because of "Republicans as well as Democrats who were willing to fight for principles before these principles became obvious to everyone." It was risky business, and it turned out to be more popular in retrospect with the public and historians than it was at the time.[6]

Truman considered himself a man of the people in the spirit of the homespun Andrew Jackson and Abraham Lincoln and the combative progressive Theodore Roosevelt. He said lobbyists represented 15 million Americans and the remaining 150 million had "only one man, the President," working for them.[7]

He was able to get people to trust his leadership for a while, notably through the 1948 campaign, but in the end he exhausted the country with his initiatives, such as the global fight against communism and the Soviet Union, and his program for relief of Europe after the ravages of World War II.

"Although more Americans heeded Truman's warnings about the Soviets, many still harbored doubts about him as president," writes historian Gil Troy. "Meanwhile, Truman's popular approval sank to 32 per cent amid paralyzing strikes, rising inflation, mounting meat shortages, and the vexing challenge of reintegrating sixteen million soldiers into society. From the left, labor leaders condemned the president for betraying them and Franklin Roosevelt's legacy by confronting striking miners and railroad workers. From the right, Southern Democrats angered by Truman's stance in favor of black civil rights stopped donating to the Democratic National Committee.

In 1946, the year after Truman stepped up to the presidency, Republicans won both houses of Congress for the first time since 1928. It was considered a referendum on the country's new leader. Truman barely campaigned and Democrats desperately played recordings of various Franklin Roosevelt speeches to remind people of their political heritage. The Republicans declared, "To err is Truman," and their winning campaign slogan asked bluntly, 'Had enough?'" When Truman returned to Washington from his hometown in Missouri after the balloting, only Undersecretary of State Dean Acheson greeted him at the train station.[8]

*   *   *

BUT TRUMAN'S FAITH in the "common man" (and woman) was restored during his famous "whistlestop" tours by train during his 1948 campaign, which he won in a remarkable upset over Republican Thomas Dewey.

Truman felt "detached and cut off" in the White House, and he decided the best remedy was to get out of town and speak to the public as often as he could. Truman wanted to get his message across personally, making fun of his Republican opponent Thomas Dewey as out of touch and lacking compassion, and mocking the "do-nothing" Congress.[9]

He decided that harsh, populist attacks on his opponents would resonate around the country, especially in the agricultural areas with which he was most familiar. It turned out that Truman had a better sense of everyday America than the pollsters and some of his own advisers did, based on his middle-class upbringing and his understanding of farm states, which he knew from his background in Missouri. His experience illustrates a major premise of this book—that the intuition and personal background a president brings to the White House can be more important than all the pollsters, focus groups, advisers, and constituent letters in the world.

"It was in the farm states that Truman made substantial gains," writes historian Zachary Karabell. "With Iowa, Wisconsin, and Ohio, he obtained 101 electoral votes in the Midwest, 26 more than Roosevelt had. He also defeated Dewey in agriculture-rich California. In pre-election surveys, Dewey was picked to win California, Idaho, Washington, Oregon, Montana, Wyoming, Ohio, Iowa, Indiana, and Minnesota, as well as the Republican belt of North Dakota, South Dakota, Nebraska, and Kansas. Of these fourteen states, he won only six. All of these states had large numbers of farmers, agricultural workers, or people who lived in cities but were connected in some way to the business of farming. Here Truman did far better than anyone had predicted.

"In that respect, Truman's populist, anti–Wall Street rhetoric was vindicated. He understood better than his advisers or adversaries the deep currents of distrust and fear of big business that ran through the areas of the United States that were defined by farming. He knew how potent these people could be if aroused. In many respects he was like them, and though he had learned how to maneuver in the East Coast worlds of money and power, he never modified his personality to fit in. Even as president he continued to view politics through the lens of a farmer from Missouri."[10]

Truman said the whistlestops gave the country a clear idea of what he wanted to do as president but also deepened his understanding of the people he was trying to lead. He told his biographer Merle Miller,

> I just got on a train and started across the country to tell people what was going on. I wanted to talk to them face to face. I knew that they knew that when you get on the television you're wearing a lot of powder and paint that somebody else has put your face, and you haven't even combed your own hair.
>
> But when you're standing right there in front of them and talking to them and shaking their hands if it's possible, the people can tell whether you're telling them the facts or not.
>
> I spoke I believe altogether to between fifteen and twenty million people. I met them face to face and I convinced them, and they voted for me.[11]

Truman's average "whistlestop day" would run from dawn to dusk. His train would rumble into a station and if there were enough people on the platform, he would stop and make a speech from the back of the last car. Sometimes the audiences were as few as ten people, Truman said later; sometimes there were thousands, and the numbers grew as the campaign progressed. Sometimes he would chat with people who gathered near him, and sometimes he would get off the train and mingle.[12]

Truman added, "You get a real feeling of this country and the people in it when you're on a train, speaking from the back of a train, and the further you get away from that, the worse off you are, the easier it gets for the stuffed shirts and the counterfeits and the fellas from Madison Avenue to put it over on the people. Those people are more interested in selling the people something than they are in informing them about the issues."[13] In Cleveland, Truman called the public-opinion polls "sleeping polls," apparently a joking reference to "sleeping pill," his daughter recalled, and said that he was sure the people were not being fooled by them. "They know sleeping polls are bad for the system," Truman noted. "They affect the mind. An overdose could be fatal." Truman felt that the massive crowds that he saw every day at his speeches were a better indication of public sentiment than the polls.[14]

He traveled 31,700 miles during the campaign; gave 356 speeches, averaging 10 a day; and addressed about 15 million people (Truman's estimate was higher), his advisers said.[15]

His daughter traced his effectiveness to a speech he gave in the spring of that election year. She wrote, "On April 17, 1948, a time when his statistical popularity had sunk to an all-time low—George Gallup said only 36 per cent of the people approved of his performance as President—he gave a speech to the American Society of Newspaper Editors in Washington. His prepared address drew no more than a flicker of polite applause from the crowd. But instead of sitting down, he started telling this very important and influential group of men exactly what he thought of the national and international situation in his own vigorous down-to-earth language." The crowd loved it, and from then to the end of the campaign, Truman talked at least partly off the cuff and let his true feelings show—especially his disdain for the "do-nothing" Congress and the Republican party for having "no program and no interest in the little fellow."[16]

Looking back, President Truman said, "Well, the feeling I got in that campaign was that most of the people in this country are not only, like I said, decent people, they want to do the right thing, and what you have to do is tell them straight out what the right thing is."[17]

*   *   *

OF COURSE, the idyllic experience of Truman's fabled train rides can never be replicated. In the wake of the assassination of President John F. Kennedy in 1963, and the attempts on the lives of President Gerald Ford and Ronald Reagan, the Secret Service would never allow what would now be considered dangerous mingling with strangers in a predictable way, day after day. Neither would a president's family, friends, and advisers. The conditions under which a president meets with everyday people today are far more controlled and insulated.

*   *   *

WHILE TRUMAN did pay attention to the news media, reading as many newspapers as he could, polls were another matter. He was always suspicious of public-opinion surveys because he didn't think pollsters selected representative samples of the electorate to test, especially by overlooking the electorate in farm states. This skepticism about polls hardened after surveys showed him losing to Dewey in 1948, only to have Truman win solidly. He took 49.5 per cent of the popular vote and 303 electoral votes to Dewey's 45.1 per cent and 189 electoral votes. Other candidates, including third-party hopefuls Henry Wallace and Strom Thurmond, split the remainder of the popular vote. Wallace carried no states and Thurmond carried four Southern states—Alabama, Louisiana, Mississippi, and South Carolina.

"In the 1940s, polling was a relatively new science," writes Karabell. "Elmo Roper, Archibald Crossley, and George Gallup promised that through rational, careful sampling, they could accurately predict how people would vote in the upcoming election. In the past few elections, Gallup had been right within four percentage points. By May 1948, Gallup reported that Truman's popularity ratings were within 4 per cent of the lowest they had ever been. Only 36 per cent of voters thought that he was doing a good job as president. In the meantime, other surveys were showing that Truman would lose head-to-head with Dewey in traditionally Democratic states such as Illinois and Pennsylvania. The press seized on these figures as conclusive proof that the president was no longer a reasonable choice for the Democrats, and George Gallup didn't mind one bit."[18] Unlike Dewey, who believed the polls saying he would win, Truman basically ignored these surveys.

After the election, Truman continued to ignore the polls as he was again weighted down by the crush of events.[19] There was the takeover of China by communists led by Mao Zedong, the Korean war, increasing confrontation with Moscow, fears of communism at home, labor strife, and economic troubles.

One area where he defied public opinion but made historic progress was in his controversial support for civil rights and desegregating the armed forces. He felt it was a matter of elemental fairness, and this made it easier for him to go against public opinion or his own racist heritage. He told anti–civil rights advocates in 1948 when he was under enormous pressure by Southern Democrats to back off his civil-rights stance,

> My forebears were Confederates. I come from a part of the country where Jim Crowism is as prevalent as it is in New York or Washington. Every factor and influence in my background—and in my wife's for that matter—would foster the personal belief that you are right [about backing off from civil rights].
>
> But my very stomach turned over when I learned that Negro soldiers, just back from overseas, were being dumped out of army trucks in Mississippi and beaten.
>
> Whatever my inclinations as a native of Missouri might have been, as President I know that is bad. I shall fight to end evils like this.[20]

He also defied the then-resurgent liberal wing of the Democratic Party. In September 1946, Truman forced liberal icon Henry Wallace to resign as secretary of commerce after Wallace drifted too far to the left in advocating cooperation with the Soviet Union. "To most Americans on the left, Wallace was the representative of a pro-Soviet policy they were convinced FDR would have carried over into the postwar era," writes presidential historian Robert Dallek. "Wallace was outspoken in his opposition to what he openly described as the belligerence of those in the United States and abroad who wanted to fight a war with the Soviet Union. He characterized Soviet actions in Europe, Asia, and the Middle East as not acts of aggression but as a response to American hostility to Moscow."[21]

But Truman publicly rejected Wallace's views. And privately he said Wallace and "the Reds, phonies, and 'parlor pinks'" were "a national danger," people who couldn't or wouldn't see the menace in Moscow.[22]

His philosophy was that "our country has never suffered seriously from any acts of the president that were truly intended for the welfare of the country. It's suffered from the inaction of a great many presidents when action should have been taken at the right time." He said a president must not be "afraid of controversy" or of offending his critics, and he expressed an idealistic faith that "reasonable people will always go along with the man who has the right ideas and leadership."[23]

During his final years in office, Truman's willingness to go his own way caused his approval ratings to plummet to the levels of late 1946, and he became the butt of jokes by comedians who referred to him as "the little man from Missouri." He declined to seek another term in 1952.[24]

* * *

THE TRUMAN LESSON is that a president can try all he wants to understand the country, but in the end, he will rise or fall depending not on how much he comprehends public opinion, but rather on the extent to which he keeps public opinion on his side. Some presidents see where the public is headed and rush to lead the parade, such as Bill Clinton did in some cases. Others, such as Truman, formulate their own views and try to persuade the country to follow them. Truman's failure was not that he misunderstood the country, but that he was unable to move Americans to adopt his ideas on too many issues, ranging from civil rights to war in Korea.

Truman felt that the best way for a president to avoid isolation is to always remain grounded in the limitations of power, and committed to testing the effectiveness of his own policies to guard against any sense of arrogance or omnipotence. In his natural modesty and self-deprecation, Truman had the right idea.[25]

*   *   *

TRUMAN was a very unpopular president when he left office. He had gotten the United States into the Korean War, had involved the country in an expensive and dangerous cold war with the Soviet Union, and seemed harsh in dealing with his critics over domestic issues such as strikes and demands for federal aid. Today, historians consider Truman a great or near-great president, bold and prescient when it counted most. There is little doubt that he tried to keep in contact with regular people not and taking an interest in their lives, through voracious reading, and through his earlier life experiences, especially with business success and failure in Missouri. His problem was that he ran too far ahead of public opinion.

CHAPTER EIGHT
RONALD REAGAN

MIDDLE-CLASS ROOTS

Ronald Reagan never forgot his middle-class roots in small-town Illinois, and this helped him stay in touch. He was always acutely aware and proud of his background.

As the magnitude of his victory became clear on election night in 1980, he was asked what Americans saw in him. "Would you laugh if I told you that I think, maybe, they see themselves and that I'm one of them?" he replied. "I've never been able to detach myself or think that I, somehow, am apart from them."[1]

The power of his life's experience was central to Reagan's approach to leadership. He believed deeply that America was a land of opportunity for anyone with talent and a willingness to work, and he saw himself as a quintessential example of that. "Reagan's own parents had been too poor to own a home, let alone a second car or a boat, and Reagan believed himself to be a most typical American," writes Reagan biographer Lou Cannon. "He had the advantage over other politicians of never thinking himself special, despite all the special things that he had done. He accepted the presidency as his destiny ... his due, and viewed his extraordinary career as vindicating the promise of America. In his own eyes, Reagan was Everyman, or at least every American. He credited his success to a system in which 'everyone can rise as high and as far as his ability will take him.'"[2]

Adds Cannon, "Reagan was personally closer to Main Street than to Wall Street. He remained a secure, old-fashioned man who fed the White House squirrels, related anecdotes to aides whose names he often could not remember, and reminisced about his life in the movie business.... [T]he greatness of Reagan was that he carried a shining vision of America inside him. He had brought that vision with him from Dixon and learned in Hollywood and on the GE circuit to play the role of the wholesome American who would set things right. It was a most natural role. Reagan may not have been a great president but he was a great American who held a compelling vision of his country.... In rejecting an era of limits, Reagan expressed a core conviction of the nation."[3]

Frank Donatelli, who was Reagan's political director in the White House, said, "No matter how successful he became, he never forgot his upbringing. Most of his life was a struggle, and he always remembered that. That's something a pollster can't give you. You either have it or you don't."[4]

An incident from his successful 1980 campaign was instructive. Reagan was booed and shouted down during an appearance in the superheated slums of the South Bronx. A crowd of about 100 African Americans, whites, and Hispanics contained many hecklers, and some chanted, "Down with Reagan!" and "Go home!" His temper flaring, Reagan said, "I can't do a damn thing for you unless I am elected."

After boarding his air-conditioned limousine, his 12-car motorcade pulled out and Reagan was asked by a journalist whether he planned to visit any more urban areas. He said yes, he would continue to take his message everywhere, including places such as the South Bronx where his reception would be hostile. "There we were, driving away, and you think of them back there in all that ugliness and they have no place to go," Reagan said. "All that is before them is to sit and look at what we just saw." A supporter said, "He truly felt bad about the plight of the poor, perhaps because the memories of his own deprivations during the Depression were deeply etched in his psyche."[5]

*   *   *

REAGAN CAME OF AGE politically as an admirer of Democrat Franklin Roosevelt, and even though he eventually became a Republican after many years as a Democrat, Reagan emulated Roosevelt in trying to stay connected to plain folks. Following Roosevelt's example in his "fireside chats" on the radio, Reagan made a habit of giving addresses on television directly to the American people, weaving the stories of everyday people into his speeches and public statements rather than simply reciting dry statistics or talking in generalities and abstractions. As with FDR, this brought him closer to the public.

Nancy Reagan, his wife, wrote, "Before he was elected, Ronnie had always regarded the presidency with great respect, even with awe. But when he became president, he had trouble believing that other people could be in awe of *him*. Unlike, say, Lyndon Johnson, he never looked at his position in terms of 'I am president.' Instead, he would refer to the presidency as 'the office I now hold,' or even 'this job.' Some people saw this as an affectation, or even a calculated pose that allowed him to appear distant from government while he was still part of it. But it was genuine. For Ronnie, it would have been presumptuous to view his job in any other way."[6]

He had what columnist George Will called "a talent for happiness," and he wouldn't allow the presidency to intimidate him or change his habits. In private, he was a plain and courteous man, considerate of those around him, a fellow who liked the simple pleasures of a basic meal of meatloaf and macaroni and cheese, and enjoyed spending evenings with his wife Nancy watching television in the White House residence, clad in his pajamas.[7]

When he was shot and nearly killed in an assassination attempt on March 30, 1981, only weeks after he took office, he exhibited enormous grace amid adversity and remarkable recuperative ability. This added to Americans' admiration for him. It also enhanced his persuasive powers on Capitol Hill and helped him push his agenda of tax cuts and slowing the growth of spending through Congress. Reagan also drew an important conclusion from his brush with death—that God had spared his life so he could bridge the gap with the Soviet Union, end communism, and make peace.[8] He made surprising progress in all these areas via his remarkable partnership with the new, reform-minded Soviet leader, Mikhail Gorbachev.

Reagan carefully read the polls and realized that he didn't have a mandate to completely turn the country upside down. But he realized that he did have some special influence to move in a more conservative direction, to cut taxes, reduce the growth of federal spending, and fight communism—all the while showing an amiable disposition and an optimistic attitude. It matched the country's mood.

Reagan also knew the power of storytelling, and he did this exceptionally well. The narrative of his presidency was that a charismatic and principled Washington outsider had arrived to clean up the capital, and

Americans liked the tale. "The American electorate seeks from its national leadership this sense of shared values, this reaffirmation of traditional American beliefs," Reagan declared in 1983. "They do not want a president who's a broker of parochial concerns; they do ... want a definition of national purpose, a vision of the future."[9]

Even amid the Iran-Contra scandal of 1987, in which illegal aid was sent to anti-Marxist "Contra" rebels in Nicaragua and partly financed with an arms-for-hostages deal in the Middle East, his aides still were looking for a positive story to tell. "We must opportunistically create events where the President exhibits his diverse qualities: leadership, compassion, identity with real people and real emotions and on behalf of the country," one White House strategist, William Henkel, asserted. Urging his colleagues to "find heroes," Henkel noted that "springtime means baseball, families, patriotism, parades, festivals, feel-good wishes." To a large degree, this positive image-making distracted the country from the Iran-Contra scandal and enabled Reagan to survive and recover his popularity.[10]

*　*　*

REAGAN RELIED heavily on polls to update himself about public attitudes and shape his message.

When he took office, he was far from a neophyte in the world of polling and assessing public opinion. His understanding had deepened when he successfully ran for governor of California and was re-elected, but he had been something of a student of polls even when he was out of elective office.

In a radio commentary on August 7, 1978, two years before he won the White House, Reagan said, "[W]e should know more than we do about how about how the questions are phrased by the pollsters and whether a certain public relations result is the goal of the organization or individual paying to have the poll taken." He displayed a nuanced understanding of how polls are done. His topic was gun control, and he cited one poll sponsored by the Center for the Study and Prevention of Handgun Violence that found that "apparently 84 per cent of Americans favor stringent hand-gun control & registration. A third of those polled would even ban the manufacture of such weapons." But Reagan went on to cite another poll a year earlier, commissioned by the anti–gun control Second Amendment Foundation, that found that "54% of Americans believe the answer to violent crime lies in stiffer punishment. Only 10% would outlaw handguns. In fact when the question was asked: 'Do you think gun controls have helped to reduce crimes committed with guns?'

67% said no." He said the best guide to public opinion on gun control isn't polling but what happens when voters decide directly on gun-control measures on the ballot in the form of initiatives or referenda.[11]

* * *

IT'S SIGNIFICANT that Reagan turned to his pollster, Richard Wirthlin, as well as in-house strategist Richard Beale, to guide him as he prepared to take office in the fall of 1980. In October, Wirthlin and Beale developed an "initial action plan" that urged Reagan to immediately claim a "mandate for change" and to act boldly in the first ninety days, reports author Hedrick Smith.[12]

The report said, "The window of opportunity opens and closes quickly; therefore, the President needs to take the initiative early and decisively."[13] Wirthlin and Beale went on to show how Reagan's predecessors Franklin Roosevelt, Dwight Eisenhower, John F. Kennedy, Richard Nixon, and Jimmy Carter had operated week to week through their first hundred days in office. Wirthlin and Beale described these presidents' legislative proposals, speeches, press conferences, foreign trips, meetings, television addresses, and sudden developments such as the failed Bay of Pigs invasion of Cuba in 1961. Reagan followed their advice, and moved boldly to win congressional approval for a massive tax cut, the centerpiece of his agenda, slowing the rate of growth of government, and more spending for defense, and he succeeded in doing so.

* * *

AS PRESIDENT, Reagan received regular polling updates, sometimes as often as once a week but not less than once a month for fifteen minutes, directly from his chief pollster Wirthlin, who wasn't a member of the White House staff but remained one of Reagan's confidants.

"The Reagan polling apparatus employed many of the same pollsters and staffers as the previous Republican administrations and, as a result, improved on the Nixon and Ford White Houses in both style and understanding," writes political scientist Diane J. Heith. "The continued usage of the same pollsters and staff members provided continuity and increasing specialization in applying opinion analysis to White House decision making. As with the Nixon administration, the Reagan White House staffers possessed sophisticated knowledge of public opinion analysis. The most frequent user of poll data, Richard Beale, worked for

Wirthlin's polling firm prior to White House employment. The Reagan White House employed individuals extremely skilled in public opinion analysis. By the time of the [first] Bush administration [immediately after Reagan's two terms], the Republicans were quite skilled and accustomed to incorporating public opinion into the White House structure. Public opinion usage was habitual and expert."[14] The pollsters included Wirthlin and Robert Teeter, and the staffers included David Gergen.

Reagan's strategists used polls to identify and track Americans in terms of their support for the president. They found some who were core supporters who would stay with Reagan through thick and thin, and "peripheral" voters who backed him based on what Reagan did on issues important to them, such as abortion and school prayer. These peripheral supporters required constant monitoring so they could be re-motivated if they started to slip away.[15]

Reagan supporters were dissected in remarkable detail. The profile of Americans in a "strong support group" included college-educated whites, 35 to 54 years old, with income above $20,000 annually, Protestant and non-union. Those in a "mixed support group" were 55 to 64, with high-school degrees and postgraduate educations, with incomes between $10,000 and $20,000, and also blue-collar workers and some white Catholics. Those in a "low support group" were people over 65 years old or under 24, "nonafflu-ent," with less than four years of high school, less than $10,000 in income, union members, ethnic Americans, women, and African Americans.[16]

The Reagan strategists also paid close attention to a "gender gap" that the pollsters were finding. On that score, women were more concerned than men that Reagan seemed too bellicose and wondered whether his policies were fair to working women.

White House aides followed up with plans to reach out to those in the low-support group and those that were considerable potential supporters. At one point, the Office of Public Liaison under Elizabeth Dole, along with White House senior adviser Jack Burgess, worked on a coalition-building program aimed at ethnic Americans. They even wanted to break down ethnicity, which they said "would enable us to track the opinions of Italian-, Polish-, Lithuanian-Americans, etc."[17]

Reagan's aides also tracked more religious categories than ever before, Heith says, "distinguishing among Presbyterians, Methodists, Lutherans, Baptists, other Protestants, Catholics, Jews, and agnostics; there was no direct reference to Islam, but a follow-up question inquired into born-again status. These categories were used frequently to classify supporters on the social issues of abortion, school prayer, gun control, a balanced budget, and tuition tax credits.... Moreover, the Reagan strategists recognized the value of specific single issues to certain supporters regardless of party affiliation. Information about public opinion empowered presidents to reframe their actions and decisions based on the possible shifting constituent support found in survey data."[18]

Wirthlin used "dial groups," which have now become common in survey research. Collections of voters were assembled to watch Reagan speeches and evaluate them using dials, numbered from one to seven, on which they indicated their reactions. The most positive reaction called for turning the dial to seven and the most negative only a one or less. The responses were tallied and charted by a computer. Wirthlin was looking for "power phrases" in Reagan speeches, moments that prompted positive reactions. If he found them, Reagan would use these words and phrases again in future addresses. Wirthlin also concluded that people often responded more to the president's facial expressions, body language, and tone of voice than to what he was saying—which became an important part of Reagan's approach to communication.[19]

Reagan, with his skills as an actor on television and in movies, was a natural on TV, and his aides were deft at arranging backdrops and scenes that reinforced his words, such as placing him in front of American flags and groups of soldiers or police to demonstrate patriotism and strength. This reached its height in his successful 1984 re-election campaign, held during an upbeat time of rising prosperity and peace, when his slogan was taken from the title of a campaign commercial, "Morning in America."

Reagan learned something else from the polling—that Americans were turned off when their politicians got too negative. This reinforced his desire to project the image of a regular fellow who tried to get along with other leaders in Washington, the kind of guy that Joe Six Pack would want to have a beer with. He was critical of Democrats, but rarely in personal terms. "He didn't demonize his opponents," says Ken Duberstein, who was Reagan's White House chief of staff at the end of his presidency.[20]

While Reagan's aides segmented and studied the electorate more than ever, there is no evidence that Reagan adjusted his fundamental philosophy to conform to public opinion. Rather, he used such research and polling to determine how to best persuade the country that his existing views were correct.

*   *   *

THE REAGAN White House also went to great lengths to study the media and decide which outlets could be used best to reach certain constituencies. This included figuring out which networks, anchors, reporters, and columnists that their supporters preferred. As Diane J. Heith reports, as of February 2, 1982, 26 per cent of Americans preferred CBS, 25 per cent preferred ABC, and 23 per cent preferred NBC. It wasn't a very large spread. More useful were other specifics. Among those preferring CBS were the best-educated, many African Americans, registered independents, and Southerners. Among those preferring NBC were seniors, lower-income people, and registered Republicans. Those preferring ABC were the youngest viewers, high-school graduates, blue-collar workers, many African Americans, and Democrats. This meant that NBC might be best used to reach Republicans while blue-collar voters might be best reached through ABC.[21]

*   *   *

REAGAN USED a number of non-polling techniques to keep in touch. A former actor in the movies and on television, he loved to watch films and TV shows in the White House residence, such as the soap-opera hits *Dallas* and *Dynasty,* and this kept him to some extent informed about popular culture. He read newspapers and magazines and each morning scanned a digest of news articles assembled by his staff. Most of all, he got his news from watching the evening newscasts of the three broadcast networks, ABC, CBS, and NBC, with a special interest in how they were covering him and his administration.

He relied on his key advisers, especially James Baker, Michael Deaver, and, later, Ken Duberstein, to keep him grounded in real American life and to tell him when he was getting into political hot water. "We were always straight with him," Duberstein told me. "And he always felt connected."[22]

Also useful to him was the counsel of Stu Spencer, a longtime political strategist in California who was a confidant of Reagan's and was particularly close to Nancy Reagan. Spencer, in phone calls and occasional meetings, would tell Reagan the bad news that he needed to hear.

Reagan also kept in touch with a small number of conservative commentators and journalists, in including William F. Buckley and Jack Kilpatrick. This was especially true during his first years in office, when he was seeking as many allies as he could find. On one occasion in May 1981, he visited Kilpatrick's Virginia farm near the capital for lunch and chitchat. Kilpatrick mentioned that it was his son's birthday, and the young man was in the Navy and stationed aboard a destroyer in the Indian Ocean. Kilpatrick wondered if the president might place a call using the extensive technology at his disposal so they could wish his son a happy birthday.

Reagan was delighted to oblige. He asked his executive assistant Jim Kuhn, who was in a holding room at the farm, if this could be done. Kuhn said it would be fine, and about 45 minutes later the connection was made. Reagan wished the young man a happy birthday and his father got to talk to him for several minutes. Kuhn said later that it illustrated how much Reagan loved making personal contacts and "It was a big deal for him."[23]

But there was always a question raised by many in the public and by his critics about whether Reagan was capable of breaking out of his own conservative ideology and understanding that the world was changing. Even some of his conservative loyalists thought he wasn't very smart, and liberals ridiculed him as an "amiable dunce."[24]

Pollster Wirthlin considered Reagan "extremely gifted and extremely bright in picking up oral briefings" but believed Reagan was so focused on a handful of priorities—"relations with the Soviets, the economy, federalism"—that he paid little attention to other issues.[25] Many other Reagan advisers agreed with this assessment.

Most of his closest advisers and friends said he had a knack for drawing on his early experiences as a low-middle-class boy in Illinois to understand what most worried everyday Americans, such as inflation and the communist threat.

He could absorb information when he wanted to. But his aides quickly realized that the best way to brief him was through anecdotes and narratives rather than reciting numbers or making analytical points. This was a technique that biographer Lou Cannon said "played to the strength of his memory rather that the weakness of his analysis" and emphasized the fact that "Reagan always thought in concrete examples rather than abstractions" and "used anecdotes and experience to construct a coherent idea of the way the world works and what he wanted to accomplish."[26]

David Stockman, who was Reagan's first budget director, wrote during his former boss's presidency that "in the final analysis, there has been no Reagan Revolution in national economic governance. All the umbilical cords of dependency still exist because the public elects politicians who want to preserve them. So they have to be paid for. That is the unyielding bottom line. Economic and financial disaster is the only alternative. I joined the Reagan Revolution as a radical ideologue. I learned the traumatic lesson that no such revolution was possible. I end up giving two cheers for the politicians. But only that."[27]

Even though Reagan talked a good game about leading a conservative revolution in Washington, some of his closest associates thought the former

Hollywood actor was miscast in this role. They felt that his ideology was outweighed by memories of his family's early struggles—his father was a heavy drinker who moved from job to job—and his firsthand experiences and observations of how so many Americans needed help during the Depression.

He tried to lead a revolution. "But Ronald Reagan proved to be too kind, gentle, and sentimental for that," wrote Stockman midway through the Reagan presidency. "He always went for hard-luck stories. He sees the plight of real people before anything else. Despite his right-wing image, his ideology and philosophy always take a back seat when he learns that some individual human being might be hurt.[28]

*   *   *

ONE OF HIS favorite ways to stay in touch was through letters, a fondness he shared with many other presidents. Anne Higgins, his chief of correspondence who had held the same job under Richard Nixon, would scan Reagan's mail and pass along a sampling of letters. Reagan would read them and often write personal replies during lulls in his schedule or during nonwork hours.

It turned out that Reagan had an extraordinary correspondence with everyday citizens through his public career. He had corresponded with regular citizens since he was an actor in Hollywood many years earlier, and he enjoyed the practice and felt that it kept him in touch with the public.[29] His replies were deeply sensitive and articulate, with a homey touch. Obviously he paid close attention to what the letter-writers were saying and was eager to respond in a meaningful way

Every month, Higgins would give Reagan about 30 letters chosen by her and her assistants from the thousands sent to the White House every day. Some of the letters were laudatory but others were highly critical both of Reagan and of his policies. "Perhaps the toughest letters to answer came from the mothers and fathers of young men and women who had died after being ordered into battle by Reagan," wrote a team of Reagan biographers who compiled thousands of Reagan letters in book form. "There were also letters from old friends, who spoke directly and frankly; these letters he seemed to cherish, even though some of them stung. His replies tenaciously defended what he had done or what he was doing. Usually the tone of his letters was calm, often sympathetic, but on occasion his anger flared and he could not resist taking a swipe at some of his tormentors."[30]

"The letters he received were carefully chosen by Higgins to spare him an overload of bad news and, since Higgins was an ardent antiabortionist, the sentiments of citizens who believed that abortion was a matter of individual choice," writes Cannon. "Both Higgins and [senior aide Michael] Deaver considered Reagan a sucker for hard-luck stories and tried to limit the number of letters he received from people undergoing hardships, to which the president would often respond with advice and a small personal check. Some aides were appalled that a president who dealt lightly with critical memoranda devoted so much time answering the letters of persons he had never met. But the aides, knowing it would have been unavailing, never registered their complaints with Reagan. The president liked fan mail, and he was so scrupulous about answering the letters given to him that he often took them along with him to Camp David [the presidential retreat in Maryland] on the weekends."[31]

Reagan took offense when letter-writers accused him of being out of touch. This happened when he received a note from Gail E. Foyt of Dayton, Ohio, whose husband was forced by the poor economy in 1982 to work in Florida while she stayed alone in Ohio. She wrote in July that she had voted for Reagan but was having regrets. She said he was "very wealthy" and didn't pay attention to "people like me—not rich, nor poor—worth nothing except to each other."

Reagan was hurt. He wrote to Mrs. Foyt on August 20, 1982:

I wish I could tell you there is some instant answer to the economic problems besetting us but I can't. However it is my strong belief that we are on the right track and the economy is turning up.

I hope and pray by the time you receive this your own situation is improved and that you are or soon will be united with your husband.

Mrs. Foyt your sentence with regard to my not being able to understand the real world touched a tender nerve. I grew up in poverty, although in a small midwestern town you didn't think of yourself as poor. Maybe because the government didn't come around and tell you, you were poor. But I do understand very well what you were saying. I've been making speeches for about 30 years on the fact that the forgotten men and women in America were those people who went to work, paid their bills, sent their kids to school and made this country run.

You said you'd pray for me and I'm grateful. I have a great faith in prayer and I intend to pray for you.

Sincerely,

Ronald Reagan[32]

Reagan was also offended whenever someone accused him of being biased or insensitive to the problems of blacks and women. Dina Merrill, an actress who knew the Reagans, made this accusation in an interview with *Women's Wear Daily* published in February 1983, and Reagan wrote a letter in response on February 10:

> If you were quoted accurately in *WWD* you are concerned about our policies regarding treatment of women and blacks. Dina, nothing has frustrated me more than the unfounded propaganda on this subject. Our record with regard to blacks is probably better than any previous administration in responding to civil rights complaints, directing government contracts to minority owned businesses, appointment to executive positions in government etc.
>
> On the matter of equality for women, we have a task force that has been combing regulations and laws for any trace of sex discrimination. We've made considerable progress with those things we can change administratively and are proposing and have proposed bills where legislation is required. We have secured the cooperation of all 50 states in doing the same thing at their level. And of course I'm sure you know our record with regard to high level appointments in government.[33]

But while the letters and his keeping track of news coverage made him well aware of pervasive criticism that he was insensitive and uncaring in dealing with gender and racial issues, Reagan believed this was due not to any failings of his own but to attacks by his critics and biased news media.

Often, he saw in the letters, even though they were carefully filtered by Higgins and others, evidence of the idealized America he had admired all his life and praised so often in his speeches. An example was a note he received from Andy Smith, a seventh-grader from Irmo, South Carolina, in 1984 that seemed to suggest an Ozzie and Harriet lifestyle still pervaded the country. "Today my mother declared my bedroom a disaster area," the 13-year-old Smith wrote to the president. "I would like to request federal funds to hire a crew to clean up my room."

Reagan saw the humor in the situation but also used it to convey a fatherly lesson mixed with his own brand of conservative philosophy. He wrote this reply:

> I'm sorry to be so late in answering your letter but as you know I've been in China and found your letter upon my return.

Your application for disaster relief had been duly noted but I must point out one technical problem; the authority declaring the disaster is supposed to make the request. In this case your mother.

However, setting that aside I'll have to point out the larger problem of available funds. This has been a year of disasters, 539 hurricanes as of May 4th and several more since, numerous floods, forest fires, drought in Texas and a number of earthquakes. What I'm getting at is that funds are dangerously low.

May I make a suggestion? This administration, believing that government has done many things that could be done by volunteers at the local level, has sponsored a Private Sector Initiative program calling upon people to practice voluntarism in the solving of a number of local problems.

Your situation appears to be a natural. I'm sure your mother was fully justified in proclaiming your room a disaster. Therefore you are in an excellent position to launch another volunteer program to go along with the more than 3,000 already underway in our nation—congratulations.

Give my best regards to your mother,

Sincerely, Ronald Reagan[34]

In another letter, a young girl named Rachel Virden of Dallas, Texas, expressed concern that she had to wear eyeglasses, and Reagan replied on November 23, 1983:

Rachel I know how you feel about glasses. I have been nearsighted all my life and when I was young I felt as you do about wearing glasses but I wore them. Being able to see clearly was more important. Now maybe seeing me on TV or my picture in the paper you wonder where my glasses are. I'm wearing them—contact lenses. Wear your glasses now and in a few years when your eyes have reached their full size you might look into the idea of contacts. It's very simple and easy to wear them. I've been wearing them all my adult life. But in the meantime don't deny yourself the joy of being able to see things clearly.[35]

And Petre Teodorescu of Scottsdale, Arizona, wrote Reagan to express his pride at having immigrated to America from Communist Romania. Reagan replied on February 4, 1983,

Sometimes those of us who were born in this country tend to take things for granted. It takes someone like you who has only recently come here to remind us how lucky we are. Like you, I dream of the day when all over the world people can know this freedom and escape from communist rule. I promise you, I shall do everything I can to preserve the freedom that you have found here.[36]

The stream of letters also served another function—sometimes giving White House planners ideas for events or for recruiting people to publicly support the president or his policies. In late 1983, Higgins scoured the letters to the president from medical students who had been rescued by U.S. troops, on Reagan's order, in the invasion of Grenada, and the staff viewed videotapes of their homecoming to the United States "to find the most eloquent students to speak at the South Lawn celebration" of the successful mission, Reagan's former executive assistant Jim Kuhn recalled. The research paid off as the students who spoke were appropriately grateful to the president and the U.S. military.[37]

The staff kept track of Reagan's outgoing letters as best they could to make sure he was adhering to his own policies, in case the correspondence became public. Peter J. Wallison, a longtime Reagan aide, gave an insight into this system when he wrote the following:

> One morning in late July 1986, David Chew, the White House staff secretary, brought me a few sheets of yellow legal-size paper on which the President had written several letters in response to letters he received at the White House. Chew's purpose in bringing these draft letters to me was to have me review what the President had said in response to a writer's criticism of the Supreme Court on the abortion issue. We both wanted to be sure that Reagan's letter conformed to what he had said in the past; these informal letters, after all, were not the place to break new policy ground.
>
> I learned later that Reagan carried on an active correspondence with a number of people to whom he had been writing before he became president, and in some cases before he became governor of California. The letters from these old friends—ordinary people he had met during his travels—were flagged by the White House Correspondence Unit and were sent directly to him along with letters from others who were writing about matters that the head of the Unit thought would be of particular interest to him. In these cases, he wrote out his responses on yellow paper, and they were typed and sent out. In the few cases where the President got into policy issues in these letters, his secretary ran them by appropriate member of the White House staff.[38]

On June 6, 1984, Reagan used the correspondence to stage a dramatic moment at the celebration marking the 40th anniversary of the D-Day landings at Normandy during World War II. Higgins had discovered a letter from Lisa Zanatta Henn, whose father, Private First Class Peter Robert Zanatta of the 37th Engineer Combat Battalion, had been one of the first Americans to assault the beaches early that morning in 1944.

"He made me feel the fear of being on that boat waiting to land," Lisa Henn wrote Reagan. "I can smell the ocean and feel the seasickness. I can see the looks on his fellow soldiers' faces, the fear, the anguish, the uncertainty of what lay ahead. And when they landed, I can feel the strength and courage of the men who took those first steps through the tide to what must have surely looked like instant death. I don't know how or why I can feel this emptiness, this fear, or this determination, but I do. Maybe it's the bond I had with my father.... All I know is that it brings tears to my eyes to think about my father as a twenty-year-old boy having to face that beach."[39]

Henn described how her dad had seen many friends die, and said, "You did what you had to do, and you kept on going."

Lisa Henn concluded her letter by saying she promised her father, who had died in 1976, that she would someday see the beaches and put flowers on the graves as her father wanted. "I'll never forget what you went through, Dad, nor will I let anyone else forget. And, Dad, I'll always be proud."

Reagan read from the letter at the D-Day event, his voice quavering. Lisa Zanatta Henn, who was in the front row, wept openly, as did many of the veterans in attendance.[40] That moment, and the images described of the heroes who had stormed those beaches and climbed those cliffs—whom Reagan called "the boys of Pointe du Hoc"—were captured by television. It was largely because of that letter that Reagan, who had never served in combat, gave one of the most moving presidential addresses in history.

His aide Jim Kuhn said the letters grounded and inspired Reagan. "He was far more comfortable writing letters than talking on the telephone," Kuhn wrote in a memoir about his White House years. "In fact, he was an enormously prolific letter writer and found it enjoyable to convey his thoughts on paper. In fact, as eloquent as he was verbally, his writing was just as articulate. He penned hundreds of letters a year—to supporters, opponents, world leaders, Hollywood friends and ordinary citizens who wrote either to praise or to criticize him."[41]

One letter led to a remarkable five-year pen-pal relationship between the president and Rudolph Hines, a precocious student at Congress Heights Elementary School, later renamed Martin Luther King, Jr. Elementary School, in southeast Washington, D.C. During his visit to the school in March 1984, Reagan asked that a student there be selected to correspond with him, and the principal chose "Ruddy," who was six years old. It led to a series of letters between the president and the African American pupil, and several visits by President Reagan and his wife to the school and trips by Ruddy to the White House over the years.[42] In their correspondence and meetings, the president and his young pen pal discussed their adventures as boys, in addition to acting, friendships, summer camp, school work, and learning how to ride horses.[43]

In 1984, the boy invited Reagan to his house for dinner but advised in his letter, "You have to let us know in advance so my mom can pick up the laundry off the floor."[44] The dinner took place on September 21, 1984, at the two-story brick apartment building where Ruddy lived with his mother. They ate fried chicken, salad, and rice from TV trays, and the president and first lady brought gift-wrapped jelly beans and front-row tickets to a Michael Jackson concert that night at RFK Stadium.[45] Several months, later, the president invited Ruddy and other children from the school to attend the circus with him. They sat together and seemed to have a wonderful time.

Moments like these make a president treasure his correspondence and the insights it gives him into life outside the White House bubble.

*   *   *

REAGAN DELIGHTED in assessing the public mood from even the smallest details of his daily life. When he traveled in his armor-plated limousine, preceded and trailed by his Secret Service bodyguards, police vehicles, and staff cars, he would look out the window and observe the crowds. He always waved. "If they took the time to see me, I need to acknowledge that," he told an aide.[46]

When he sped through New York City, it seemed like someone on the street would always make a rude gesture as he raced by. Reagan would laugh and call it "another New York City wave."

He also watched the people passing by when he went abroad. On a trip to Moscow, he noticed that people were waving half-heartedly, with their hands barely above waist level, when he arrived. After his conciliatory meeting with Soviet leader Mikhail Gorbachev, however, the people who lined the streets waved vigorously with both hands, and many women jumped up and down in excitement.

*   *   *

DESPITE HIS EFFORTS to stay in touch, Reagan was in some ways a loner who would confide fully in only his wife. And he could lose track of important developments in the life of the country either because he wasn't paying close attention or because no one in his orbit pointed out what was going on. One egregious example was the AIDS epidemic. Even though the rate of infection and death from the disease was growing fast, Reagan wasn't aware of the depth of the problem. His White House physician, John Hutton, said Reagan viewed AIDS as though "it was measles and it would go away."[47] He didn't take much of an interest until actor Rock Hudson, a Hollywood friend, died of the disease on October 2, 1985. As so often happened with Reagan, it was the personal story that hit close to home that made all the difference, not statistics or briefings.

Hudson's death—and his appearance at the end when he had transformed from a handsome leading man to a gaunt, hollow-eyed specter—prompted Reagan to ask Hutton about AIDS, and from then on he supported substantial federal funding for AIDS research to find a cure and federal efforts to encourage prevention. Still, critics said none of this was enough. They argued, with considerable justification, that if Reagan had used his bully pulpit to candidly inform the country about the nature of AIDS and how to avoid the disease, he might have saved lives.[48]

*   *   *

FOLLOWING THE PATTERN of other first ladies, including Eleanor Roosevelt and Rosalynn Carter, Nancy Reagan sometimes played a key role in keeping her husband in touch. "The first lady is often exposed to perspectives and viewpoints that the president never gets to hear," Mrs. Reagan wrote in a memoir. "Time after time, I was approached by White House aides and elected officials who gave me valuable information, warnings, and insights. 'I wish you'd go in and tell my husband,' I'd say. But something happens to people when they walk into the Oval Office. They just freeze up, and they tell the president only what they think he wants to hear. There are times when his wife may be the only person who can be honest with him. If he's lucky, and when it's necessary, she'll be able to tell him the bad news. Or at least give him another point of view."[49]

Mrs. Reagan did this in two important instances. She felt that White House Chief of Staff Donald Regan wasn't serving her husband well enough because he was too controlling and because his arrogance was offending many influential leaders in Washington, D.C. So she helped to turn her husband against Regan, who was forced to resign.

And Mrs. Reagan became increasingly upset because so many Americans and people around the world considered her husband bellicose and eager to confront the Soviet Union. She campaigned privately to persuade her husband to make overtures to Soviet leader Gorbachev and work with him to lower tensions. In the end, that's what Reagan did in a partnership that helped to end the Cold War.

*   *   *

REAGAN used all the modern methods of staying in touch, and some old-fashioned ones, throughout his eight years in office. He paid close attention to the polls. He scoured the news media, especially television, the dominant medium of his time. He had regular contact with everyday people through letters and maintained a remarkable group of pen pals. Most of all, he relied on his life experience as a young man growing up in Middle America to inform his judgments as president. He was a nostalgist, and his memories were not always accurate. But his belief in the striving, patriotic, good-hearted America that he fancied from his youth tapped into an important strain in the country's psyche.

CHAPTER NINE
BILL CLINTON

Escapes from Disaster

Bill Clinton relied on polls perhaps more than any other president in history to keep him grounded in American life. He also was a student of popular culture, paid close attention to movies and television, and maintained a large network of friends and associates, all to help him stay in touch.

When he was governor of Arkansas, he was always eager to learn what he could about the mood of the public, especially how he was doing in their estimation. Democratic pollster Stan Greenberg recalls meeting with Clinton in 1990 when he was governor. "He was intensely interested [in public opinion]," Greenberg recalls. "He viewed it as part of *being,* to understand people and what was going on in their lives. He thought he could connect with people and he was always talking to people.... He believed you couldn't be a leader if you didn't have that connection."[1]

Clinton also urged his advisers to talk to him candidly. After a few months as president, he told his senior staff that everyone had been giving him "an awful lot of what they thought I wanted to hear" and not enough of what they really thought. He felt that his official meetings didn't give him information about what was going on around the country because they were organized to make a point or argue a case, not to simply educate him. He resented the feeling of isolation, and he began calling the White House "the crown jewel of the federal penitentiary system."[2]

One evening, a steward opened his elevator door on the wrong floor of the White House residence, and Clinton stepped out and found himself in the middle of a reception for about 30 people that he didn't know. The steward quickly apologized and offered to take the president to the correct floor, but Clinton, looking around at the crowd, decided to stay and mingle. "Don't worry about it," Clinton told the steward. "I used to be a human once upon a time, too." He had a wonderful time talking to these strangers, who were delighted to converse with their unexpected visitor.

*   *   *

CLINTON REACHED out to the world beyond the White House in many ways. "From the beginning of his presidency, Clinton was under an all-out assault from Republican leaders and their acolytes and mouthpieces in the conservative media," writes political scientist Norman J. Ornstein. "He was also remarkably accessible to a wide range of allies and adversaries—constantly in contact with a mind-boggling collection of people to get ideas and gauge performance."[3]

"Clinton's uncanny ear for the American zeitgeist saved him from many perils and has made him a popular ex-president," writes historian Gil Troy. "But as president, Clinton was too mired in the center and anxious for Americans' approval. Abraham Lincoln, Theodore Roosevelt, and Franklin Roosevelt sought the popular center to move America forward. All three occasionally adjusted their own stands to broaden their support, but each risked popularity to defend core principles when meeting pressing challenges. Although Clinton could be as inspiring as Lincoln or the Roosevelts, he failed in policy making. Clinton's don't-rock-the-boat governance proved that moderation can lead to mediocrity if the president lacks the backbone to push his agenda and his constituents."[4]

Most important of all, increasingly he came to rely, perhaps over-rely, on his pollsters. At meetings, "The pollster was the first person to talk at White House meetings," says a prominent Democrat who attended some of the sessions. "The pollster was anointed with the special formula and the special stature."[5]

Says Dick Morris, Clinton's chief pollster and all-around political guru for part of his first term, "Bill Clinton did care what America thought. He cared not just so he would get reelected but because he too recalled Vietnam and knew that without popular support no policy would work. He was not, in this respect, a prisoner of polls. He rarely consulted them to decide what foreign policy should be. He used polling instead to discover what arguments would be most persuasive in getting popular support for a decision. In Bosnia, for example, he led America to the right conclusion despite adverse polling data that warned against American involvement."[6]

Clinton was also the first president to cope with the full range of changes in the media, which some called a revolution. There were no longer only three television networks—ABC, CBS, and NBC—that dominated the news flow of the country. CNN brought the news on cable 24 hours a day, and other "new media" added to the relentlessness of the news cycle, which was no longer geared to the evening news but to constant updates and one breaking story after another all day long. Talk radio took hold, especially conservative shows dominated by glib, entertaining, and hard-right commentators led by Rush Limbaugh. Unfortunately for him, Clinton became a celebrity politician in the sensational, 24-hour media age, a president who was of intense interest to the media and the public. And the stories flowed endlessly, stories about his taste in fast food, his jogging, whether he preferred boxers or briefs as underwear, even his sexual past and whether he had been faithful in his marriage.

The media, ever alert for the possibility of scandal and unwilling to give the president the benefit of the doubt, jumped onto stories about state troopers in Arkansas who alleged that they had facilitated adultery while Clinton was governor. Other stories speculated on whether Bill and Hillary Clinton got special treatment in a land deal, known as White-water, in which they invested years before he ran for president. It was an extraordinarily difficult environment in which to operate as president, especially for a baby boomer such as Clinton who had experienced the lifestyle, cultural, and political changes of his generation, which included opposition to the Vietnam War and a new, anything-goes era of media scrutiny that seemed to provide a salacious rumor a day.

All this also made it more difficult for a president to make a fair assessment of public attitudes toward him from the "mainstream media," from amidst the rising babble of the Internet community, and from partisan media such as conservative and liberal talk radio.

* * *

CLINTON FALTERED badly during his first two years, and he was informed about his slide every step of the way in a series of blunt memos from his chief pollster at the time, the brilliant and professorial Stan Greenberg. The problem was that Greenberg and other senior White House advisers couldn't agree on what to do about it, so Clinton was at sea.

In a confidential memo on January 6, 1994, entitled "The First 1994 survey," Greenberg wrote to President Clinton, First Lady Hillary Rodham Clinton, Vice President Al Gore, and four other senior advisers, "This first national survey of 1994 is just frustrating. In the last half of the year, the administration had won the respect of the American people—grudging, to be sure, in a period of great cynicism. An uneasy public had set aside many of its doubts about the president personally, focusing instead on his determination, hard work, intelligence, compassion and, most important, growing effectiveness.... The events of the past few weeks have taken their toll on your personal standing, though voters are discriminating about the charges and, for now, uncertain about their meaning. The news reports have deprived us of a very good Christmas and have reinforced the distrust that has always plagued us. People are asking themselves, 'is he real,' is he genuine, can we believe him—not about Whitewater, but about his vision and hopes for the country."[7]

Greenberg went on to say that Clinton's proposal to overhaul the healthcare system was in danger of failing in Congress (which, in the end, it did, resurrecting the charge that Clinton was too liberal and a weak leader). There also was widespread sentiment that Clinton had not done enough to improve the economy and that his policies for fighting crime, a major issue at the time, were ineffectual.[8]

As the midterm campaign advanced, Greenberg's internal memos painted an increasingly negative picture of how the November election would turn out for Clinton and fellow Democrats. The pollster said there was a likelihood of big losses in the House and Senate as Clinton's public image took a battering day after day, week after week.

In a memo on September 12, entitled "1994: Strategic Concepts," Greenberg started off with another warning. "The Republicans have effectively defined our current political environment and are on the verge of defining the 1994 contests in their own terms," he wrote. The GOP was portraying the Democrats, who controlled the White House and both houses of Congress, as unable to govern, advocates of big tax increases and big government, and a much bigger government role in the healthcare system, a measure that ultimately failed. Greenberg added, "The President's job approval is at 40 per cent according to the public polls, which needs to rise to 50 per cent to make possible an acceptable off-year result."[9]

On October 6, with the election only a month away, Greenberg sent another private memo, entitled "The 1994 Race Defined," to "The Political/Communications Team." He said, "The Republicans, with some success, have already tried to put their definition on the election: The

Democrats are for big government and higher taxes. The Republicans are for smaller government and lower taxes. If the Republicans succeed in making the election about that definition Democratic candidates will run at a strong disadvantage. That definition has allowed the Republicans to run as a protest party—opposed to what is happening in Washington." He said the GOP had given the Democrats an opening, however, by promoting a "Contract with America"—an agenda that they pledged to carry out if they took control of Congress and that included lower taxes on the wealthy, less government, and increased military spending. Greenberg suggested condemning the contract as "old policies that people believe put this country in a hole."[10] His argument was that these GOP ideas had been tried before and made matters worse.

On October 20, Greenberg sent President Clinton and seven senior advisers a confidential memo entitled "Strategic Issues—Final 3 Weeks." He tried to sound hopeful, but there was an undertone of dismay. "Our current course is making a difference, particularly for the President, and has the potential to make a difference in the election." But Greenberg said there were still serious problems for Clinton and the Democrats, including the fact that Clinton's approval ratings remained poor on the economy, taxes, and the deficit. "The 1994 election remains very tough, although we are beginning to have some impact," Greenberg wrote. "Overall, the partisan environment remains tilted against us.... The party is operating at a remarkable disadvantage in 1994; just 35 per cent of the public express a 'warm' sentiment about the Democratic Party; 44 per cent express such sentiments about Republicans—putting our candidates at a 9-point disadvantage."[11]

Greenberg urged the president and fellow Democrats to emphasize that they were on the people's side in terms of working for the middle class and wanting to "go forward," while the Republicans favored the rich and the powerful and wanted to take the country back to failed conservative policies of the past. These were themes that the Democrats had used frequently over the years (and would use again in the 2012 campaign to re-elect Barack Obama). But it turned out that the voters didn't believe the Democrats this time.[12]

*   *   *

IN NOVEMBER 1994, Clinton's Democratic party lost control of Congress in a shattering rebuff, partly because the president was so unpopular as the top Democrat. This seemed to be an ominous sign for Clinton's re-election in 1996, and it triggered an almost obsessive effort by Clinton to reach out and fix what had gone wrong.

In sum, Greenberg wrote confidentially to Clinton and handful of other top aides on November 22, "The nagging doubts about the President formed the backdrop of the 1994 election. People did not vote those doubts [Clinton, of course, was not on the ballot], but they contributed powerfully to the sense that Democrats could not change the country for the better. They undermined the morale of many who would otherwise support Democrats in the congressional and state elections. The Clinton Presidency cannot succeed, nor can Bill Clinton be re-elected, when less than 40 per cent of the electorate say he makes them feel confident (37 per cent in our latest survey).

"The root of the problem is the sense that Bill Clinton is not strong enough to deliver on his promises.... The failure to deliver has led voters to a number of conclusions and feelings about the President: you can't believe in him, he has broken his promises, he is weak, he's not honest. It has produced a number of powerful emotions; disappointment, resentment, distrust, indeed, a sense of betrayal."[13]

And in a passage within that November 22 memo that was sent only to the president and first lady, Greenberg sagely noted, "Voters are quite conscious that there is a question of morals associated with the President. About half of the college-educated women, seniors and older non-college women mentioned the issue in their open-ended comments about the President. Indeed, 'questionable morals' was the highest single attribute selected in the word choice exercise (19 mentions, though overwhelmed by the range of responses on effectiveness and leadership). The discussion in the groups, not surprisingly, centered on 'fools around,' 'running around with women,' 'sexual escapades,' 'unfaithful to his wife,' 'plays around with women too much.'"[14]

*   *   *

IN LATE DECEMBER, Clinton and his wife Hillary convened a group of self-help authors, motivational speakers, and communications specialists at the presidential retreat at Camp David. He wanted their evaluations of his first two years as president and how he could recover his luster.

Among the attendees were authors Anthony Robbins, Marianne Williamson, and Stephen R. Covey. The names of these well-known self-help gurus were leaked to the media. Two others were also there—Jean Houston, an author and self-styled expert on psychic experience, and Mary Catherine Bateson, a colleague of Houston's and anthropology professor at George Mason University. It seemed to Clinton critics that he was desperately casting about for answers to explain his lack of leadership.

At one point during the hours of discussion, the president was asked to describe his best qualities. "I have a good heart," he replied. "I really do. I hope I have a decent mind." He was eager to do what was best for the country, he said, and it was clear he would seek counsel and insight from anyone he could in order to achieve that goal.[15]

Clinton also brought controversial political consultant Dick Morris back into his inner circle. Morris had worked for Clinton in his first run for governor of Arkansas in 1978, which he won. Clinton and Morris soon parted ways, but after Clinton lost his bid for re-election in 1980, he hired Morris again and won the governorship in 1982. "From that point on, the two men had maintained a Svengali-like relationship," says consultant Doug Schoen, who worked with both of them after Clinton won the White House.[16]

But Morris's role was kept quiet at first, partly because he was also working for conservative Republicans and didn't want to be labeled a mercenary. Morris, realizing the magnitude of the challenge he was facing, quickly enlisted his friend and fellow pollster Doug Schoen to work with him on his new rescue mission at the White House.

"I did our first poll for Clinton in December 1994 on the issue of targeted tax cuts," Schoen recalled. "Our polling showed clearly that, for Clinton to get reelected, he would need to take dramatic steps to repair his image. He was perceived as a cultural and social liberal and his approval rating was well below 40 per cent. Things needed to change, but the working arrangement itself was decidedly odd. The president was clearly listening to me—a national television address on the subject of targeted tax cuts made that clear enough, and yet we hadn't officially been hired. As far as the world knew. Stan Greenberg remained Clinton's pollster. I was breaking out my rusty French to track Morris down [while he was vacationing] in France to talk strategy, and just when I'd begin to suspect that this was not what Morris said it would be, Clinton would go public with one of our ideas. The situation was intriguing but unsatisfying."[17]

In January 1995, Morris paged Schoen and told him they were scheduled to meet with Clinton at the White House on February 6. It would be a memorable session.

"I was shocked by the man I saw there," Schoen recalled. "The president of the United States is the most powerful man in the world, yet when I first met Bill Clinton, he appeared defeated. He was physically in the room, but mentally he was somewhere else. I knew Clinton to be powerful, brilliant, and famously charismatic, yet the Bill Clinton I found that night seemed disengaged from his own administration. The way he told it, others were making decisions in the White House, and he was only one of the many voices.[18]

"I wanted to get up, walk across the room, grab him by the shoulders, start shaking him, and tell him to snap out of it. It was my first meeting with a sitting president, but, far from being awed, I was dismayed. Still, Clinton's analysis of the situation was right on. 'I'm way out of position,' he complained. He had run as a moderate Democrat in 1992 but was now seen as a cultural and social liberal. In particular, he was bitter about the advice given to him by his pollster, Stan Greenberg, who had counseled him to pursue healthcare reform but later criticized the decision and said it was the reason Democrats had lost the 1994 midterm election."[19]

In addition to firing some of the liberals, a frustrated Clinton told the two pollsters that he needed to do one other thing. "I've got to get back with the people," the president said. He felt too isolated in the White House. He added, "How can I make policy if I don't know what the public thinks? . . . If I don't know what the people think, what good will I be?" Schoen concluded that Clinton was talking past the American people and, at that point, wasn't relevant to their lives.

Only about 38 per cent of voters approved of Clinton's job performance, according to Democratic polls, a dangerously low level. The president explained to his new pollsters that he was really a fiscal conservative and in some ways a cultural conservative, but the public wasn't perceiving him that way, partly because he was following the lead of liberal members of Congress such as then–House Speaker Tom Foley and then–Senate Majority Leader George Mitchell, in developing legislation. Another problem, Clinton said, was because some of his key advisers, such as Greenberg, were liberal. Clinton also said he was seen as a big spender and a creature of the left-wing celebrity culture of Hollywood. He said he needed to change all that, and that meant a change in his inner circle.

Schoen told him he would never win fiscally conservative voters, such as those who supported billionaire businessman Ross Perot in 1992, unless he showed he also was a fiscal conservative. Clinton said he agreed with that assessment.

After deciding to bypass Greenberg, who from then on did most of his White House–related work for the Democratic National Committee, Clinton began a series of initiatives that were widely considered conservative if small-bore "values issues," such as advocating school uniforms to increase the sense of discipline and pride in public schools, and allowing prayer in school. He also advocated a balanced budget, rare for a Democratic president.

From then on, there was virtually no limit to the polling that Clinton sought and got, his key aides said. His pollsters briefed him at least once a week and often several times a week during the runup to the 1996 election, which he won handily. Schoen and his partner Mark Penn did 50 to 60 polls a year. "His bottom line was the pollsters drove the bus," a senior Clinton aide told me. Penn and Schoen said they didn't think of themselves as policy-makers, only as advisers who could tell Clinton what the public wanted, how his ideas were going over, and how to sell them to the public.

Other Clinton aides recalled that, shortly after the devastating Democratic losses in the congressional elections of November 1994, the president began meeting at 7 or 7:30 p.m. every Wednesday with his political advisers on the second floor of the White House residence.

Morris said Clinton complained, "Greenberg never told me what to do," and Clinton wanted his pollster to provide clarity about his course of action.[20] Morris was different. After he supplanted Greenberg as Clinton's chief public-opinion analyst, Morris did tell Clinton what to do. That seemed to be his main goal.

Clinton's approach was to have his pollsters brief him directly on their research, including confidential analyses of their findings and how they might shape administration decisions, especially how to keep Clinton's job-approval ratings high. Many of the polls and memos today reveal an intense preoccupation with survey research on virtually every conceivable aspect of policy and politics. The topics of the polls, financed by the Democratic National Committee, included public attitudes toward major Clinton policies such as balancing the budget, abolishing welfare, promoting free trade, and helping parents use technology to control what their children watched on television.

Summarizing their counsel, Schoen writes, "Morris and I were agreed on our prescription for the president. He needed to first and foremost present himself to the country as a fiscal conservative. Otherwise, he would never be able to escape the tax-and-spend label. My solution was clear: present a balanced budget. In January, Clinton had sent a budget to Capitol Hill that called for massive budget deficits in both the near- and long-term. Not only was it dead on arrival, it was ridiculed by congressional Republicans who were pushing hard for both an end to deficits and a constitutional amendment that would force Congress to balance the budget. They had the American people on their side. According to our polling numbers, 80 per cent of Americans wanted Washington to get its fiscal house in order."[21]

Morris recognized that his new client was suffering from the historical problem of presidential isolation:

> As a president sits in his office, he may easily be overcome by the day-to-day details," Morris wrote. "He therefore relies on his staff to present him with possible courses of action; he has no time to develop them himself. He can issue whatever orders he wants to issue, but the alternatives are suggested to him by the staff. This—as I have said—is how the staff controls the president. He can't easily fire his people because they might turn around and savage him from the outside and give him even bigger problems than he started with. Besides, at least in Clinton's administration, each staffer represents a constituency, and by firing the staffer, the president would also fire the voters, or the donors or the politicians the staffer represents.
>
> This is why Clinton is such an avid reader of magazines, journals of opinion, editorials, and columnists in preference to reading the news. After all, he *was* the news. He needed his reading hours to canvass advisers, and get opinions that amplify options.[22]

Morris, glib and ever ready with a new idea, urged a new path for Clinton—promoting "bite-size" initiatives such as urging the use of school uniforms to promote discipline and pride, raising the minimum wage, increasing scholarships, encouraging the use of technology through the "V" chip to allow parents to block child-unfriendly TV shows, and asking Congress to fund 100,000 new cops on the beat nationwide to fight crime. He urged Clinton to emphasize "compromise, reconciliation, values, and healing" and to speak "the new language of opportunity-responsibility" rather than use "class-warfare" rhetoric that would divide the country and lead to policies that Morris contended would fail the middle class. Morris said Clinton should "take a middle course," and "triangulate, create a third position, not just in between the old positions of the two parties but above them as well."[23]

In his 1996 State of the Union address, Clinton, following Morris's advice, sounded Reaganesque when he declared, "[T]he era of big government is over."[24]

*   *   *

THE WHITE HOUSE was deeply divided between centrists such as Schoen, Morris, Penn, Treasury Secretary Bob Rubin, and Vice President Al Gore on one side, and liberals including Chief of Staff Leon Panetta and senior aides George Stephanopoulos and Harold Ickes on the other side. "Having come from the outside into this political maelstrom, I quickly realized that Morris and I had entered a brutal battle for the president's soul," Schoen recalled. "In early 1995, it wasn't clear who was going to win—or even if we were going to be around when that moment arrived, not to mention the next week."[25]

The issue that provoked most internal feuding was a balanced budget. Morris and Schoen pushed for it, and the liberal advisers such as Ickes, Panetta, and Stephanopoulos opposed it.[26] Morris and Schoen produced polls showing that most Americans favored a balanced budget, but still the liberals were against the idea, saying it would alienate congressional Democrats and violate liberal principles because social programs would have to be cut. For many weeks, Clinton, who sometimes vacillated on controversial issues, wouldn't commit.

Finally, on June 13, 1995, he gave a speech to the nation pledging to balance the budge in ten years, three years sooner than what the Republicans called for in their plan. He also set forth a list of spending cuts, including reductions in Medicare that were less severe than what the Republicans supported but still represented a break from Democratic orthodoxy. Clinton had sided with the pollsters over the liberal ideologues.

"Dick [Morris] liked to call it triangulation—taking the best from both parties," writes Schoen. "To him, it was the most effective way not only to redefine the Democratic Party but also to respond to the more centrist mood of the electorate. In fact, I never truly bought into the triangulation theory. In my view, the reality was more complicated. The country was trending to the Right. For Clinton to survive, he had to move closer to conservative political positions—because quite simply, they better reflected the mood of the electorate. But he had to talk in terms of values—effectively speaking a new language that many Democrats did not understand and appreciate. By late June, Clinton's poll numbers were already inching upward."[27]

Hammering at the issues of fiscal responsibility, fighting crime, and protecting the middle class, at the urging of the pollsters, Clinton's re-election campaign started a massive advertising blitz in mid 1995, more than a year before the 1996 election and far earlier than was customary. The main message was that Clinton was willing to cut taxes but at the

same time he would defend Medicare, Medicaid, education, the environment, and programs to fight crime.

Schoen says, "From the summer of 1995 until Election day, in
November 1996, we bombarded the nation's airwaves with ad after ad.
In crafting these ads, we were careful to always start on a positive note,
first emphasizing that the president was a positive campaigner who shared
and understood voters' concerns and values, and only then responding
to Republican attacks with counterattacks that, say, excoriated congressional Republicans for their 'heartless' budgetary plans. The swing in the
president's poll numbers was immediate and extraordinary. Within a short
period, Clinton's favorabilities were cresting.... [T]he early advertising
blitz was probably the single most important factor in turning public sentiment in the president's favor. Without the ads, I'm convinced Clinton
would not have been easily reelected."[28]

* * *

THE ROLE OF THE POLLSTERS during the government shutdown
in the summer of 1995 was crucial, and provided insight into how much
Clinton came to rely on survey research.

As Schoen recounts, he sat with Clinton in the Map Room of the
White House in August 1995 and they discussed how one poll after
another indicated that Clinton should stand and fight the Republicans
over the budget rather than knuckle under to draconian GOP demands
for cuts. Schoen told Clinton that his approach was working, but the
president wasn't so sure and he realized his presidency was on the line.
"Poll it again," the president said. "I just don't believe it. Test five or six
more hypotheses."[29] They did, and the results were the same as they had
been in previous surveys—58 per cent of Americans would blame the
Republicans if the government were shut down; only 25 per cent said
they would blame the president.

The confrontation was not resolved, and there was a partial government
shutdown. It lasted only a few days, but Clinton came out of it with an
enhanced reputation as a fighter and a defender of the middle class. In addition, Clinton was coming across to more people as strong and principled.

Then the Republican leaders in Congress shut down the government
again rather than give in to the president. This time the shutdown lasted
more than a month. Morris polled every night, trying to determine how
Clinton could win the public-relations battle with the GOP, and the
president and his senior staff were briefed on the polls every morning.[30]

Huge majorities approved of Clinton's handling of the crisis since Clinton's poll-guided stance seemed more reasonable, and most disapproved of GOP tactics to reject compromise, which seemed harsh and overly belligerent. Clinton again came out ahead.

* * *

A COMMON COMPLAINT by Clinton to his staff—some of his advisers thought it was an obsession—was his treatment by the news media. He said they were too critical, always looking for faults, seemingly eager to hurt his presidency or declare him a failure. "He talked about the press more than anything else," recalls pollster Greenberg.[31] For extended periods, this caused him to read the newspapers and magazines and watch the TV news less and less. It only upset him.

He gave his closest friends a special fax number they could use to send him private communications about how he was doing and discuss other topics that were on their minds. He promised they would always be kept private. These faxes would arrive in his executive assistant's office just outside the Oval Office, and Clinton made a point of reading them all.

He would also talk to friends on the phone, sometimes in the wee hours, just as Lyndon Johnson had done, or have them meet with him at the White House. He had a long list of people inside and outside Washington whom he would contact.[32] If they talked about the sessions publicly or to the media, they wouldn't be asked over again or he wouldn't call back. Former White House Chief of Staff Leon Panetta observed, "This guy is like a hungry lion who searches for every morsel of information he can get." He was always reaching out to people for suggestions, ideas, and advice.[33] But Clinton found that his friends and associates were still so deferential and supportive that as a rule he didn't get much candor.

When he had some free time, Clinton would play golf and chat about contemporary events with trusted friends, including Washington, D.C. power broker Vernon Jordan.

He would pay close attention to anything he felt would give him a reading on the public mood, even to the point of noticing how many bystanders gave him the finger when his motorcade passed by (a rude sign that Ronald Reagan also had looked for to gauge his public standing). He was careful to note how friendly people were when he shook their hands after speeches or at rope lines when he was traveling, and how they reacted when he hugged them.

He was perpetually late, talking to people he met at speeches and rallies after the official program was over, making him behind schedule for his next appointment. He was not only energized by the contact; he felt he was learning, up close and personal, and in a highly textured way, what Americans were thinking and feeling. To a large extent, this was true because of the intensity and frequency with which reached out.

*   *   *

CLINTON'S INTEREST IN polling only intensified. In 1995, Morris even polled for him, without being asked, on where he should go on vacation, which Morris later admitted was "the ultimate in carrying polling to a mindless extreme."[34]

"We learned that hunters were, of course, for [Senator Bob] Dole [Clinton's eventual Republican opponent], MTV viewers for Clinton," Morris said. "But baseball fans were swing voters. So were hikers and people who love technology. Camping out was a favorite of swing voters." So Morris told a meeting of the highest-level White House strategy group that he had a list of "approved presidential activities for his coming vacation. I urged that he take a mountain vacation, that he hike and camp out in a tent." Golf, though it was a sport that appealed to Republicans, was also judged by Morris to be "a presidential activity," partly because he knew Clinton had become an avid duffer and wanted to play golf on his vacation. Morris said, he "compensated by noting that we would have to publicize the high-tech gear the president would be using" as an outdoorsman.[35]

Clinton wasn't pleased and he began to mock Morris's recommendations. "Can I golf?" the president asked sarcastically. "Maybe if I wear a baseball cap? ... What if I hike, set up my campsite, and go fishing but I don't catch anything? Will that be OK?"

But on his next vacation, Clinton did what the pollster recommended—he went camping with his family, and he hiked in a national park.

The following year, just before the fall election campaign, he vacationed in the Rockies. But he called Morris and asked, "I want to take Chelsea [his daughter] rafting. She really likes it. Do you think it's OK?"

Morris asked, "Is it dangerous?"—missing the point.

"No," Clinton replied, "There's no danger, but do you think they'll make a joke of it?"

He was referring to white-water rafting and the potential of its being linked to an ongoing investigation into an investment that Bill and Hillary Clinton had made years ago in an Arkansas land deal called Whitewater.

Morris advised him to not to worry. "No sir, go rafting," Morris said. "Even if they joke about it, they'll have to write that you went rafting and that will be good for you politically."[36]

After he was safely re-elected, Clinton never again went on a hiking or outdoors vacation. He went where he had the best time, to Martha's Vineyard, Massachusetts, a playground for the rich and famous where he loved to be surrounded with adoring celebrities.

In early 1998, Penn and Schoen even polled on the dog that the Clintons had just brought into their household. In a confidential January 6 strategy memo for the president, the pollsters wrote, "The gang did not want us to share some holiday fun for fear it would get out, but the number one story is in fact the acquisition of a dog, edging out the Bosnia troop visit by one point." Eighty-five per cent of Americans were "aware of the new puppy," the pollsters reported, and 56.7 per cent approved of the name given to the canine, Buddy. "Only 16 per cent think the Clinton family should get another pet," the memo said. The fact that the pollsters saw fit to test these propositions, and then present their findings to the commander in chief, shows how deeply Clinton craved polling information on virtually every topic.

The memos sometimes seemed designed to lift the president's morale, which became a common role for White House pollsters over the years. "The mood of the country is exceptional," the pollsters wrote on January 6, "and the holidays (including a visit to U.S. troops), a strong economy, have all continued to keep the administration's numbers at a zenith." Sixty-eight per cent of Americans approved of the job Clinton was doing, and 66 per cent said the economy was on the "right track," a key finding that indicated voter optimism.

But there were some warning signs. The public was starting to pay attention to allegations of sexual impropriety swirling around the president. Seventy-eight per cent were "aware of President Clinton being deposed by Paula Jones' lawyer in a sexual harassment case against him (16 per cent unaware)," the pollsters wrote. Twenty-eight per cent were "more favorable" toward Clinton's denial and 40 per cent were "less favorable." This was the case that eventually led to charges of perjury against Clinton that would result in his impeachment.

On January 21, the pollsters asked this question in another survey, which they summarized in a memo: "Paula Jones has accused President Clinton of making sexual advances in a Little Rock, Arkansas, hotel room in 1991. President Clinton has denied the accusations. Who do you think is right—President Clinton or Paula Jones? 33 per cent President Clinton.

28 per cent Paula Jones." It was not an overwhelming show of trust in the president, who got the nickname "slick Willie" when he was governor of Arkansas and who also had a reputation as a womanizer.

Week after week, the pollsters gave Clinton this rich diet of survey research. The pollsters' briefing sessions became very popular with the White House staff, and many clamored to attend because they knew the president was so interested in the topic and they wanted to be close to the action. Nearly every polling memo started off with a summary of whether Americans thought the country was headed in the right direction, how people assessed the state of the economy, and Clinton's job-approval rating, which held up remarkably well even during his most difficult times.

Clinton's worst crisis began on January 21, 1998, when news broke that he had engaged in an affair with White House intern Monica Lewinsky. As multiple investigations continued, including several by the news media, by Congress, and, most important, by independent counsel Kenneth Starr, the furor grew. In August 1998, Clinton testified before a grand jury. Clinton was impeached by the House of Representatives in December 1998 for lying under oath and acquitted by the Senate in February 1999.

Throughout the episode, Clinton relied heavily on polls to determine his course of action and his public stances. The conclusion that the pollsters gave Clinton was that the public was "willing to forgive you for adultery, but not for perjury or obstruction of justice." Since Clinton had already denied the affair under oath, the president at first decided to continue lying about it rather than admit his earlier deception.[37]

As the impeachment saga intensified, Clinton needed every public-relations advantage in his desperate struggle with Starr, who was investigating a variety of charges against Clinton, including whether he had lied under oath about having an affair with Lewinsky. As the controversy turned white-hot, Clinton had to face the possibility that the Senate might remove him from office, and his pollsters gave him extensive survey research on how he could best persuade the country that congressional Republicans were on an unfair witch hunt to destroy his presidency. In weekly, and sometimes more frequent, poll briefings held in the president's East Wing residence, Penn showed him how, with the proper spin and public-relations techniques, his policies could remain popular even if his private failings were the objects of scorn and ridicule.

Penn's advice, which Clinton accepted, was to hammer home the idea that he was sorry for his adultery and his lies, which he eventually admitted, but they had nothing to do with whether he was a good president. Clinton's refrain was that he got up every morning to work for the American people, and he would continue to do his job no matter how much embarrassment he suffered from the Lewinsky disclosures. Clinton knew, based on Penn's research, that the American people would be receptive to this message. Among his most effective strategies was portraying Starr as obsessed with his personal life.

One of the most important developments in the Clinton presidency, in fact, was his success in persuading the country to separate his private character, which most people thought was deeply flawed, from his public leadership, which most people admired.

Not only did Clinton's poll-tested strategy save his presidency; it also boosted his approval ratings. By insisting that it was important for him to continue working for the American people as president during a time of peace and prosperity, Clinton saw his approval rating soar to 60 per cent in January 1998, and it never dropped below that level for the remainder of his time in office.[38]

* * *

CLINTON was one of the most empathetic presidents in history. He stayed in touch with the country in every way imaginable, and was proud of how close he was to the people. After an unpopular flirtation with liberalism during his first two years, he moved to the center after his party suffered serious losses in the 1994 congressional elections. After that, he was even more obsessed with polls, and they helped him win re-election in 1996 and to survive impeachment. His policies matched the public mood and gave Americans the kind of helpful, modestly activist government they wanted in the 1990s.

CHAPTER TEN
BARACK OBAMA

BEYOND THE BELTWAY

Barack Obama recognizes more than most of his predecessors the problem of presidential isolation, which he calls, with disdain and disappointment, "the bubble." Shortly after taking office, he said, "It's the hardest thing about being president. I mean, how do you stay in touch with the flow of everyday life?"[1]

Adding to the dilemma is the fact that he is surrounded by aides who see him as a "transformational" leader and a major historical figure because he is the first African American president and has set an ambitious agenda for change. He not only finds it difficult to escape from the rarified atmosphere of the White House, but he is treated with a special deference every hour of the day by his aides and his friends. He does attempt to get other views and he takes various steps to break out of the White House cocoon, but he recognizes that the results have been mixed.

An insight into his plight came in October 2012 when Obama revealed a "secret" to TV talk-show host Jay Leno on NBC's *Tonight Show*: He had overruled the Secret Service and actually driven a car on the White House grounds. His bodyguards frowned upon such a thing because he was so exposed to view from outside the gates and because of concern that he might get into an accident. But, like a child with a new toy, Obama jumped at the chance to familiarize himself with this new plaything. His life had gotten so far from normal that even something as common as driving a car had become a big deal.

So Obama said he got behind the wheel of a Chevrolet Volt, a semi-electric car, when a friend drove the vehicle to the White House and asked him, "Why don't you take it for a spin?" That's what he did, on the spur of the moment. "I was really getting into it," Obama said. The Secret Service closed the gates to discourage him from driving outside the grounds, and he had to content himself with a very limited itinerary. "That was my big joy ride," Obama said ruefully. "Three times around the South Lawn driveway. It was wild."[2]

* * *

ADDING TO his aura of apartness, at least in official Washington, Obama has kept his distance from many other influential people in the capital, and he seems aloof even from his allies who increasingly are puzzled by it or resent it.

For a while, Obama felt badly misunderstood and maligned by his critics—an occupational hazard for any president going through a rough patch, as was happening to Obama in 2010 when the economy was sinking and his approval ratings were dropping. He spent more time with his small circle of friends from his hometown of Chicago whom he had appointed to key jobs in his administration, including White House senior adviser Valerie Jarrett, and senior advisers from the glory days of his 2008 campaign, such as senior strategist David Plouffe. It was a "bubble within the bubble" and a "self-imposed exile" as Obama's closest associates promoted the idea that "the American public just did not appreciate their exceptional leader."[3]

He seemed cut off from Capitol Hill, where legislators, even powerful ones who could help him advance his agenda, would go for months without hearing from him. "I don't think he really likes politics," said veteran Democratic pollster Peter Hart, who admired Obama but felt that the president was isolating himself too much, at least from Washington insiders. "He likes performing. He likes crowds." In describing the Obama White House in 2012, Hart said that early efforts by Obama to reach out had mostly ended. "It's closed. It's insular. It's shut out," the consultant said. "This is not a person who is interested in getting the maximum amount of information from the maximum amount of people."[4]

To many in Washington, he seemed arrogant. The story spread of how a senior legislator asked Obama in 2008 if he could truly fill the football stadium in Denver where he was supposed to give his speech accepting the Democratic presidential nomination. Obama dismissed the concern. "There's not a venue in America I can't fill," he said with supreme confidence. Many of his political colleagues said he hadn't changed in his desire to stand apart from the capital's insiders.

But he makes no apologies. Journalist Fareed Zakaria asked him in a January 2012 interview about his cool, aloof style, especially in dealing with congressional Republican leaders, and Obama replied, "You know, the truth is, actually, when it comes to Congress, the issue is not personal relationships. My suspicion is that this whole critique has to do with the fact that I don't go to a lot of Washington parties. And as a consequence, the Washington press corps maybe just doesn't feel like I'm in the mix enough with them, and they figure, well, if I'm not spending time with them I must be cold and aloof. The fact is, I've got a 13-year-old and 10-year-old daughter."[5] His friends say he prefers to spend time with his family rather than schmooze with the capital's power brokers. And he is particularly sensitive to his daughters because his own father was an absentee parent and the young Obama always missed having a paternal presence in his life.

He addressed the issue again in a November 2012 interview with CNN. "Sometimes Michelle and I not doing the circuit and going out to dinners with folks is perceived as us being cool," he said. "It actually really has more to do with us being parents." He added, "Sometimes on weekends, we may turn down the invitation to this or that or the other just because we're trying to carve out family time."

His aides say there's another reason he hasn't warmed to the capital's social circuit. He thinks Washington has become so divided and partisan that his adversaries won't compromise with him no matter how charming he is or how much he reaches out to them. This is a valid point, given how much of his agenda opposition Republicans blocked in his first four years.

*   *   *

OBAMA ACTUALLY has tried in many ways to avoid isolation. He was the first president to make extensive use of the new technologies of social media. He refused to give up his BlackBerry, even though his Secret Service bodyguards thought the device could enable terrorists to track his movements. But Obama was very eager to remain in touch with friends around the country, to whom he had given his private contact information. He kept using his device, albeit with extra security precautions. Obama also surfed the Internet at the White House residence each night, checked his email using various techniques, and took a look at sports news. "He wanted to stay in contact with the outside world and break out of the bubble," says Cornell Belcher, a Democratic pollster who did survey for the Obama campaigns and the Democratic Party in 2008 and 2012.[6]

Obama tried some new techniques. He used his iPad, on which he scanned newspaper reports and other news items (he rarely watched news on TV, considering it too superficial and sensational). He held town-hall-style meetings with some questions posed via Facebook and Twitter, two popular outlets of social media. The topics were similar to those asked by people at in-person town-hall meetings, but Obama friends said he missed the engagement of such in-person sessions when he could see people eye to eye, observe their body language, and perhaps shake hands with them. But he thought it was worth the effort because he was experimenting with potentially valuable new forms of presidential communication and he was showing Americans that he was reaching out in creative new ways.

*   *   *

IN A MORE traditional approach, Obama often refers to the importance of letters from everyday citizens as a lifeline to the world outside Washington. He receives 10 communications a day, selected by his staff from an estimated 20,000 letters and emails that arrive at the White House daily, and reads them in his residence after work. Obama is not, of course, the first president to use this method to stay in touch. Ronald Reagan and Franklin Roosevelt did it, too, and they frequently wrote handwritten responses, as Obama does. But Obama takes it particularly seriously.

First Lady Michelle Obama has said her husband is absolutely devoted to reading the letters, demonstrating the same level of commitment to the public she has always seen in him. And she has explained that her husband is trying his best to live a normal life in the White House. "He's the same man who, when our girls were first born, would anxiously check their cribs every few minutes to ensure they were still breathing, proudly showing them off to everyone we knew," she told the Democratic National Convention in Charlotte, North Carolina, on September 4, 2012.

"That's the man who sits down with me and our girls for dinner nearly every night, patiently answering their questions about issues in the news, and strategizing about middle-school friendships.

"That's the man I see in those quiet moments late at night, hunched over his desk, poring over the letters people have sent him.

"The letter from the father struggling to pay his bills ... from the woman dying of cancer whose insurance company won't cover her care ... from the young person with so much promise but so few opportunities.

"I see the concern in his eyes ... and I hear the determination in his voice as he tells me, 'You won't believe what these folks are going through, Michelle.... It's not right. We've got to keep working to fix this. We've got so much more to do.'

"I see how those stories, our collection of struggles and hopes and dreams, I see how that's what drives Barack Obama every single day."

And like his predecessors, Obama sees the letters, delivered to him six days a week during the evenings in a purple folder, as a lifeline to reality. His aides told me he often forwards the letters to his senior advisers and other government policy-makers after he has read them, and he frequently annotates them with his comments or with orders to look into their complaints. In other cases, he calls his aides to ask them to follow up. Sometimes he also calls the actual letter-writers or writes out replies by hand. In other cases, he reads them to his wife before bed.

He isn't troubled, his aides said, that the tone of some letters is derisive or even insulting, addressed to "Dear Jackass" or "Dear Moron."[7] Obama believes the tone reflects people's understandable stress and dissatisfaction during very difficult times.

In June 2011, Charles Oliver, a carpenter in Portland, Maine, wrote Obama that he was unemployed and the economy was in trouble, and asked the president, "Are we as Americans going to be all right?"[8] Obama took the letter to heart—it was a familiar refrain in the correspondence he had received from day one in the White House—and he tried to be honest with Oliver. "I know things are tough right now, and I won't lie to you," Obama replied on White House stationery in a hand-written scrawl, "—it will probably take another year or two to fully dig our way out of this hole." But Obama added, "But yes, we will be ok. Because America has gotten through tougher times before, and because of good people like you."

Obama also uses the letters for political purposes. In July 2012, the Democratic National Committee sent out a fund-raising letter from Obama that opened, "Each night, I get the chance to read about 10 letters from people across the country. Some are inspiring. Some are heartbreaking. But each one compels me to keep moving forward on this journey we started together.

"And as I read the stories, hopes and fears of people nationwide, I'm also reminded of what I told you and the American people when I was sent to the White House. I cannot do this alone."[9] He went on to ask each recipient of his letter to send "a membership contribution of $25, $35, $50 or more to the Democratic National Committee.

On January 8, 2010, his purple folder contained what his aides called the usual "10 pieces of unvetted correspondence" addressed to the president. "Inside, Obama found crumpled notebook paper, smudged ink, sloppy handwriting, and misspelled words—a collection of ten letters from constituents that he considered his most important daily reading," said a journalist who was given access to the correspondence on that day. "One letter was from a grade-schooler asking for help on his spelling homework; another was from an unemployed mother demanding a job."[10]

Obama called attention to the letters in his first news conference after the 2012 election, which he easily won partly because he had managed to stay more in touch than his opponent. Addressing reporters on November 14, 2012, in the East Room, Obama said he had received an email from Steve Wise of Brentwood, Tennessee, who expressed admirable sentiments about the importance of compromise, views that the two of them shared. Wise wrote on November 11, "I am hoping this email does reach you but am realistic that it most likely will not. So whoever reads this I hope you handle [its] content in the way it was intended." Wise admitted he had not voted for Obama in 2012 but added, "[G]iven that we have elected you to another term I stand ready to support your efforts to move the U.S. forward and deliver solutions that will solve our important issues, especially as they relate to the economy. I am starting a new business so I expect I will be impacted by any solutions put in place. My hope is that we can make progress in light of personal and party principles, special interest and years of business as usual. We've got to work together and put our differences aside."[11]

*　*　*

SOMETIMES Obama has personal contact with a regular citizen that gives him a vivid impression of the world outside the White House. In September 2010, he was brought up short at a town-hall meeting on the economy in Baltimore, Maryland, when an African American woman named Velma Hart told him, "Quite frankly, I'm exhausted. Exhausted of defending you, defending your administration, defending the man for change I voted for, and deeply disappointed with where we are right now." She added that the recession had badly hurt her family and had caused her and her husband to sink deeply into worry about their financial situation. "And quite frankly, Mr. President, I need you to answer honestly—is this my new reality?" she asked.[12]

Obama replied, "As I said before, times are tough for everybody right now. So I understand your frustration." He said his administration was doing its best to help families get by.

Afterward, Hart, of Upper Marlboro, Maryland, said she still supported President Obama and felt that the economy was slowly improving but she found the possibility of unemployment "scary." Two months later, Hart was laid off from her job as chief financial officer for AmVets, a veterans' service group based in Maryland, in what was described by AmVets officials as a cost-cutting move.

Friends of the president said this personal contact makes a big difference and has much more impact on a president than other forms of communication with citizens.

*   *   *

OBAMA brought more of a sense of the middle class with him into the White House than his critics acknowledged. He was not raised as a liberal elitist, as some critics charged, but in a thoroughly middle-class household. "If there is a representative teenager's life, Barry Obama lived a version of it in Hawaii in the late 1970s," writes biographer David Maraniss. "Several things stood out—he went to a prestigious school, he lived with his grandparents, his father was gone, his mother was infrequently present, he was a *hapa* black in a place where most people were a light shade of brown—and those traits helped shaped his particular character, but they did not make his life odd or mysterious. He smoked pot with his Choom Gang and goofed around outside the classroom, where he came across as smart and mature if not notably studious, but the central activity of his high school life was basketball. With equally strong roots in the Kansas of his ancestors and the playgrounds of black America, basketball connected the disconnected parts of him—and he was good enough to play with 'the best bunch of guys' [his words] on the best team in Hawaii, one of the best teams in the nation."[13]

He has remained a sports fan throughout his life, and kept track of sports teams throughout his presidency, partly to relax and partly to stay in touch with popular culture because sports are where so many Americans find common ground. His favorite teams are those from his home city of Chicago, especially the Bulls of the National Basketball Association.

A senior Obama adviser told me that Obama has a deep connection to the middle class because of "the upbringing he had, the way he was raised." He was taught by his mother and his grandparents that education and hard work were keys to achieving the American Dream of prosperity and upward mobility. He was a striver, but his means were modest, and he wasn't able to pay off his student loans until well into his adulthood, which is common among young college graduates today. The aide also said Michelle Obama lived "the great American story" in which her father worked at a filtration plant in Chicago and imbued in his children the desire to make their lives better by getting good educations and working hard.

*   *   *

AS PRESIDENT, OBAMA makes effective use of associates and people he learns about in the news in order to stay in touch. In September 2011, two days before giving a speech to Congress on jobs, Obama contacted Starbucks chairman and CEO Howard Schultz, who had drawn the president's interest when he was named *Fortune* magazine's "Business Person of the Year." Obama was intrigued because Schultz had gone public with his criticisms of the dysfunction in Washington, and his concerns were similar to Obama's. Schultz also had said he was so disgusted that he would stop making campaign contributions to incumbents, whom he held responsible for the capital's atmosphere of bickering and gridlock. Obama had to be a bit concerned about this decision since Schultz had been a big contributor to fellow Democrats.

Their half-hour telephone conversation focused on their mutual concern for the country and the budget problems faced by the federal government and the states. They agreed there was a profound crisis of confidence in America, according to *Fortune*'s account of their talk.[14] The chat, reinforced by private and public polling data on the nation's sour mood, contributed to Obama's feeling that America needed him to convey a sense of optimism and hope. He tried to do that in his address to Congress two days later.

Obama also has relied on scholars to connect him with the larger world of history. He has held several private dinner parties with historians and other scholars to give him a sense of how he can emulate his successful predecessors and avoid the problems of others. Among those who have attended are historians Douglas Brinkley, Robert Caro, Robert Dallek, and Doris Kearns Goodwin, and law professor and author Kenneth Mack. Members of the group met with the president at the White House in May 2009, June 2010, July 2011, and January 2013.[15]

One point that came out of these dinners was the danger in keeping the nation involved too long in foreign wars or military ventures such as Vietnam and Korea. Several of the historians said Iraq and Afghanistan could easily fit into that danger zone, and Obama seemed to agree, although he was noncommittal about his own plans there. By the end of Obama's first term, however, he had extracted nearly all U.S. combat troops from Iraq, a nation his predecessor had invaded under questionable circumstances, and a military commitment that Obama had opposed as a candidate in 2008. And he announced that he would withdraw U.S. combat troops from Afghanistan by 2014, ending another war his predecessor had started, but one Obama had supported.

At the January 2013 dinner, held less than two weeks before his second inauguration, Obama gathered seven scholars at the White House: Brinkley, Caro, Dallek, Goodwin, Mack, historian H.W. Brands, and political scientist Norm Ornstein. Among the staff members attending were White House senior adviser Valerie Jarrett, then–chief of staff Jack Lew, and speechwriter Jon Favreau.

Over a dinner of salad and pastry-wrapped beef, Obama discussed history with his guests for two hours. He was particularly interested in their thoughts on how he could ensure a successful second term and what kind of legacy he could create. One guest called it "a free-flowing exchange." During the discussion, Obama said his second-term goals included strengthening the economy, reducing the deficit, reforming the immigration system, curbing gun violence, and minimizing climate change. The scholars were impressed that Obama was reaching out to them to solicit their ideas, and participants said he listened carefully to their opinions.

Continuing his outreach, Obama hosted a group of top economists in the Oval Office in late 2011 to solicit their advice on how to fix the economy. He asked them for their candid assessments of what needed to be done, not whether their suggestions *could* be done. "I'm not asking you to consider the political feasibility of things," he said. Nearly all replied that he should develop a comprehensive plan to forgive part of the mortgage debt owed by millions of homeowners whose houses had declined in value. It was a bold idea, but very unrealistic politically, and Treasury Secretary Timothy Geithner said so. "How do we get this done through Congress?" he asked. There was no answer, but the discussion itself showed Obama's willingness to consider big options from outside his inner circle.[16]

And Obama has reached out to his critics. After the Republicans took over the House of Representatives in November 2010 in what Obama admitted was in part a repudiation of his leadership, he invited Matthew

Dowd, a Republican strategist and former pollster and senior adviser to George W. Bush, to the White House for a private chat about what was going wrong.[17] During the first week in December 2010, Dowd talked with Obama in the Oval Office for an hour, one on one, with no one else in the room. Dowd's impression was that Obama had arranged the get-together himself without the knowledge of his aides. This was very understandable to Dowd because he was well aware, from his experience with Bush, that some presidential aides—in Bush's case, Deputy Chief of Staff Karl Rove—want to control the information that flows to the president as much as possible, partly to enhance their own power.

Dowd's impression was that Obama was concerned about getting too insular and that he recognized his need for diverse opinions, not just the advice he was getting from his top staff members. He requested of Dowd, "tell me where you think I messed up and what to do about it." Dowd obliged. And while Dowd wouldn't disclose the details—which he considered confidential—Dowd said Obama "listened and pushed back on some things."

Dowd told him that he wasn't communicating adequately the problems he faced in "the means of governing" and was too focused on "goals and ends." Americans wanted "the means fixed in Washington," Dowd said, such as the bitterness and partisanship. Obama agreed.

* * *

ANOTHER METHOD that Obama uses to learn about the country is to take bus tours and to talk as much as possible with everyday people at diners, barbeque stands, schools, town-hall meetings, and other venues. Obama told aides he learned a lot about the depth of America's frustration and anxiety about the economic downturn during his bus trips in August 2011, when he visited Illinois, Iowa, and Minnesota, and in October 2011, when he toured North Carolina and Virginia. Part of the reason for these trips was to argue for his job-creation proposals, which were stalled in Congress, and to generate support for his re-election in key battleground states. But White House Press Secretary Jay Carney said there was something more. "It is a very positive thing for the president—and I would argue any president—to get out of Washington and to talk to Americans around the country," Carney told reporters. That's something Obama has tried to do with increasing frequency.

A side benefit was picking up practical ideas for government initiatives. At one event in the Midwest, Obama heard from a military veteran who said he was carefully trained and highly skilled in triage on the battlefield, but couldn't find work in the medical industry back home. Obama told aides that they needed to find ways to help such people, and an initiative was born. A few weeks later, the president announced a plan for the federal government to encourage the healthcare industry to hire such military veterans.

*   *   *

OBAMA DOES keep up with the news media's reporting about him and his administration. Each day, he reads or at least browses through several newspapers, including the *New York Times,* the *Washington Post,* the *Wall Street Journal,* and his hometown papers, the *Chicago Sun-Times* and the *Chicago Tribune,* in print and sometimes on his iPad in the morning and just before he goes to bed at night. He also reads blogs and Twitter, sometimes telling aides of articles or comments he likes and dislikes.

He gleans information about popular culture in various ways. "I don't watch a lot of TV news," Obama told *Rolling Stone* in 2012. "I don't watch cable [news] at all. I like *The Daily Show,* so sometimes if I'm home late at night, I'll catch snippets of that. I think Jon Stewart's brilliant. It's amazing to me the degree to which he's able to cut through a bunch of the nonsense—for young people in particular, where I think he ends up having more credibility than a lot of more conventional news programs do. I spend a lot of time just reading reports, studies, briefing books, intelligence assessments.... I'll thumb through all the major papers in the morning. I'll read the *Times* and *Wall Street Journal* and *Washington Post,* just to catch up."[18] Obama added that he reads "all of the *New York Times* columnists," including economics specialist Paul Krugman, and "a handful of blogs," such as Andrew Sullivan's in the *Daily Beast.* And he reads essays in some publications such as the *New Yorker* and the *Atlantic,* which he said "still do terrific work." He added, "Every once in a while, I sneak in a novel or a nonfiction book."

Obama has developed a detailed critique of the news media, which he feels aren't as reliable as they used to be. He complains that political coverage focuses too much on winners and losers rather than on substantive discussions of policy, and he isn't happy with the "false balance" in which two opposing sides are given equal weight regardless of the facts."[19] Obama's views on the media are shared by many media critics from academia and elsewhere.

He draws another important conclusion from his assessment of the media—a critique of his own lack of understanding that he needed to establish a "narrative" of his presidency in order to explain to the country most effectively what he was doing. "The mistake of my first term—couple of years—was thinking that this job was just about getting the policy right," he told Charlie Rose of CBS in July 2012. "But the nature of this office is also to tell a story to the American people."[20]

Obama also finds it valuable to meet with journalists who he considers serious about ideas and whose views he finds interesting, rather than hold more news conferences with the White House press corps, which he considers preoccupied with trivia and too eager to play "gotcha." Among the journalists with whom he has met for extensive conversations are columnists E.J. Dionne and Ruth Marcus of the *Washington Post,* David Brooks of the *New York Times,* and Peggy Noonan of the *Wall Street Journal* (who is a former speech writer for Ronald Reagan).[21]

*   *   *

AND AS WITH so many of his predecessors, Obama relies on his wife and children to keep him grounded. First Lady Michelle Obama privately tells him when a speech doesn't go over well or when she thinks a policy needs revision. And the president clears his schedule nearly every day to have dinner with his family and to hear daughters Malia and Sasha talk about their activities. He tells friends that this gives him a firm attachment to his daughters' lives. This contact in turn reduces any tendency he may have to be self-important or self-indulgent, his aides say, because his daughters are quite irreverent in dealing with their father's shortcomings. For example, they tease him about his ignorance of the singers and movie stars favored by the young. "It grounds him in the real world of fatherhood," says an adviser.

*   *   *

BEYOND HIS personal efforts to stay in touch, polling is very important to Obama, dating back to when he first decided to run for president. His advisers arranged for polling and focus groups to be done secretly to test his potential appeal and assess the vulnerabilities of the front-runner in the 2008 cycle, senator and former first lady Hillary Clinton of New York.

In late 2006, Obama's aides commissioned focus groups and polls in Iowa, which would hold the first nominating caucuses in the 2008 cycle. The polling found that Obama was in third place behind Clinton and former senator John Edwards of North Carolina, but within reach of the leaders.[22]

"More striking were the focus groups, which were conducted in Des Moines and Cedar Rapids," wrote journalists John Heilemann and Mark Halperin. "Almost uniformly, the people in the groups reacted favorably to Obama—to his 2002 speech opposing the [Iraq] war, his rhetoric of change and unity, his freshness and sense of promise. Rarely did they express grave misgivings about his race or his exotic background. The more they knew about his biography and bearing, the more they liked him."[23]

The focus groups also found nagging doubts about Hillary Clinton. She was liked and respected but seemed too much a creature of the status quo, and she reminded voters of the messy divisions of the past, especially the polarization and the partisanship in Washington, D.C. during the presidency of her husband, Bill Clinton, and his embarrassing impeachment because he lied about having an affair.[24] All this was instrumental in persuading Obama to run for president and in shaping his decisions on the path to take as the tribune of change.

Another key moment that reinforced Obama's belief in survey research came in February 2007, when he met with campaign advisers in the eighth-floor conference room of the Washington, D.C. office of his lawyer, Bob Bauer. Obama heard from David Binder, a focus-group leader based in San Francisco who described the voter discussion sessions he had recently conducted in the first four states scheduled to hold nominating contests in 2008—Iowa, New Hampshire, Nevada, and South Carolina. Obama was largely unknown to the voters, Binder said, but they liked his sincerity, his freshness, and his emphasis on change, and the fact that he gave a speech opposing the Iraq war in 2002.[25]

Joel Benenson, Obama's lead pollster, then took the floor and said that his surveys in New Hampshire found that Obama was only four points behind Clinton, and among voters following the race closely, he led by ten points. Voters were seeking change over experience by a two-to-one margin, Benenson said, and they wanted a president who could move beyond the polarization and bitterness of the Clinton years.[26]

All this was music to Obama's ears. He had intended to run his campaign as a change agent and a conciliator, and the survey buttressed his belief that his strategy was a winner.[27] It deepened his respect for polling and focus groups as a way to keep him in touch with the country, a respect that he retained after entering the White House. He is briefed regularly on the latest survey research about the country's mood and his own standing.

Benenson remains a key figure. (See Chapter Eleven.) "In 2008, this campaign kind of reinvented campaigns by using the available technology," says David Axelrod, Obama's chief strategist. "But we're light years ahead of where we were in 2008. We had to reinvent ourselves, and think about all the tools that were available to us—that provided much richer data, much more surgical means of talking to voters.... We knew a lot more about the electorate than we did in 2008. We could make much more precise judgments about the attitudes of voters, about what was important to individual voters, about who was likely to participate and who wasn't likely to participate. So we had great confidence in our numbers. I got reports every night—all the senior people did—from our analytics guys about where all these battleground states were. And they were remarkably close [to the actual result]—Benenson's polling, within a tenth of a percentage point in the battleground states."[28]

The depth of Benenson's research was extraordinary. In addition to polls and focus groups, he conducted what he called an "ethnology project"—a "deep dive" into the lives of "up-for-grabs" voters through an exhaustive series of web questionnaires and interviews. When combined with polls and focus groups, it probably amounted to the most extensive look at the American voter ever undertaken by a campaign.[29]

The results were passed along to President Obama, who devoured them. The goal was to "give him a very in-depth picture of how people were viewing their lives" at a time of deep economic stress, Benenson said.[30]

One finding was that most Americans didn't blame Obama for the economic hardships they were enduring, but held George W. Bush, his predecessor, more responsible. This is something the Republicans never seemed to understand. As a result, the GOP presidential nominee Mitt Romney never made it clear how he differed from Bush on economic policy, which deepened public skepticism that Romney had any new economic answers. (See Chapter Eleven.)

* * *

BUT SUCH RESEARCH wasn't the be-all and end-all for Obama. He sometimes defied the polls, making decisions that ran against public opinion even when they seemed likely to hurt him politically.

One was his decision to bail out the auto industry as it neared collapse during his first term. "I was in the room when we made the decision," Axelrod recalled. "And I got to tell you, I had the polling data in front of me: Even in Michigan [home of the auto industry], people were opposed to the auto bailout. I wasn't trying to influence the president's decision, but I felt it was my obligation to tell him what the politics were. In fact, I always joke that I like him so much because he listens to me so little. There are so many decisions on which the polling said one thing and he said another, and this was one."[31]

In response to Axelrod's feedback, Obama noted, "We're in the middle of the worst recession since the Great Depression. How do you just let the American auto industry collapse? There are a million or more jobs you're going to lose. As long as there's a plausible way forward that has a reasonable chance to work, we ought to pursue it."[32] As time went on, the public came around, and the recovery of the auto industry vindicated Obama's original decision to go for the bailout. This was crucial to his victories in states that were heavily dependent on the auto industry, especially Michigan and Ohio.

Obama stuck to his guns on healthcare legislation, as well, despite angry public opposition. In the summer of 2009, demonstrations by conservatives upset at his proposal swept the country; they said it amounted to a federal takeover of healthcare. Axelrod went to the Oval Office and reported the situation to Obama, noting that the administration was being pummeled and there would be no letup. Obama let Axelrod finish sounding the alarm and then said, "Look, I know you're right. I'm sure we're taking on water on this. But I just got back from Green Bay, and I met a woman who was 36 years old, two small children—her husband and she both have jobs. They have insurance. But she has Stage IV breast cancer now. She's hit her caps. And she's just terrified that she's going to leave her family bankrupt—that she's going to die and leave her family bankrupt. That's not the country we believe in, so let's just keep on fighting."[33] Obama and his Democratic allies in Congress succeeded in passing the healthcare law, but it remained a divisive issue throughout the country.

*   *   *

BEYOND THE POLLS, Obama's personal outreach in Washington, D.C., or lack of it, is still criticized. Some feel that he is surrounding himself too often with idolizers, not people who tell him their real concerns and voice their criticisms.

One of the leading idolizers is Valerie Jarrett, a senior counselor at the White House and a longtime friend of Barack and Michelle Obama from their years in Chicago. She is one of the few aides who goes on vacation with the Obama family and often dines with them in the White House residence at night.[34] Jarrett's title is assistant to the president for intergovernmental affairs and public engagement, but she is in many ways his closest confidante outside of his family.

"Jarrett is supposed to be the point person for the administration's effort to keep in touch with the outside world—everyone from senators to foreign dignitaries," writes author Edward Klein. "Obama sent her to talk to the Dalai Lama before he visited China. However, if you talk to Democratic donors, businessmen, congressmen, and African-Americans, as I have, it turns out that Jarrett is far better at giving people the cold shoulder than at welcoming them with open arms. Like Obama, she has a fundamental lack of respect for businessmen. In a typical blunder that sent shudders through the business community, she dismissed Tom Donohue, the highly regarded CEO of the U.S. Chamber of Commerce, as irrelevant, saying that she preferred to deal with 'real' industry executives."[35]

And Jarrett has gone too far in limiting others' access to the president, according to a number of White House and congressional sources. Her goal is to keep Obama in a cocoon of admirers who won't, in her mind, shake him up too much or present views that might be contrary to her understanding of Obama's positions.[36]

This insulation extends to most of the audiences that Obama addresses. "The only audiences he sees are audiences that like him and his administration, or love him, or adore him," said Republican pollster Frank Luntz in April 2012 as that year's presidential campaign was gearing up.[37] This can easily lead to the impression by a president that he is more popular than he is, and that his critics are in a tiny minority or are motivated by irrational hatred. Luntz also saw signs that Obama was dismissing virtually all media criticism and wasn't dealing with people personally. "With the security, it's almost impossible to engage people in a personal way," Luntz told me. "There's no way for interaction." This is true for nearly all modern presidents, he added.

*   *   *

ON THE OTHER SIDE, 2012 Republican presidential nominee Mitt Romney was trying to make the point that he, not Obama, was really in touch. The Democrats ridiculed this claim—one senior Obama aide told me in June 2012 that it was "laughable"—pointing out that Romney was one of the wealthiest people ever to seek the presidency and had very little contact with everyday people for most of his life. But Romney's aides said he took seriously the need to keep in touch and he learned what it was like to struggle in the troubled economy by chatting with everyday people, privately and off the record. His advisers wouldn't reveal the circumstances or the names of his citizen associates, but Romney at one point said he met with families "almost every day."[38] At a rally in Pittsburgh on May 4, 2012, he said, "Before I begin an event like this, I typically am able to sit down with a few people on an off-the-record kinda basis. I agree not to say who they are to the members of my media." He also told CBS News on May 1, "So far during my campaigns one of the highlights for me has been sitting down with three or four families almost every day without the camera there. Most of them are done privately—that is a wonderful way for me to understand how people are really feeling."[39] Among the people he liked to meet with were small-business owners and entrepreneurs. "I'm amazed by the hard work and the entrepreneurial spirit of the American people," Romney said in Pittsburgh.[40]

Romney enjoyed such private meetings with everyday citizens, although his staff wouldn't divulge how many times he did it and who the other participants were. On one rare occasion when reporters were allowed to watch such a session for a while, Romney aides were displeased when they focused on minutiae, such as how the candidate misidentified a bear claw as a donut. The staff resolved to allow reporters into these sessions only rarely for the remainder of the campaign, but they told me in the spring of 2012 that Romney had resolved to find ways around the barriers to staying in touch.

Romney aides said that he also tried to stay in contact with political leaders across the country, including Republican senator Rob Portman of Ohio. Romney felt it was important to get out of his campaign routine as frequently as he could, such as by going out with his family to the movies, to ice-cream parlors, and to restaurants. He didn't trust the media enough to rely on them for news or information about the country, his aides said. But he did talk frequently to his pollster Neil Newhouse about the state of the country and about campaign strategy.

* * *

IT WAS CLEAR that both Obama and Romney had another goal in mind when they talked about staying in touch—the public-relations value of having it known that they were talking and listening to everyday Americans.

Creating an image of being in contact was important to both of them as the 2012 campaign proceeded. As journalist John Dickerson wrote for *Slate*, "At the start of the general election where each candidate is trying to define their opponent in the race for middle-class support, both have settled on the same message: My opponent is 'out of touch.' The candidates will talk about jobs, tax rates, and the deficit, but those dry policy issues aren't going to stir the passions. Campaign strategists want to gall—or at least frighten—people into thinking that the other party's candidate is so bubble-wrapped in privilege that he is incapable of understanding the problems of real people."[41]

Romney used the perks of the White House to score political points against Obama. "Years of flying around on *Air Force One*, surrounded by an adoring staff of true believers telling you what a great job you are dong, well, that might be enough to make you a little out of touch," Romney said after winning the Wisconsin Republican presidential primary in early 2012.[42]

Vice President Joe Biden argued, "Governor Romney calls the president out of touch. Hey, how many of y'all have a Swiss bank account? How many of you have somewhere between $20 million and $100 million in your [retirement account]?"[43]

For most of the campaign, Obama won the faceoff over who was closer to the public. A *Washington Post*/ABC News poll in the spring of 2012 found that 49 per cent of Americans thought Obama "better understands the economic problems people in this country are having." Only 37 per cent believed Romney did. It amounted to a serious empathy gap, to Romney's great disadvantage.[44] And it plagued Romney to the last as Obama won a solid victory with just over 50 per cent of the popular vote and a huge majority in electoral votes, 332 to Romney's 206.

Polls showed that Obama was trusted to stay in touch with Middle America while Romney was not. "It's pretty clear," said pollster Stan Greenberg, summing up the election trends, "that to most voters what defines the Republican Party and Mitt Romney is that they are totally for the rich and out of touch with average people, which is key when you have an election about the middle class."[45] "The strongest theme in voters' reasons to vote against Romney," Greenberg said, "centered on the fact that he was out of touch with ordinary people and for the rich—because of his comment about the '47 per cent,' corporate policies, and support for more tax cuts for the wealthy."

*   *   *

IN THE WEEKS prior to his inauguration in January 2013, Obama endured a fresh wave of criticism that he was too insular and that he was surrounding himself with yes-men. What triggered the negative assessment at that time was Obama's naming of three white males to his cabinet— Senator John Kerry of Massachusetts as secretary of state, former senator Chuck Hagel of Nebraska as secretary of defense, and national-security official John Brennan as director of central intelligence. Feminists and other Obama supporters from his 2012 campaign were particularly displeased because Kerry was replacing the popular Hillary Rodham Clinton, who was resigning after four grueling years. Naming Kerry struck many as hypocritical after Obama had made a point during the campaign of saying he was sensitive to the need for diversity in government.

At a news conference on January 14, Obama addressed the concerns directly. Expressing pride in his record of naming women to government, he said, "If you think about my first four years, the person who probably had the most influence on my foreign policy was a woman. The people who were in charge of moving forward my most important domestic initiative, healthcare, were women, The person in charge of our homeland security was a woman. My two appointments to the Supreme Court were women. And 50 per cent of my White House staff were women. So I think people should expect that that record will be built upon during the next four years."[46]

At the same press conference, Obama seemed miffed when asked directly if he and his staff were too insular. He didn't deny that he could be personally aloof, but he said it didn't matter; Washington was so polarized and partisan that no amount of socializing would change the harsh environment. He explained that only if the American people rejected "uncompromising positions or sharp partisanship or [politicians who are] always looking out for the next election," and only if the public rewarded "folks who are trying to find common ground, then I think you'll see behavior in Congress change. And that will be true whether I'm the life of the party or a stick-in-the-mud."[47]

Then he made a rather poignant comment that echoed what Harry Truman had said more than a half-century earlier about the loneliness he felt at the White House when his family was away. "Now that my girls are getting older, they don't want to spend that much time with me anyway," he said. "So I'll be probably calling around, looking for somebody to play cards with or something, OK, because I'm getting kind of lonely in this big house."[48]

*   *   *

THE WEEK BEFORE his second inauguration, the gun-control issue erupted, as it had a decade earlier when Congress last considered comprehensive legislation to reduce gun violence. Obama announced an ambitious package that included renewal of the ban on assault weapons that had lapsed in 2004, ensuring that anyone who bought a gun had to go through a background check, and a variety of executive orders to limit the purchase of guns by people who might want to harm others. Obama was trying to seize the moment after the nation was outraged by the massacre of twenty children and six adults by a gunman at a Newtown, Connecticut, elementary school in December.

Even though stronger gun controls were supported by most Americans, according to the polls, emotions quickly boiled over on all sides. The National Rifle Association ran a video on its website calling Obama an "elitist hypocrite" for allowing Secret Service protection for his two daughters at school but expressing skepticism about using armed guards to protect other children at their schools. White House Press Secretary Jay Carney condemned the NRA video as "repugnant" and "cowardly" because it brought Obama's daughters into the debate. But conservatives said Obama was guilty of using kids as political pawns because his staff arranged to have on stage with him at the gun-control announcement children who had written him letters advocating limits on weapons.

It was a sign of how deeply polarized Washington had become. And it showed how even a president who understood national opinion and tried to reflect it could encounter furious resistance from a well-organized minority.

*   *   *

OBAMA, despite the criticism of his personal aloofness in dealing with Washington insiders, has kept as close to the country as any president in recent history. He knows the importance of not becoming trapped in the White House and he works hard to avoid it. He uses almost all of the tools at his disposal, including what he learned about American life growing up in a middle-class household, polling, letters from citizens, the social media, his family and friends, and keeping track of popular culture. His success at staying in touch is a big reason he won a second term in 2012.

One area of regret for him, however, is that he didn't spend enough time traveling around the country during his first term. He says he missed the contact with regular people, and he hopes to do more traveling in his second term to escape the White House bubble.

One part of staying in touch that he has shown little interest in is forging relationships with members of Congress, the news media, and others who consider themselves Washington movers and shakers. He says it just isn't worth the effort because schmoozing won't improve his ability to govern. And he is more interested in spending time with his wife and daughters, which severely curbs his availability for other socializing.

IV

FROM WIZARDS TO CHICKEN PEDDLERS

CHAPTER ELEVEN
THE WIZARDS OF THE WHITE HOUSE

In the past four decades, the role of the presidential pollster has grown exponentially. As a group, these advisers have been some of the most interesting characters to ever work in government. And in some cases, they established a mystique as experts in the art of assessing public opinion, which, combined with their self-promotional skills, made them seem indispensable to their bosses. The history of the pollster is an important, if little-understood, part of presidential history.

It was Franklin D. Roosevelt who started using polls to determine public attitudes, if in a relatively limited way.[1] His successors, Presidents Harry Truman and Dwight Eisenhower, showed little interest in opinion research.[2]

"Polling was not institutionalized in the White House until after the high-level intelligence gathering exhibited during John F. Kennedy's 1960 run for the presidency," says political scientist Diane J. Heith. "The Kennedy and Johnson administrations vastly expanded presidential interest in and use of the presidential polling apparatus," both for re-election and for governing. "However," adds Heith, "none of the administrations from Roosevelt to Johnson received a continuous flow of public opinion data. The Kennedy and Johnson White Houses did place a greater emphasis on public opinion than their predecessors, but could only obtain partial, piggybacked control over their poll questions and surveys; subsequent presidents achieved complete control.... In stark contrast, the administrations of Nixon, Ford, Carter, Reagan, Bush and Clinton devoted substantial time, money, and attention to a White House public opinion apparatus."[3]

*　*　*

WHAT DIFFERENCE does polling make in the White House? A lot, partly because the polls, public and private, are considered reliable indicators of American opinion. "Our poll measurements have become so frequent and have received so much attention that they are accepted as reality—not only by political actors, but by many journalists who interpret polls for the public," says Kathleen Frankovic, director of surveys for CBS News.[4] The same is true for the polls conducted for the White House.

Some presidents value polling very highly but prefer to use non-pollsters, especially trusted political strategists, to interpret surveys and keep them informed about real life outside the White House. This can be an effective way of keeping in touch.

Among those who used this technique were George H.W. Bush with his chief strategist Lee Atwater; George W. Bush and his political "architect" Karl Rove; and Barack Obama and strategists David Axelrod and David Plouffe.

The question is whether presidents pay too much attention to public opinion. "Students of voting behavior have long disagreed over whether citizens have the intellectual capability and wherewithal to participate effectively in voting and governing," writes Heith. "In *Public Opinion,* Walter Lippmann argued that it would take too much effort and work by the citizen to remain informed enough to provide useful feedback to government. For the public official, the debate can be framed in terms of behavior. A president or member of Congress can either respond to the will and whims of the people (act as a delegate) or rely on his or her own judgment (act as a trustee)."[5]

My instinct is that the more contact a president has with the outside world, whether through polls or direct interactions with real people, the better.

*　*　*

IT'S DIFFICULT for us today to fathom how suspicious presidents, members of Congress, and other politicians were regarding polls and pollsters for most of American history. As recently as the late 1940s, Harry Truman made a strong case against polls. And he had good reason. In his 1948 campaign, the polls had famously pointed to a Truman loss and a victory by Republican Thomas Dewey, but, as discussed earlier in this book, Truman scored a spectacular victory. Truman later said in his memoirs, "[I] never paid any attention to the polls myself because in my judgment they did not represent a true cross section of American opinion.... I did not believe that the major components of our society such as agriculture, management, and labor, were adequately sampled. I also know that the polls did not represent facts but were speculation, and I have always placed my faith in the known facts.... A man who is influenced by the polls or is afraid to make decisions which may make him unpopular is not a man to represent the welfare of the country."[6]

It took a long time for polling to gain legitimacy as a tool for campaigning and governing. At first, political leaders accepted the idea fostered by columnist Walter Lippmann, that citizens' opinions were "fickle, untrustworthy, and therefore not to be taken into account when making policy decisions," observes political scientist Robert M. Eisinger. "This view, combined with the fear that polls created a bandwagon effect, helps explain Congress' initial aversion to polls."[7]

On February 8, 1957, the *Washington Star* published an article on the executive branch's efforts to gauge public opinion, causing a backlash from members of Congress. Some legislators "saw executive polling as a usurpation of their powers"; others were bothered because the operation was kept secret. As a result, the House Government Operations Committee held a hearing on State Department polls, which were widely considered inappropriate because legislators felt that foreign policy should be beyond politics.[8] The committee report criticized the State Department for what was called the illegal use of appropriated funds and for the department's evasive testimony before the committee.[9]

In the late '50s and early '60s, polling, though still suspect among many, gained more respect among politicians. The case was eloquently made by pollsters George Gallup and Saul Forbes Rae in an argument aimed mainly at members of Congress but that applied just as much to the president. "Instead of being attempts to sabotage representative government, kidnap the members of Congress, and substitute the taxi driver for the expert in politics, as some critics insist, public-opinion research is a necessary and valuable aid to truly representative government," they wrote. "The continuous studies of public opinion will merely *supplement,* not destroy, the work of representatives. What is evident here is that representatives will be better able to represent if they have an accurate measure of the wishes, aspirations, and needs of different groups within the general public, rather than the kind of distorted picture sent them by telegram enthusiasts and overzealous pressure groups who claim to speak for all the people but actually speak only for themselves. Public-opinion surveys will provide legislators with a new instrument for estimating trends of opinion, and minimize the chance of their being fooled by clamoring minorities. For the alternative to these surveys, it must be remembered, is not a perfect and still silence in which the Ideal Legislators and the Perfect Expert can commune on desirable policies. It is the real world of competing pressures, vociferous demonstrations, and the stale cries of party politics."[10]

Today, polls "have become an essential part of the politician's tool kit," writes Eisinger.[11] "The interplay between politics and public opinion is so intertwined into the fabric of governmental decision-making, that one cannot imagine a politician who dismisses or ignores citizens' views."

One goal of survey research today is to shape what political scientists call "crafted talk," defined by Heith as "the art of employing public opinion polls and focus groups to choose words and phrases that resonate with the public, even when the policy does not."[12]

Among the examples of this technique, pioneered by Republican pollster Frank Luntz for congressional Republicans, is defining tax increases as "revenue enhancements," calling changes in Social Security "reforms" instead of "privatization," and labeling the "estate tax" the more ominous-sounding "death tax" in order to undermine support for such levies.

Polls are used to strengthen a president's position by releasing the results publicly to show how popular an incumbent is or how much favor his policies are drawing. John F. Kennedy and his staff pioneered this approach more than 50 years ago when they spread the word about favorable polls to "those we hoped to sway," according to former Kennedy aide Theodore C. Sorensen.[13]

* * *

DESPITE CONGRESSIONAL cynicism, for many years Franklin D. Roosevelt used polling to circumvent his own Democratic Party and the news media. One pollster whose studies he monitored was Emil Hurja, who worked for the Democratic National Committee (DNC). DNC Chairman James Farley "found Hurja's maps and statistical analyses invaluable political instruments," especially after Farley became postmaster general and used Hurja's analyses of areas containing high levels of FDR support to reward local Democratic leaders with patronage jobs or contracts.[14] FDR was aware of Hurja's work in the middle and late 1930s, and encouraged the DNC to keep using him to provide advice and to keep tabs on Roosevelt's popularity.

But eventually, Roosevelt turned to another pollster as his personal guide to public opinion.

HADLEY CANTRIL

Hadley Cantril, director of the Office of Public Opinion Research at Princeton University, was the first White House pollster.

Born in Utah, he held a doctorate from Harvard and was the former chairman of the Department of Psychology at Princeton University. In 1940, he founded Princeton's Office of Public Opinion Research and starting that fall he polled for FDR in secret.

Cantril began by assessing public opinion for Roosevelt on a burning issue of the day—the U.S. role in the European war and how much America should aid Great Britain. He found "growing receptivity toward lending war materials to the British," and this deepened FDR's determination to provide those materials because he believed he could build support among Americans and get them to accept the program.[15]

But the polling itself was so controversial that it was kept under wraps, almost as if the whole process were a form of espionage. Polling information was disseminated by Cantril and his partner Gerard Lambert to White House advisers at Lambert's house in Washington, D.C.[16] Cantril later wrote that they "deliberately made a point of being seen as little as possible in government offices or agencies in order to minimize curiosity and preserve the informality of our relationships."[17]

Cantril secretly conducted several surveys for the State Department in 1943, funded confidentially from a discretionary fund for "emergencies in the Diplomatic and Consular Service."[18] All told, the State Department commissioned polls for 13 years starting in 1944.

Cantril wrote to FDR adviser Samuel Rosenman, "No doubt you have told Mrs. Roosevelt that because of the confidential nature of our work we are anxious to soft-pedal the fact that we have our own privately financed polling mechanism and that we never want this fact published."[19]

Cantril said the polls were designed to "guide the president and other civilian war leaders in bracing people for the long, hard road ahead and for occasional setbacks." Cantril polled on sensitive matters, such as how the bombing of Rome might affect U.S. Catholics' morale and support for World War II, and whether the United States should create refugee camps for people persecuted by the Nazis.[20] It's likely that the sensitive nature of these topics contributed to the White House's desire for secrecy; FDR didn't want his critics to know he was having these issues poll-tested because it might have raised questions about whether he was too driven by public attitudes of the moment.

"Cantril's polls gave Roosevelt more than a snapshot of the public mood; they increased the autonomy of the presidency by assuming within the executive branch a traditional function of Congress, that of assessing public opinion," Eisinger says.[21]

"Polls became Roosevelt's independent mechanism for measuring citizens' attitudes," Eisinger writes. Cantril "frequently accompanied his poll numbers with advice on how to market policies, including specific recommendations on how to advance the president's agenda by increasing FDR's exposure and popularity. Specifically, some of Cantril's reports explicitly were designed to assess public opinion as it related to the president's communicating with the public."[22]

On September 17, 1941, less than three months before the Pearl Harbor attack brought the United States into the war, Cantril compared "opinions of those who do and do not listen to the president's radio talks." He found that radio listeners had more money, were more interventionist, and were more likely to believe they would personally feel the consequences of a German victory in World War II than nonlisteners and more likely to support Roosevelt's wartime policies.[23] In a memo to FDR advisers, Cantril wrote that it seemed "safe to conclude that the President's talks do have some influence. If more effort were made to publicize these speeches in advance, especially among the lower income groups, the effect might be more noticeable."[24]

Another sign of Cantril's wide-ranging influence came in another memo, dated September 30, 1944. "Incidentally," he advised FDR on the timing of a speech, "I think it is a mistake to have a major broadcast on Saturday night. It's a poor night for coverage."[25]

PATRICK CADDELL

At the age of 25 Patrick Caddell became Jimmy Carter's campaign pollster in 1975. The two developed a very close relationship and after the 1976 election victory, Caddell went into the White House as Carter's official presidential pollster. He gained unprecedented authority and access to the president and his senior staff as Caddell made his way into Carter's inner circle.

Caddell had been the chief pollster for Democratic presidential nominee George McGovern while still a Harvard undergraduate in 1972.[26] He made a habit of mixing polling data with his own interpretation of social, cultural, and political trends, and could produce compelling analyses of contemporary society on short notice, even if his critics said they were often over the top.

"Caddell's lengthy poll summaries often arrived at the White House immersed in strategy and advice to the president," writes Eisinger. "At times these included outright suggestions for policies, and in one case, Caddell composed a memo based almost entirely upon theories about leadership. In this regard, Caddell functioned as a confidant and political consultant who employed both quantitative poll data and abstract reasoning to counsel and engage the president."[27]

Caddell polled on both domestic and foreign policy, such as voter attitudes about the volatile Middle East where Carter had a special interest, and he sometimes sent his findings directly to the president without going through intermediaries. He attended many White House meetings and phoned or got together with Carter on a regular basis. Caddell also traveled frequently with the president aboard *Air Force One* and the president's *Marine One* helicopter, a sign of his status.

Caddell's influence over polling and assessing the public mood was unparalleled, so much so that no one had the power or the credibility within the White House to argue with him or balance out his views. This was a dangerous situation for Carter because it concentrated the power over polling information in one person's hands.

A rumpled academic type, Caddell exhibited a haughty and dismissive quality when challenged that intimidated his potential rivals. He asserted himself immediately after the election during Carter's transition to power. Caddell reminded the president-elect in a December 1976 memo that he was elected to remove the insiders and "clean house in Washington." To appease the grumbling from party loyalists, Caddell recommended that an inaugural party for the DNC include "a gathering of your state coordinators and other key political people." The president personally noted in the margin a directive to top aide Hamilton Jordan, "Try to do this or equivalent."[28]

Over time Caddell consolidated his power even more. "Patrick Caddell bypassed the Democratic National Committee (DNC) to send information to Carter and his staff directly," Heith says. He also prepared a large volume, *An Analysis of Political Attitudes in the United States of America,* for both Carter and the DNC.[29]

Caddell and his firm, Cambridge Survey Research, provided the Carter White House with poll data at least four times a year for four years. These analyses (generally six to eight chapters, and well over 300 pages) contained questions and analyses of public opinion on all the significant issues and attitudes pertaining to the Carter presidency, Heith says, adding, "Although a large number of staff members and Cabinet members had easy access to Caddell's polling data, that access did not necessarily imply sophisticated understanding of public opinion techniques or limitations."[30]

"The events leading to the infamous Carter 'Crisis of Confidence,' or 'Malaise,' speech underscore the devastating consequences of novice opinion users relying on polls and pollsters," Heith adds. In late 1978 and early 1979, Caddell sent several urgent memos to Carter on "the state of America." In January 1979, Caddell wrote to Carter that his most recent survey "may well be the most significant and disturbing survey I have looked at in the ten years I have been conducting polls." The country, he said, was suffering from a crisis of confidence.

Caddell littered his later reports with alarmist rhetoric. And there was no one in the Carter administration capable of challenging Caddell's dogmatic assessments, such as, "One can only conclude from these figures ... that all the legislative initiatives, programs, foreign policy efforts, while being good and important governmental actions, are essentially irrelevant to solving this deeper, more fundamental, more demanding problem." Pushed by Caddell, Carter eventually agreed to give a "crisis of confidence speech."[31]

Eisinger writes that on April 23, 1979, leading up to that address, Caddell provided to Carter a 75-page essay entitled "Of Crisis and Opportunity," in which Caddell elevated his role of presidential pollster to a new level. Caddell explained his perception of growing pessimism and dwindling confidence in the America body politic. "He quoted liberally from James MacGregor Burns' book, *Leadership,* and offered inspiring words about the president's opportunity to join the ranks of Lincoln, FDR, and Woodrow Wilson," Eisinger notes. "Marked by a dearth of poll numbers and an overflowing of theory and narrative, this essay represented a departure from the presidential pollster's traditional role as analyst and informal adviser.... Caddell's theorizing marked a novel foray into the presidency. Caddell, accepted into Carter's official family to assess the public mood with polls, had now framed his version of public opinion by expressing his own political ideas and ideals to the president."[32]

In an April 28 entry in his diary, Carter wrote that he met with Caddell, his press secretary Jody Powell, and wife Rosalynn and discussed the "basic deep-seated and growing concerns among the American people about the future, and what I as president might do about it." In his 2010 book *White House Diary*, Carter elaborated, "Pat Caddell's penetrating opinion polling revealed that our country was still affected by the assassinations of Martin Luther King, Jr., John Kennedy, and Bobby Kennedy, embarrassed by our military defeat in Vietnam, Watergate, and Nixon's impeachment; and felt vulnerable due to the effective Arab oil embargo. I was particularly interested in what the polling revealed about our efforts to promote energy conservation; until this time, the Congress had not been able to overcome the powerful interest groups and pass my comprehensive energy policy. Caddell's polling helped us understand that additional speeches about energy would not be effective but we still did not know how best to advance our agenda."[33]

Carter accepted many of Caddell's ideas, as contained in what was called Caddell's "Apocalypse Now" memo from April. And eventually he settled on giving what became known as the "malaise speech" on July 15, 1979. The initial reaction was favorable. But within a few weeks, the impression shifted and Carter was criticized for taking a downcast and overly pessimistic view of the future. This caused Carter's popularity to plummet, never to recover amid Cabinet resignations and the Iranian hostage crisis.[34]

*   *   *

CADDELL WAS a potent inside player. He knew how to make the most effective and dramatic case for action based on his polling data, but he was also adept at maneuvering within the government. It's significant that he went to First Lady Rosalynn Carter and White House Press Secretary Jody Powell to marshal support for his positions and circumvented the doubters, including Vice President Walter Mondale and domestic-policy adviser Stuart Eizenstat.[35]

While he was a creative thinker, Caddell could wander down some theoretical cul de sacs where he would go unhindered. At one point, he came up with the notion that Americans who used oil to heat their homes had different attitudes on energy than people who used natural gas, coal, electric, or other energy sources. And he began researching the opinions of people based on that, such as their views on the need for energy conservation and whether they favored or opposed a tax on imported oil.

At one point, he asked in a poll, "Do you favor or oppose a tariff (tax) on imported oil that would raise the price of gasoline 10 or 15 cents per gallon if it would end our dependence on foreign oil?"[36] But no significant new patterns were found. In fact, the polling found that Americans didn't believe the oil shortage was a crisis requiring sacrifice, no matter what kind of energy they used for home heating. Caddell eventually dropped the concept of a "home heating" constituency but only after wasting a considerable amount of time and energy in the process.

RICHARD WIRTHLIN

Richard Wirthlin, a soft-spoken Mormon with a professorial air, held a doctorate in economics from the University of California at Berkeley. He chaired the economics department at Brigham Young University for five years. But he left the academic world to conduct polls for Ronald Reagan's 1970 run for governor of California, for Reagan's unsuccessful 1976 presidential campaign, and for his victorious 1980 and 1984 presidential runs. During the Reagan presidency, Wirthlin was one of Reagan's closest advisers.[37]

Wirthlin didn't have a formal job in the government. Explaining why he turned down Reagan's offer to join the White House staff in January 1981, he said, "On the one hand, I was deeply honored by the offer and my heart was saying yes. However, after analyzing the issue more closely, I wasn't so sure that was the best way to serve the president. For one thing, presidential pollsters have not historically been on the federal payroll. Instead, their services are usually routed through their respective political party machinery. But there was another, more strategic reason why I decided to turn down the president's request. I wanted Reagan to know that my counsel was independent of any ongoing turf battles that might arise within the White House."[38]

Wirthlin instead got Reagan's approval to create a White House Office of Planning and Strategy, headed by Wirthlin ally and confidant Richard Beale. "This gave me the best of both worlds," Wirthlin said later. "I would have White House information resources at my disposal and the ability to keep an ear to the ground, while at the same time I could avoid getting caught in any circular firing squads."[39] He also persuaded Reagan to give him "unfettered" access, and the two met hundreds of times during Reagan's eight years in the White House.[40]

At the start of Reagan's presidency, Wirthlin was a key player in the early debates over economic policy and how best to sell it to Congress and the American people. Wirthlin, in league with White House Chief of Staff James Baker, warned Reagan about the dangers of promising too much. They insisted on a pared-down agenda that they felt was achievable, led by severe budget cuts and tax reductions to stimulate the troubled economy. Other issues, such as regulatory reform and limiting abortion, would have to wait because the economy was in such trouble and so many Americans were suffering from a combination of high inflation, high unemployment, and a high degree of pessimism about the future.

Wirthlin wrote an initial "action plan" for Reagan, formulated just after he won the election in November 1980, that said, "A plan to permanently reduce the size of the federal budget must be launched within two or three weeks of the Inauguration and must be the lead element in the total economic package. Professional economic opinion and Wall Street sentiment could run against a major tax cut in the absence of real spending restraint."[41]

Wirthlin, using data from his firm Decision/Making/Information (DMI), also told Reagan that his polls revealed that the public "much preferred" cutting federal spending to cutting taxes because people feared that tax cuts without "significant" budget cuts "will accelerate the rate of inflation."[42]

Reagan decided to go for huge cuts in both spending and taxes, coupled with an equally massive flow of money to the Pentagon for national defense, and he masterfully won congressional passage of legislation to do both.[43]

⋀   ⋀   ⋀

WIRTHLIN WOULD meet with Reagan at least once a month in the Oval Office. Sometimes one or two other senior advisers were in the room, such as the White House chief of staff. Sometimes Reagan and Wirthlin met alone.

As the White House correspondent for *U.S. News & World Report*, I struck up a relationship of trust with Wirthlin, and he gave me many interviews, deepening my understanding of Reagan's agenda, what Wirthlin felt the public would eventually embrace, and Wirthlin's own important role in advising the president.

He described his role this way:

> I would almost always present to the President first. Sometimes I would give the Councilor to the President or the Chief of Staff a verbal heads-up. It was

customary that the Councilor and the Chief of Staff would be in the Oval Office when I reviewed the political environment with the President. On some occasions, when the information was particularly sensitive, I briefed the President alone.... Then when there were some key issues that might pertain to the Director of Communication, a member of the cabinet, etc., I would give follow up briefings. Simultaneously, I would present most of the results to the Chairman of the Republican National Committee and his key staff. I also addressed virtually every gathering of the RNC [Republican National Committee] and the Republican Governor's Association. On more than one occasion, I briefed the entire cabinet. I frequently, both before the 1980 election, during, and after the election, gave briefings to the Republican Congressional leadership, some of the members of the key committees, and after the 1980, 1982, 1984, and 1986 elections I briefed the newly elected congresspersons. During this period many of the Republicans running for office were our clients. If a major speech was being prepared on a specific topic that I had reviewed I would present that data to the White House speech writers. The data would then be separated by topics and I would prepare a memo on each topic that had fairly wide distribution in the White House and the RNC. These memos were drafted against the criterion that nothing should be put in these writings that would cause embarrassment to the White House or the Republican Party.[44]

Wirthlin sent Reagan and other senior advisers a stream of data and interpretation. "In the fall of 1981," Wirthlin wrote, "I reviewed how the president's economic policy and the tax cuts had been perceived by the American people. Three out of every four Americans felt that at least half of the Reagan economic program had been implemented. Overall, his policies had been well received. Fifty-nine per cent believed his economic plan would reduce inflation, 58 per cent called the plan 'fair,' and 57 per cent said it would increase productivity. A strong majority of Americans also felt Reagan had 'the strong leadership qualities this country needs,' was 'trustworthy,' and would continue being 'effective in getting things done.'"[45]

"But most importantly," Wirthlin added, "Reagan's ability to communicate matters of dollars and cents had begun erasing the negative stereotypes Republicans had been battling for years. A large random sample of Americans were asked whether they thought the statements 'shows too much business favoritism' and 'does not care enough about the needs of the elderly and poor' applied to Ronald Reagan. Almost every category of voter rejected these two descriptions. The reason? Reagan spoke from the heart. He cared about the poor because he had grown up poor himself.

Moreover, he understood that for most Americans economic policy isn't some abstract, academic exercise. It's personal. It's immediate. When he spoke about such things he did so in ways that were intensely relevant—ways that showed he cared."[46]

*   *   *

AS THE 1984 re-election campaign swung into high gear, Wirthlin used his survey techniques to keep Reagan in touch and to show Americans that he had their best interest at heart. "With map in hand," he recalled, "we set out to create a series of television advertisements that would neutralize [Democratic candidate] Walter Mondale's 'lock' on the 'Security for Oneself/Children's Future' rectangle.... I would then test them to gauge audience reactions.... Challenging the fairness of Mondale's plan to raise taxes—the team had created a thirty-second spot that asked the question, 'Are you willing to work harder to pay for Walter Mondale's campaign promises?' It scored well."[47]

But another ad tested even more favorably, and became Ronald Reagan's favorite commercial of the 1984 cycle. Called the "Bear Ad," the thirty-second spot showed a grizzly bear roaming through a forest while a narrator said, "There is a bear in the woods. For some people the bear is easy to see. Others don't see it at all. Some people say the bear is tame. Others say it's vicious and dangerous. Since no one can really be sure who's right, isn't it smart to be as strong as the bear? If there is a bear."

Wirthlin says, "Test audiences went wild; they loved it. Viewer recall rates were remarkably high (68 per cent). The number of individuals who remembered the central message of the ad was exceedingly high as well (56 per cent). More importantly, people understood the central message: Strength is the best way to achieve peace."[48] The ad was used extensively in the campaign.

*   *   *

AS THE REAGAN presidency progressed, Wirthlin's role deepened on domestic policy, foreign policy, and politics. On April 10, 1985, he wrote Reagan a memo offering advice on how to win a congressional vote on aid to Nicaragua. He argued that Reagan should tone down his rhetoric and lobby Congress in a low-key way: "By raising the political stakes and the public salience of this particular issue, you would not only put into jeopardy the favorable job approval you now enjoy, but, more important, you will generate more public and congressional opposition than support.... I, thus, strongly recommend, Mr. President, that you not take your case concerning aid to the Contras to the public in some dramatic and/or symbolic fashion."[49]

Reagan rejected his advice and took the Nicaragua issue to the public in an aggressive way. He didn't manage to sway Congress, however, and aid to the anti-Marxist Contras was rejected.

Wirthlin's advice regarding whether to fight for a balanced-budget amendment to the Constitution was the opposite—full-speed ahead. "If this analysis is correct," he wrote in an October 1983 memo to the White House, referring to his analysis of polling data, "... an aggressive program of presidential events, statements and surrogate support for a balanced budget amendment would improve the approval rating for the President's handling of the deficit, restore the conviction that he will follow through on his campaign promises and renew confidence in his handling of the economy."[50] Reagan pushed for the amendment, but, again, Congress rebuffed him.

Wirthlin conducted focus groups to get a deeper sense of public opinion and how to sell Reagan's policies to swing voters.[51] When the 1984 re-election campaign began, Wirthlin and aides devised what he called "a quantitative instrument," which one of his own advisers dubbed a Hierarchical Values Map (HVM). "Ronald Reagan's rhetoric spun on the axis of values," Wirthlin wrote. "After years of analyzing this dimension of Reagan's communication, I began researching the scholarly literature on how values influence human behavior and, more specifically, the attitudes people hold. Tom Reynolds, a leading scholar on the issue, devised a theoretical model capable of mapping voters' decisions based on three factors: issues, policy program traits, and values. The HVM itself looked like a spider web with rectangles sprinkled throughout. It allowed me to monitor which candidate, Mondale or Reagan, 'owned' which issues and which values, and to understand the linkages between them. For example, in August of 1984, Mondale owned the rectangles that led to the value of 'Security for Oneself/Children's Future.'"[52]

Based on that finding, Wirthlin concluded that Reagan's television ads needed to challenge the fairness of Mondale's proposed tax increase; the Reagan campaign had to "connect the need to strengthen national defense with the preservation of world peace," and the HVM suggested that the campaign needed to "continue reinforcing the president's image as a strong, effective leader."[53]

During Reagan's second term, Wirthlin also developed what he called PulseLine. Wirthlin described it this way: "Whenever the president was to deliver a major policy speech, I would gather a group of between thirty-five and one hundred Americans. Selection of these individuals was based on the target audience we were interested in studying. For example, if we wanted to gauge how males under 50 years old reacted to the president and his rhetoric, we could arrange for a group of men fitting this description to participate in our study. Participants would be handed a small handheld electronic box with a rheostat (dial) on its face that ran from zero to ten. Each of these devices was connected to a central tabulation unit. Participants were then told they would watch a speech. When the speaker said something they responded positively to, they were to turn their dial toward ten to indicate their level of agreement. Conversely, negative reactions were to be registered by turning the dial toward zero."[54] This technique, known today as "dial groups," has become widely used in the survey research industry and in politics.

Wirthlin continued,

After the speech was finished, the central tabulation unit would average the participants' overall ratings as well as provide a measure of the degree of consensus in the rating of the group. The printout looked like a mountain range, complete with peaks and valleys. I could then go back and pinpoint the exact phrases and segments from the president's speech that had produced the most and least favorable responses, matching the speech's highs and lows against the actual videotape of the event. This allowed me to trace how the audience had responded almost to the president's every word. Mind you, this was all done with the full understanding that PulseLine, like any research instrument, was limited in what it could and couldn't measure. Nevertheless, the tool could help provide us with a context for understanding the magic of the Reagan message.

Also—and this is important—we would then hold focus groups with these same individuals to tap into the *reasons* for their responses. We wanted to understand the emotional dimensions behind why a viewer had dialed toward ten or toward zero. The result was something I called "power phrases," which were those lines or phrases from the speech that had garnered the highest response from the audience. I saw to it that subsequent speeches on similar issues contained these power phrases, and statements by White House surrogates of daily talking points could also benefit from their use.[55]

Wirthlin cites as an example a speech Reagan gave to a joint session of Congress in November 1985, after he returned from his summit meeting with Soviet leader Mikhail Gorbachev in Geneva. The original PulseLine study had been conducted to study his speech to the United Nations General Assembly in New York in October 1985, a month before the Geneva speech. Wirthlin found three "power phrases" in that October speech—"fresh start," "escape the prison of mutual terror," and "peace and progress." At Wirthlin's urging, Reagan included the first and second power phrases in his congressional address, and it was judged a big success.

Reagan saw Wirthlin's PulseLine as a way for him to get feedback on his speeches that went beyond the immediate reaction of the crowds before him. "He saw the value of being able to pinpoint areas of strength and weakness in his speeches," Wirthlin recalled. "What's more, he was confident enough in his own abilities not to take it personally when the trend lines dipped. The way he saw it, it was better to know what areas needed improvement. He wanted to make sure that his audiences received his messages clearly."[56]

Wirthlin was also instrumental in persuading Reagan to bluntly address the biggest scandal of his administration—the Iran-Contra affair of 1987, in which U.S. operatives sold arms to Iran in exchange for help in freeing hostages being held in Lebanon, and using some of the profits to finance the anti-Marxist Contras in Nicaragua. This happened at a time when Congress had banned such assistance and when Reagan had pledged never to negotiate with terrorists.

In March 1987, Wirthlin met with Reagan in the Oval Office and told the president that his job-approval ratings had plummeted. Americans, the pollster said, didn't believe that Reagan had been unaware of the diversion of funds and they didn't believe that he opposed the exchange of arms for hostages. Wirthlin said Reagan's credibility was at stake and he urged the president to "consider admitting clearly and openly to the American people that the policy was a mistake."[57]

Two days later, Reagan accepted Wirthlin's advice, shared by other senior Reagan advisers, and made the key admission. "A few months ago, I told the American people I did not trade arms for hostages," the president said. "My heart and my best intentions still tell me that's true, but the facts and evidence tell me it is not." Reagan took responsibility for the error and said, "As angry as I may be about activities undertaken without my knowledge, I am still accountable for those activities. As disappointed as I may be in some who served me, I'm still the one who must answer to the American people for this behavior." He concluded by explaining that he hoped to move beyond the scandal because, "My fellow Americans, I have a great deal that I want to accomplish with you and for you over the next two years."[58]

Reagan endured; his job-approval ratings rebounded, and he left office as a popular president who was widely regarded as a success.

ROBERT TEETER

Robert Teeter, a laid-back Midwesterner from Michigan, was not a self-promoter and he never achieved the notoriety of other White House pollsters. But he was an invaluable adviser to three Republican presidents—Richard Nixon, Gerald Ford, and George H.W. Bush—a track record spanning more presidencies than any of his predecessors or successors. The pattern is for a pollster to work for only one president, let alone three. But Teeter had a way of inspiring trust in those around him, partly because he was so congenial and willing to share credit with others.

Teeter was among the pollsters who worked for Nixon in the 1970s. And any pollster who worked for Nixon had some serious challenges. One was Nixon's penchant for secrecy; he restricted access so severely that the polling results were kept in a safe.[59] So Teeter had to be vigilant not to spread his surveys too widely at the White House.

As director of Market Opinion Research (MOR), Teeter was named polling director for Nixon's 1972 re-election campaign and did most of his surveys directly. But Teeter magnanimously suggested that the Committee for the Re-Election of the President [known to Nixon's critics as CREEP] hire several other firms to poll for Nixon and the Republican Party, to get a diversity of results and backstop him. "Using more than one vendor has several advantages," Teeter wrote to attorney general and campaign manager John Mitchell. "It gives the President's campaign access to large amounts of trend data, experience, and expertise [that] these firms have built up in certain states. It gives us access to more of the advanced thinking and new techniques that have been developed within the party during the past few years."[60] At Teeter's suggestion, CREEP hired, in addition to MOR, Opinion Research Corporation (ORC) and DMI.[61]

As Eisinger says, "The breadth of the ORC and MOR polls, the staffers' diligence in getting advances of poll data, the tight reins over access to poll data by [White House Chief of Staff Bob] Haldeman, the secrecy underlying the internal polls, the tacit agreement by the RNC to accept a subservient role, the use of polls to alter schedules and produce propaganda, and the constant drumbeat of publicity that surrounded poll data were proof that Nixon's polling operation surpassed all other presidents [up to then] and that his polling served in part to replace the power of his own party. Presidential polls were no longer piggy-backed surveys that included information that was of peripheral interest to the president. They were now fortnightly instruments designed to see what the public knew about current events and to shape public opinion, both about the president's image and policies."[62]

After Nixon resigned in 1974, Teeter worked for his successor, President Ford, in an expanded role when he and his firm MOR were hired by Ford's election campaign to conduct surveys for the 1976 campaign. Teeter became a prime adviser to Ford. For example, in discussing Ford's upcoming State of the Union address in January 1976, Teeter argued for and won a special emphasis on fighting inflation.[63] He worked closely with Ford's White House chief of staff, Dick Cheney, and didn't mind it when Cheney periodically suggested the wording of poll questions for Teeter's surveys.

Teeter gave advice on how to improve Ford's television performances, advising him to appear in more-formal settings and to carefully rehearse his words to demonstrate gravitas. The intensity of Ford's commitment to and interest in polling was less than Nixon's had been, but it was still an important part of the White House operation. Teeter met with Ford thirty-eight times in 1976 as the role of the president's pollster became institutionalized. Cheney or his assistant Foster Chanock made a habit of reviewing Teeter's private polls.[64]

As the 1976 campaign wore on, Teeter pioneered some techniques that became widely used in the polling business. He began to use daily tracking polls and "response meters" and dial groups (invented in the 1930s by Paul Lazarsfeld and Frank Stanton, and also used by Wirthlin) to determine how Ford's message was going over. Particularly important was his use of tracking polls—daily snapshots of where his candidate stood in the race—to determine whether Ford or Republican challenger Ronald Reagan was ahead in key states and to adjust Ford's message. Ford won the nomination.[65]

Later in the 1976 campaign, Teeter developed a "Rose Garden strategy," which called for the incumbent to stay at the White House or in other presidential venues to demonstrate his stature in comparison to the lack of national experience of his opponent.[66] Ford came from behind but narrowly lost the general election to Democratic challenger Jimmy Carter. Still, Teeter's reputation as a master of public opinion and strategy was enhanced.

Teeter once described a key element of his philosophy of presidential elections. He said voters cared less about issues than about how they sized up the candidates as people and leaders. "They don't line up eight issues and decide which one they line up with more," he said. "They want someone they trust to make value judgments for them."[67]

Reviews of polls had become "normal functions of the president, his pollster, and his senior advisers" and "a White House bureaucracy had evolved to ensconce polling in the presidency," Eisinger writes. "Second, presidents' private polls were now unadulterated political vehicles designed to help the president get elected. The maturation of presidents' private polling operations meant that gauging public opinion had increasingly become a political endeavor [not solely a function of public policy]. Questions were asked about issues and personality characteristics. Underlying these questions was a common goal—identifying how people wanted to vote for their political preferences. In this sense, the line between public opinion and public relations was blurred as polls became an important vehicle from which the president marketed himself."[68]

After Ford lost the 1976 election, Teeter left presidential polling, since the Democrats were now in charge. When Republican Ronald Reagan took office in January 1981, he brought in his own pollster, Richard Wirthlin, as noted above. But when another Republican, George H.W. Bush, took office in January 1989, it was Teeter who emerged again as the prime public-opinion guru for the White House.

As an adviser to George H.W. Bush, Teeter continued the practice of taking polls and giving advice on a very wide range of topics. In 1990, Teeter began seeing signs that Bush would have trouble winning re election in 1992. Teeter and his associates "warned President Bush and his advisers that his high approval ratings were encouraging, but still not an accurate indicator that Americans were overly sanguine about the Bush presidency."[69] In December 1991, Teeter gave Bush and a handful of his senior advisers polling data showing that 70 per cent of voters thought the nation was heading in the wrong direction and only 23 per cent thought the country was on the right track.[70] It was another alarming sign.

When Bush formally started his campaign for re-election in 1992, he named Teeter as his campaign chairman. But the decisiveness as well as the organizational, diplomatic, and political skills needed for that role were not the same as those required of a pollster, and many Bush loyalists felt that Teeter was not the man for the job.

Things got progressively worse for Bush. In a memo from aide Ron Kaufman to Bush on July 21, 1992, the president was told that he wasn't seen as favorably by voters as Democratic challenger Bill Clinton was, and Bush wrote in the margins, "Ugh!"[71]

When he finally realized how much trouble he was in, it was too late to stop Clinton's momentum, and Bush lost his bid for a second term.

STAN GREENBERG

Stan Greenberg, a short, bespectacled intellectual, had the air of a professor, very analytical and serious. Greenberg felt that his role as the presidential pollster was twofold: to keep Bill Clinton informed about public opinion and to serve as a caretaker of Clinton's promises from the 1992 campaign—"what put him in the White House," Greenberg said. This meant steering as close as possible to the wants and desires of the middle class.[72]

He met with President Clinton at the White House for 15 minutes each week. "It was just us," Greenberg recalled, and the two of them would resist bringing others into these sessions, even though many other staffers wanted to attend.[73] Greenberg wanted to solidify his personal relationship with the president and he didn't want anyone else in these briefings who might interrupt his presentation, cause him to limit his candor, or distract the president.

Greenberg would go into the meetings with detailed notes outlining what he wanted to say, and often brought along graphs and charts to illustrate his points. Afterward, he would send a memo to Clinton and about a dozen of his senior aides, including Vice President Al Gore and First Lady Hillary Rodham Clinton, summarizing what went on. Each memo was numbered, like a formally classified national-security document, so it could be kept track of and wouldn't slip into the hands of unauthorized people.

At his focus groups, which Greenberg conducted frequently, he developed a special technique that was particularly fascinating to Clinton. At the end of these sessions with about a dozen voters, after sometimes-detailed and -emotional discussions of issues and trends, Greenberg would ask each participant to fill out a postcard to the president. The idea was to pass along something that the participants were eager to share with the man in the Oval Office. Greenberg would later give these postcards directly to

Clinton, and he always looked forward to reading them as a sort of direct line into the mind of the nation.

Often, especially at the rocky start of Clinton's presidency in 1993, the messages were tough to take, along the lines of "You're letting us down," or "You're spending too much time on allowing gays in the military" when the economy should have been his main concern, as he pledged it would be during the campaign. When he read such comments, Clinton wasn't offended; he was grateful for the information on public attitudes.

The White House suffered some embarrassment early on when the *Wall Street Journal* revealed that the Democrats had spent nearly $2 million on polling and other opinion research in 1993 compared to about $200,000 spent by the Republicans for Clinton's predecessor, George H.W. Bush, during a comparable period.[74] Greenberg explained that Clinton wanted the polls for very good reasons—to keep informed about public attitudes and to determine how he could communicate most effectively with the American people.

* * *

UNLIKE SOME OTHER presidential pollsters, such as Patrick Caddell for Jimmy Carter; and Dick Morris, who succeeded Greenberg as Clinton's public-opinion maven; Greenberg didn't think it was his role to be a policy-maker, only a conveyor of information about public attitudes. "I didn't think it was my job to say what should be in the economy plan," Greenberg told me as an example. "That's not the pollster's job." And there were plenty of economic and political advisers to do that. His challenge was to make the case for whatever the president decided he wanted to do, such as to focus on deficit reduction rather than public investments.

There were many cases where Greenberg was the bearer of bad news, and he didn't sugar-coat it. In a confidential memo to the president and first lady on May 17, 1994, Greenberg opened with a dire warning. "The administration, the Democrats in Congress and the party face a disaster in November unless we move urgently to change the mood of the country," Greenberg wrote. "The public's current blues are rooted in questions about our leadership and capacity to move the country forward. Voters have serious doubts, but they are answerable if we move in the less than six months ahead of us."[75]

Greenberg listed many issues on which Clinton was found lacking by the public, such as fighting crime, looking out for the middle class, showing leadership in foreign affairs, having an admirable personal character, and demonstrating competence. Many voters felt he was in "over his head" as president. The pollster concluded, "We seem defensive and focused on ourselves. The administration will only make the turn to a successful 1994, if we make the turn that we executed in New Hampshire [a reference to the Democratic primary in 1992]: Bill Clinton doesn't matter; the hits don't matter compared to the hits the American people have been taking every day of their lives. The drama of the Bill Clinton Presidency must be about ordinary people and what Bill Clinton is fighting for to make sure they have better lives."[76]

But Clinton was unable to turn things around that quickly, and the Democrats lost control of Congress in the November 1994 midterm elections. It was widely seen as a rebuff of Clinton himself. Greenberg's post-election analysis recognized how much trouble Clinton was in. In a confidential memo to key senior staffers on November 29, entitled "Strategic Definition of the Clinton Presidency," Greenberg wrote, "The starting point should be the core idea of the Clinton Presidency. Right now, voters have very little understanding of our purpose and direction. That needs to be clarified and affirmed over and over again. Let me suggest a structure. Our purpose is to make this country work for the average American, not the big and powerful. That must be true for the government (cut waste and overspending, limit lobbyist influence, empower people). That must be true for the economy (better paying jobs, training, college loans, middle class tax relief). That must be true for health care (affordable and secure)."

Three days later, on December 2, Greenberg presented in greater detail his plan for how to move forward. This confidential memo was sent to the president, the first lady, and five other senior administration officials, including Vice President Al Gore. Greenberg wrote,

> While the administration must excel in many areas, the three goals outlined below constitute the most important and should structure the other decisions we make:
>
> 1. Strength. Bill Clinton must be seen as determined and strong enough to do what he says he'll do. His resoluteness and strength allows people to depend on him; without it, he seems political. The sense that the President is not strong enough to do what he promises is probably the biggest problem we face and the most important of these challenges.

2. Identification with the middle class. The President should be seen to be motivated by this passion, as he was during the campaign, when he said people who play by the rules are working harder and earning less. The Republicans are waging class warfare on taxes, welfare, immigration, spending and other issues, and we dare not let them build a phony identification with the middle class.

3. Economic vision. The President and the administration need to communicate a clear economic vision that allows people to interpret current economic news and feel positively about the future. Large portions of downscale America, particularly non-college voters under the age of 50 (the "new economy independents"), are not feeling the recovery and resent our course. It's not our accomplishments that matter here; it is our vision.[77]

But by the fall of 1994, having lost Congress in a humiliating defeat, Clinton had lost considerable confidence in Greenberg. The president concluded that his pollster was too liberal and that he needed some fresh advice or he would lose his bid for a second term. Clinton replaced Greenberg with the triumvirate of Dick Morris, Mark Penn, and Doug Schoen, with Morris starting out at the top of the triumvirate.

DICK MORRIS

Dick Morris cut a wide swath in the White House. Short in stature, his hair perfectly coiffed, fast-talking, and always ready with an idea, he was one of the most influential pollsters ever, perhaps the most influential of all for the relatively short amount of time that he worked for President Clinton. One of the reasons for his impact was that the man he was advising was such a voracious consumer of information about public opinion.

And Bill Clinton felt he had a special bond with Morris. "I think he is, first of all, brilliant, tactically and strategically," the president said in 1997, when both were in their heyday. "Secondly, with me he's always been very straightforward and honest, the bad news as well as the good and, if possible, the bad news first. Thirdly, he knows how I think, and he knows what I will do and what I won't do. Fourthly, he's full of new ideas all the time. And finally, we've been together so long that he not only understands me, I understand him."[78]

Clinton had known Morris for many years and had relied on him as his pollster while Clinton was governor of Arkansas. After he got into political trouble as president when the Democrats lost control of Congress in

1994, in what was in part a referendum on his presidency, Clinton turned to Morris again. He was worried about his re-election in 1996.

But Morris's return to Clinton's orbit presented several problems. Morris, a supremely energetic operator whose enthusiasm knew no bounds, was based in Connecticut and was then working almost exclusively for Republican candidates, so his presence would upset many Democrats. Bringing him back would also alienate many members of the White House staff, who would see him as an interloper and a self-promoter who didn't share their core Democratic values. "Morris, 47, represented a side of Clinton that the president disliked in himself—the pragmatist who knew that a candidate needed to jockey and reposition himself to gain approval and win elections," says author Bob Woodward. "But Clinton was always eager to be liked, and the attraction between Clinton and Morris was almost magnetic. They knew and understood each other so well they could finish each other's sentences."[79]

"From the beginning of our relationship, in 1977, polls have been my common frame of reference with Bill Clinton," Morris writes. "We used polling not to determine what positions he would take but to figure out which of the positions he had already taken were the most popular. I would always draw the distinction between deciding on policy and identifying certain issues for emphasis by telling Clinton, 'You print the menu of the things you want. Then I'll advise which dish to have for dinner tonight.'"[80]

Polls were central to Clinton's approach to politics and governing. "For him, a poll helps him sense who doesn't like him and why they don't," Morris writes. "In the reflected numbers, he sees his shortcomings and his potential, his successes and his failures. For Bill Clinton, positive poll results are not just tools—they are vindication, ratification, and approval—whereas negative poll results are a learning process in which the pain of the rebuff to his self-image forces deep introspection. Intellectually, polls offer Clinton an insight into how people think. He uses polls to adjust not just his thinking on one issue but his frame of reference so that it is always as close to congruent with that of the country as possible."[81]

"I have a lot of faith in polling," Morris adds. "But polling shouldn't determine what a political leader does. Much of the time he has to go against what the polls say the people want. But polls can help a leader figure out which arguments will be the most persuasive."[82]

As Morris recounts it, Clinton phoned him in October 1994 and said, "I want you to do a poll for me. I'm not satisfied that I know how to handle what the Republicans are doing to me. I'm not getting the advice I need."[83] That survey showed the depths of Clinton's troubles. "Voters believed that the president had not accomplished much and didn't stand for anything," Morris recalls.[84]

Morris had bluntly predicted the disastrous Democratic showing in the 1994 mid-terms, and this reinforced Clinton's belief that Morris had his finger on America's pulse and could help Clinton rebuild his popularity. Morris told Clinton that voters didn't identify him with any clear accomplishment and they didn't believe Clinton had substantially reduced the federal deficit, which he had. Many voters just wouldn't believe that a Democrat would do such a thing because deficit reduction was supposed to be a Republican objective. Many of Clinton's accomplishments—on federal spending, winning congressional approval for a crime bill, and other issues—didn't even register.[85]

"Clinton valued Morris not just for their long personal history together, or for Morris's tactical acumen or his notorious willingness to do just about anything to win," Woodward writes. "Morris was a *Republican* consultant. He had worked almost exclusively for the other side in recent years, and Clinton now had to understand the enemy better than ever. At the same time, he knew Morris was frequently wrong, misguided or even crazy. His ideas and proposals needed filtering, but Clinton could do that himself and act as the necessary check."[86]

As the White House correspondent for *U.S. News & World Report* at the time, I recall White House officials saying, repeatedly, that if Morris had a hundred ideas, ninety would be mediocre, five would be horrible, and five would be brilliant. The challenge was to figure out which was which. But Clinton liked the concept of Morris providing a constant stream of ideas, and the president could pick and choose.

Morris insisted that he have weekly meetings with Clinton, which he felt were "the central step in organizing his campaign."[87] They continued nearly every week from December 1994 until Morris left the campaign in August 1996, and almost always were held at the White House residence. For a while, Morris met with Clinton alone and then the group expanded to include about twenty senior Clinton advisers, with Morris chairing the sessions.[88]

One of Morris's initial recommendations was to reduce the attention that Clinton was paying to the liberal wing of the Democratic party, both in Congress and on Clinton's staff, resulting in the president's options being more limited than they should have been. "Your allies have become your jailers," Morris told Clinton.[89]

But given the sensitivity of bringing Morris on board, Clinton decided to start him out in secret, as a consultant with an office outside the White House. The two talked frequently by phone and sometimes in person, and much of what Morris said was incorporated by Clinton in what he did. After a while, White House staffers knew Clinton was talking to someone who was affecting his thinking, but they weren't sure who it was. Clinton started using a nickname for the secret adviser, "Charlie," and White House aides thought it was based on the off-camera mystery man who was directing the action in the TV series, *Charlie's Angels.* Morris says he came up with the code name himself, referring to veteran GOP strategist and Morris friend Charlie Black.[90] At first, Clinton didn't want to divulge how important Morris had become to his evaluation of how to reposition his presidency.

When White House Chief of Staff Leon Panetta figured out what was going on, he demanded that Morris be openly incorporated in the discussions at the White House so policy-making and political strategizing could be properly coordinated. Clinton agreed, and Morris began attending meetings and, at Clinton's direction, the White House staff began working with him, at least to some extent.[91] But throughout his tenure advising President Clinton, Morris still had to deal with hostility from some White House advisers, including the influential Deputy Chief of Staff Harold Ickes. They thought he was an arrogant self-promoter, that many of his ideas were wacky, and that he was at heart a Republican and wanted to move Clinton to the right.

Yet Clinton remained enthralled with Morris. In consultation with him, the president concluded that he had lost touch with Middle America in fundamental ways, and blamed it in part on the fact that real wages were declining and many families were hurting, and they didn't think the president understood their plight. Many of these voters also felt that Clinton didn't show enough respect for their traditional values, such as the work ethic, skepticism about welfare, opposition to gays in the military, and the need to fight crime. Since many of these people were swing voters, Clinton felt that his re-election was in jeopardy.

Morris came up with the theory of "triangulation," which meant Clinton should borrow ideas from the left and right and take positions between the extremes and above the orthodoxies of the past. It was essentially an argument for centrism.

Adopting the role of policy and political advocate and not simply public-opinion analyst, as Greenberg had been, Morris began sending Clinton a blizzard of ideas, what he called "bite-size initiatives," designed to move him to the center. And Morris did many polls, which he said showed that American wanted tax cuts, economic recovery, more federal aid to education, and programs specifically targeted to help families.[92] Morris said this program should be called a "middle class bill of rights."

Clinton liked the idea and he made it the centerpiece of a speech he gave to the nation on December 15, 1994. It included proposals for a $500-a-child tax cut for families; making college tuition tax-deductible; and authorizing the use of tax-free Individual Retirement Accounts for medical expenses, education, or buying a first home.[93] The speech received a considerable amount of criticism from Republicans and the media as a collection of half-measures and mini-initiatives, but it set the president on the centrist path that Morris was recommending.

*   *   *

THE HALLMARK of Morris's internal attempts to gain influence was his tenacity. As Clinton had predicted, some of his ideas were beyond the pale. In May 1995, as the president was flying home from a summit in Russia, he got a fax from Morris proposing a theme for Clinton's weekly radio address that Saturday, May 13, on Japanese trade. Morris wanted Clinton to go on the attack, to harshly condemn Japanese trade practices and threaten retaliation. It was designed in part to appeal to American workers, especially those in the auto industry, who felt under siege by Japanese products. But National Security Adviser Tony Lake was appalled. He felt the Morris text was too inflammatory and could trigger a trade war.[94]

Clinton rejected Morris's recommendation, but the incident showed that the pollster was intent on getting into as many policy areas as he could, and it was happening again and again, on issues including deficit reduction, balancing the budget, fighting crime, Medicare, communications strategy, advertising for the campaign, fighting terrorism, and now trade. He was also pushing Clinton to authorize a massive ad blitz a year before the general-election campaign to praise the job Clinton was doing and criticize the Republicans. The president approved the ad campaign, and it raised Clinton's job-approval numbers—a personal coup for Morris.

Morris's performances at meetings were breathtaking for their audacity. George Stephanopoulos, a key Clinton adviser who was often at odds with Morris, watched in near-awe as Morris went from one major issue to another, even writing radio addresses and speeches on his keyboard on the spur of the moment. Morris once wrote a complete Saturday radio address for Clinton in about 15 minutes, a remarkable feat.[95]

Lake complained to Chief of Staff Panetta about what he considered the pollster's inappropriate and wrong-headed forays into national security policy, and this confirmed Panetta's feelings that Morris was close to being out of control. He ordered the entire White House staff to report to him any dealings with, even sightings of, Morris. It was a remarkable recognition of how dysfunctional the Clinton staff operation had become when a sort of all-points bulletin had to be issued to rein in a shadowy adviser who had backdoor access to the president but little or no willingness to coordinate with anyone else.[96]

It was a high-water mark not only for Morris but for the White House pollster as an institution. Never before, not even with Patrick Caddell, had a pollster tried to range so far and so deep into presidential policy-making with so little restraint from within the West Wing. Morris had emerged as the chief strategist in the Clinton White House.

*   *   *

IN THE END, Morris was his own worst enemy. It was revealed that he was seeing a prostitute, and he was forced to resign as Clinton's pollster and leave Clinton's inner circle shortly before the 1996 Democratic National Convention. But, using Morris's blueprint for triangulation, Clinton went on to win a second term.

MARK PENN AND DOUG SCHOEN

The successors to Morris as Clinton's chief strategists, Mark Penn and Doug Schoen, were more disciplined and low-key than Morris but also extremely influential with Clinton.

Penn, a longtime pollster not only for Democrats but also for corporate clients, emphasized sophisticated analysis, such as computer models, to help him decide in which media markets to advertise in Clinton's 1996 re-election campaign. Among the factors he considered were previous voting history, cost of advertising time, estimated number of undecided or persuadable voters the ads might reach, cumulative previous pro-Clinton advertising over a given period of time, the likely impact on local House and Senate races, and how important that market was in Clinton's drive to win a majority in the Electoral College in November 1996. Penn said the program could calculate the most efficient way to determine the "cost per persuadable vote" in each market.[97]

Schoen was the less-known and less-visible partner in the Penn-Schoen polling operation but also played a crucial role.

He and Penn developed a tool of analysis to enable the Democratic Party to "reconnect with middle-class voters" over the long term, building on Morris's theories about the political importance of Middle America and also based on Penn's goal of developing a "psychological profile of the electorate."

"Mark's great insight was that it wasn't enough to understand the electorate demographically, by such parameters as age, race, gender, or even by political affiliation," writes Schoen. "Instead, he argued, we needed to look at the electorate in an entirely new way, in order to figure out what issues were of greatest concern. Lifestyle characteristics, attitudes, values, and even personality traits—all of these things were relevant." This is what Penn called the "psychological profile of the electorate."[98]

Using the same methods that worked for corporate clients such as AT&T, Penn and Schoen broke the electorate into "current customers" or supporters and "potential customers." They concluded that about 40 per cent of the electorate was aligned with Clinton and the Democrats, 40 per cent were with the Republicans, and 20 per cent were in the middle. The goal, Schoen explained, was to "develop a message that appealed to that middle 20 per cent. In elections, particularly presidential races, it is often those 'potential customers' or swing voters that make all the difference. In order to get those swing voters, we realized that we would need to segment and divide the electorate in ways that had never before been attempted. Mark called it a neuropersonality poll, and it would eventually become the defining document of Clinton's reelection effort."[99]

Penn and Schoen divided the electorate into the Clinton base (28 per cent of the electorate); the base of Republican presidential nominee Bob Dole, a senator from Kansas (18 per cent); "Swing I voters," who leaned toward Clinton but were still undecided (29 per cent); and "Swing II voters," who were more conservative and less likely support Clinton (25 per cent). Penn and Schoen concluded that Clinton needed the support of 60 per cent of Swing I voters and 30 per cent of Swing II voters to win.[100]

The next step was to do extensive polling on attitudes and the intensity of feelings within these groups. Penn and Schoen, instead of asking people if they supported cutting taxes, would pose a choice in a specific context, such as if people in a target group would support tax cuts even though they would be "irresponsible" because the budget deficit was so high. Then they would ask voters, if a presidential candidate took such a position, would they be much more likely to vote for that candidate, somewhat more likely, unaffected, somewhat less likely, or much less likely to vote for that candidate. "The point wasn't to figure out what issues were most important but rather to understand which ignited the greatest passion—in other words, what issues were most likely to impact their vote," Schoen recalled. "Equally important, we could test the messaging and see what formulations were most resonant."[101]

Schoen said the results of the polling surprised them. It turned out that income level and age were not the great defining variables in American politics, as was generally supposed. Instead, the main definer in 1996 was marital status, especially among swing voters. Having raised children was the "crucial dividing line in the electorate," Schoen concluded. This led Clinton to emphasize his views in those areas that were compatible with the attitudes and concerns of married voters who were raising children, such as limiting tobacco advertising aimed at kids, promoting crime prevention and elder care, raising the minimum wage, preventing healthcare companies from denying coverage, balancing the budget, limiting Medicare cuts, and backing voluntary school prayer.[102]

The pollsters further divided voters into subcategories to determine and measure the intensity of their views on issues. They devised nine "issues-based clusters": economic liberals, social liberals, international liberals, 1992 Clinton voters, balanced-budget swing voters, crime stoppers, young social conservatives who were also swing voters, senior-citizen conservatives, and rich conservatives.[103]

The pollsters went from there to dividing the electorate by personality traits, such as extroversion vs. introversion, sensing vs. intuition, thinking vs. feeling, and judging vs. perceiving. They also asked voters their favorite television shows and found that Clinton voters liked HBO, MTV, and Oprah, while Dole voters liked *Home Improvement* and *Larry King Live* and swing voters liked *Seinfeld* and *Friends.*

Most important, the pollsters developed an extraordinarily sophisticated breakdown of typical swing voters: "They were around the age of forty, had an income of between thirty thousand dollars and sixty thousand dollars, were married, well-educated, moderate, and nonunion. They enjoyed music, sports, the outdoors, videos, talk shows, *60 Minutes* (a favorite with both Swing I's and Swing II's), and soap operas. More specifically, Swing I and II voters were afraid. They were worried about crime, retirement, technology, pressure at work, and illness."[104]

All in all, Schoen said, "Never before had a political candidate so carefully dissected the electorate."[105]

At a meeting to discuss their latest wave of polls, Clinton asked, as he had before, why he had lost the centrist image he had earned in the 1992 campaign. He couldn't believe it was just about taxes and government spending. Penn said, "Mr. President, it's not about economics; it's about values." This crystallized Clinton's thinking and he developed a mantra that he would use through the rest of his presidency and that resonated with the public—he would justify his policy decisions in terms of what the pollsters called "all-American values" such as "opportunity, responsibility, and community."[106] Among the issues that he pushed successfully was welfare reform, in which he broke with liberal Democrats who felt he was going too far in requiring work for benefits and in supporting time limits for individuals on welfare. But neither did he give hard-line conservatives in Congress all they wanted. In the process, he rebuilt his image as a centrist, a strong leader, and a savvy negotiator, which is what the country wanted from the president. Clinton used insights from his pollsters to remake his presidency and win a second term.

In assessing Clinton, Schoen concluded, "He was and remains the best reader of polls I've ever seen—always aware of what questions to ask in order to challenge us and force Mark and me to give him better results. He went over many of the pieces of direct mail that we sent out, pored over television commercial scripts, and was a tireless fundraiser of campaign dollars. Based on the results of our neuropersonality poll, Clinton would introduce and promote a series of small programs—like tuition tax credits, V-chips for television in order to keep inappropriate content from children, school uniforms, and curfews—that responded to people's daily concerns. These were often derided in the press, but for swing voters suspicious of big-government solutions they were perfect—and they resonated."[107]

Clinton's self-indulgence and other character flaws that led to his affair with former White House intern Monica Lewinsky (see Chapter Nine) were seen by most Americans as a separate issue from his public leadership and his understanding of middle-class concerns, and he left office with high job-approval ratings.

JOEL BENENSON

Joel Benenson, President Obama's lead pollster, stays out of the limelight. He rarely makes speeches or public statements, and his media interviews are infrequent. But Benenson has had a strong impact on Obama's thinking, giving him a much better insight into the 2012 electorate than his Republican opponent Mitt Romney ever had—insight that continues to shape the Obama agenda and the Obama rhetoric to this day.

Benenson, a bearded, cerebral, and intense New Yorker, emerged from Obama's successful re-election campaign in 2012 as one of the top polling sages in the country.

Benenson didn't make a habit of briefing Obama directly on his polls, as some of his predecessors, such as Wirthlin, Morris, and Penn, had done. Most of his data flowed through White House aides, especially senior advisers David Axelrod and, after Axelrod moved back to Chicago to work full-time on the 2012 campaign, through senior White House adviser David Plouffe. But Benenson was always part of the political inner circle. "I was very fortunate to be part of the strategy team all the way through," Benenson told me.

He says his goal as a pollster is "to understand the hidden architecture of opinion," and to "probe deeply into the underlying values and attitudes that shape how people are viewing the issues of the day and the context of their lives." He adds, "I often say that what people are bringing to the table is as important if not more important than what you say to them" in a campaign or in other attempts to send them a message or persuade them.[108]

*   *   *

BENENSON, who worked for New York governor Mario Cuomo earlier in his career, takes pride in his eclectic background. He comes from a working-class family and attended the City University of New York, not some Ivy League school. While in his twenties, Benenson started working as the co-owner of a beer distributor in the city's Crown Heights section, one of the most diverse communities in America, and for a while he was a reporter for the *New York Daily News.* He believes that these experiences broadened his understanding of American culture and keep him grounded in the world outside the Washington Beltway.[109]

He said his seven years as a beer distributor brought him into contact with people of many backgrounds, including Latinos, working-class whites, Hasidic Jews, and those who were living paycheck-to-paycheck. He did tasks in those days that gave him a sense of the routines of many wage-earners: loading trucks when a regular employee was out sick; operating the cash register; and getting to know his fellow workers, their families and his customers. "You hear the voice of the people," he said. "How do you expect to solve people's problems if you don't hear the voice of the people?"

One of his guiding principles is to keep from becoming isolated himself. "I constantly ask people questions about their lives and what makes them tick," he told me. He encourages the free expression of a wide range of opinion within his consulting organization, Benenson Strategy Group, where he encourages his staff members to eat lunch together in a "break area" of his offices on the thirty-third floor of a Manhattan skyscraper. He regularly visits a property he owns near other family members in Montana, where he has gotten to know many local residents from ranchers and restaurant owners to teachers and craftsmen—"people who see things differently from the people who live in the Washington–New York corridor."[110]

It always stayed with Benenson how abnormal life had been for Governor Cuomo, who hadn't driven his own car for twelve years while he served in government because his security guards advised against it and because he was too busy for the simple activities that most Americans take for granted. Benenson says it is immeasurably more difficult for a president to have a normal life. "You can't take a walk or go to a park," Benenson told me. "You can't walk your dog. You can't move around to talk to people. A lot of things are harder to do."[111]

Benenson said Barack Obama is acutely aware of and deeply disappointed by the isolation of the White House. As described earlier in this book, President Obama is helped in his attempts to break out of the "bubble" by ventilating options with his staff and learning what others outside his inner circle have to say, Benenson explains. And Obama retains a conviction that "the American people are always ahead of the politicians, and they are," Benenson says.

One of Benenson's political innovations is what he calls the "ethnography project," designed to do "a deep dive" into the world of everyday people not only to bring out their views on politics but to "have conversations with voters about their daily lives." The project was inspired by a study conducted in 2005 by Benenson for the Service Employees International Union to find out why the Democrats did poorly in the presidential race in 2004, and particularly why the party was having great difficulty appealing to working-class and middle-class people. One conclusion was that Americans sensed that the economy was falling out of balance for them, and that the Democrats weren't representing the middle class as aggressively or as effectively as they had in the past.

In mid 2011, Benenson discussed the idea with senior Obama strategist David Plouffe, and they agreed to move ahead. So that spring, 100 "up-for-grabs" or undecided voters were selected in three battleground states—Colorado, Florida, and Ohio.[112] The voters were asked to go to a special website and answer eight to ten questions about their lives and everyday activities on six occasions over a sixteen-day period. Each respondent took an average of an hour to fill out the questionnaire each time. The topics ranged from explaining the type of community they lived in to how they were treated at work, what kind of treatment in the workplace they considered fair and unfair, their personal values, and how they were adjusting their behavior to cope with the economic downturn.

After the responses were analyzed, nine voters were chosen from among the participants in each of the three locations, and they were, in turn, divided into groups of three, or "triads," in each location. At that point, detailed interviews were conducted to learn even more about them as individuals. They were questioned, for example, about their everyday routines; their families; their concerns about the present, their hopes for the future, and how secure they felt; whether they or any family members had recently lost a job; how much risk they were willing to take to improve their circumstances, such as whether they would change jobs or move out of town; and how their work environments had changed in the past five years. Each of these sessions lasted about two and a half hours. They were also asked whether Obama deserved to be re-elected, and why.

Benenson says this information, compiled into what he called "ethno-journals," was combined with the results of polls and focus groups conducted by a veteran moderator. The ethnography project produced 1,400 pages of transcripts and data that Benenson and aides pored over. Summaries were given to President Obama and key Obama advisers at the White House and with his re-election campaign. It all amounted to a "rich resource" that the Obama campaign and the White House used through the rest Obama's first term and into the fall election campaign, Benenson says. "You've got to hear the conversations that people are having" or you can't solve their problems as a political leader, Benenson told me.[113]

Among the findings, Americans felt that the economic crisis didn't happen overnight and would take a long while to end, probably at least five years. Also, there was the finding that the economy was not undergoing an ordinary recession but a particularly harsh and deep one that indicated fundamental long-range problems.

Participants said they were using various "coping mechanisms" to deal with the economic hard times, such as putting products back on the grocery shelves rather than spending the extra money for them, and saving money on gasoline by not driving to movie theaters on the weekends. The voters also made clear that they didn't blame Obama for rising gasoline prices—a growing issue at the time—but instead blamed oil companies, oil speculators, and turmoil among oil-rich countries of the Middle East.

This research, along with similar findings of polls and focus groups, was one reason why Obama injected certain themes into his presidency and his re-election campaign, such as that he was trying to create an economy that was "built to last" and that should be constructed from the middle up, not from the top down. It was also important for Obama to acknowledge the reality that most Americans were experiencing—that the economy had improved but was still causing many hardships and strains. So he talked about how the economy had "turned a corner," that his policies had started to work, not that his policies had fully worked or that "America is back."

* * *

ALL THIS paid off in the fall campaign. Obama and his team realized that he needed to connect with voters' concern about the economy and show how his values, his vision, and his record, from the federal bailout of the auto industry to providing more aide to college students, were all aimed at promoting the middle class.

"The president's positive favorable ratings and job ratings show that the American people know he came into office facing the worst economic crisis in their lives and that in the face of fierce opposition from lobbyists and Republicans in Congress, he's made tough decisions to do what's right for America and create an economy that's built to last, not for the next boom and bust cycle," Benenson told Politico in June 2012. "Average working Americans know there's more work to do but that the president's actions like the auto rescue and investments that have created more manufacturing jobs than we've had in a decade are beginning to pay off and that's why on comparative attributes President Obama has a 20-point advantage over Mitt Romney on 'looking out for the middle class.'"[114]

But Neil Newhouse, the chief pollster for Republican challenger Mitt Romney, had a different analysis. "Obama's high favorable scores are reflective of the raised expectations and hopes that voters had for Obama when he was first elected," Newhouse told Politico. "What we're finding now in our focus groups and polling is that voters can contemporaneously like the president while at the same time believe that his policies have failed to make things better in the country and that it's time to make a change."[115]

In the end, Benenson's theories proved to be more accurate, illustrating again how the president's pollster can be invaluable in keeping the chief executive informed about public opinion. Reviewing the campaign, Benenson says, "From the start you had a theory on the Republican side:

They were going to make this a referendum on President Obama, using the old Ronald Reagan question": Are you better off today than you were four years ago?[116]

"But the American people were focused on, 'Which candidate is going to make my life better over the next four years?'" Benenson says. "Overwhelmingly, Americans viewed the economic crisis and recession as an extraordinary circumstance—not as an ordinary recession."[117] The more that Romney and the Republicans minimized the unusual nature of the recession, the more out of touch and tone-deaf they seemed.

The Republicans overplayed their hand in using the economy as a bludgeon with which to attack Obama. "They are living in a 1980s model—all you have to do is say, 'We're going to cut taxes' and the world will be fine," Benenson argues. He says middle-class Americans tended to dismiss that argument because "those at the top have benefited more than they have," and they wanted a president who would fight for them—a major Obama theme.[118]

Benenson also says that his polls didn't show Obama's support vacillating in the last several weeks of the campaign, as the Republicans claimed. Some GOP strategists said Obama made key mistakes, such as a poor performance in his first debate with Romney, and this hurt his standing. But Benenson argued that Obama maintained a lead of three to four percentage points for many weeks. "It wasn't volatile no matter what the [public] polls and chatter said," Benenson notes. "The old model that says the undecideds will break for the challenger is no longer true. We knew we would get our share.... We had a lead, we had an edge, and we never relinquished it."[119]

In demographic terms, Benenson, along with other senior Obama advisers, argued throughout the campaign that Obama could essentially reconstruct his winning coalition from 2008 by courting Latinos, African Americans, young people, new voters, and single women—all important segments of the electorate—while building support among other key groups, such as white independent women and lower-income whites. In the end, this strategy carried the day.[120]

Benenson also said, "The population changes. The Republican vote model imagined that it would be 2004 again (when George W. Bush won reelection). But America doesn't stand still. And it's not all about demographics. It's about who makes my life and my family's life better."[121]

Benenson's success shows the importance of a pollster not only in conducting fair and accurate research, but also in interpreting the data correctly and getting a president to accept his conclusions.

CHAPTER TWELVE
BREAKING OUT OF THE BUBBLE

In sum, America's presidents live in a world apart. Every president, because of the privileges and protections that envelop him, "removes himself from the company of lesser breeds who must stand in line and wait their turn on a share-and-share-alike basis for the comforts of life," writes former White House adviser George Reedy.[1]

As this book has shown, some presidents have tried to live as normal a life as they could and to minimize the imperial trappings of the office. But even President Obama, who has shown more of a commitment to staying in touch than most of his predecessors, agrees that the problem of presidential isolation remains severe.

As Reedy wrote presciently four decades ago, "It does not matter what a president wants to do if the people are unwilling to do it. A political leader who ignores the popular will is not a hero but merely a shoddy crafts-man who is not entitled to his job." Some of our leaders, such as John F. Kennedy, resisted the idea of having to "merely bow to the popular will," Reedy says, "But if he is unaware of those currents, he will be unable to pilot the ship of state to safe harbor."[2]

Historian Arthur Schlesinger, Jr., who served as a White House adviser to President Kennedy, saw the problem clearly in 1973 when Richard Nixon was trying to stonewall various investigations of the Watergate scandal. Schlesinger conceded that most presidents are elected with a respect for the Constitution and for the need to stay in touch. "Yet Presidents chosen as open and modest men are not sure to remain so amid the intoxications of the office; and the office has grown steadily more intoxicating in recent years," Schlesinger wrote. "A wise President, having read George Reedy and observed the fates of Johnson and Nixon, will take care to provide himself while there still is time, with antidotes to intoxication.... But it does mean a reduction in the size and power of the White House staff and the restoration of the access and prestige of the executive departments. The President will always need a small and alert personal staff to serve as his eyes and ears and one lobe of his brain, but he must avoid a vast and possessive staff ambitious to make the decisions of government. Above all, he must not make himself the prisoner of a single information system. No sensible president will give one man control of all the channels of communication; any man sufficiently wise to exercise such control properly ought to be President himself."[3]

And Theodore H. White, the famed chronicler of presidential politics, noted that even Nixon, who was associated with expanding the imperial presidency, realized that something was amiss in the way the presidency was conducted and the demands it put on him. He tried to reorganize the White House because the duties and burdens had become so heavy and he was feeling in constant need to stay in touch.[4] "But the problem of the Presidency, the near-impossibility of one man being both policy-maker and executive at once, remains," White observed. "Even if the purest and noblest man had sat in the White House in the Nixon years, he would have had to recognize this challenge, created by the simultaneous inflation of Presidential authority and the shortfall of any President's personal reach.... In all matters except trust, the Presidency has been an experimental office since George Washington first held it in 1789. The entire electoral process has been left by the Constitution to the trial and error of succeeding generations. But now, as the parties split and tear at each other and within themselves, one is more troubled than ever."[5]

The system was sorely tested in 2000, when Republican George W. Bush won a majority of electoral votes after a disputed 5-4 Supreme Court decision that gave him the state of Florida. This came even though Democrat Al Gore won 500,000 more popular votes nationally than Bush did. The outcome left many Democrats bitter for many months while they questioned Bush's legitimacy as president, and whether he really was connected to a majority of his fellow citizens.

President Obama is doing much better as a tribune of the people and a man who is truly striving to stay in touch and break out of the White House bubble. But it is a constant struggle, as he and his aides admit.

My own prescriptions for ending or at least reducing presidential isolation are these:

REMEMBER YOUR ROOTS

One can't overstate the importance of a president having a background that includes time living a normal life or having experiences that put him or her in contact with everyday people. Jennifer Granholm, former governor of Michigan and now a TV commentator, says she felt isolated in her government job but worked as hard as she could to stay in touch as governor. She made "specific, concerted efforts to connect with people's struggles. Experiencing the unfiltered pain of one's citizens is, I believe, the most important work a governor must do—the foundation for action."[6] She went on to argue that the same applies to the president.

The much-maligned Gerald Ford hasn't been given enough credit for trying to stay in touch with Middle America after he succeeded Richard Nixon in the White House when Nixon resigned in August 1974. Ford was the ultimate middle-class man, a humble politician who represented the Middle American town of Grand Rapids, Michigan, in the House for many years and who, like Reagan, never forgot his roots. Ford's basic decency came through in how he treated his staff with respect and how he felt that everyday Americans would do the right thing if given the facts and the opportunity.

Vacationing at a leased home in the posh mountain community of Vail, Colorado, during August 1975, Ford was shocked to find that his dog Liberty had left a mess on the floor during a family dinner. A steward rushed over to take care of the problem but Ford waved him off. "No man should have to clean up after another man's dog," he explained. Ford's problem was that such acts of consideration and decency were never fully conveyed to the American people.

American voters would be wise to carefully scrutinize all the presidential candidates and determine if their backgrounds would lead them to understand America's problems. If a candidate never lived a middle-class life, never suffered from adversity, or never was in touch with everyday concerns, those facts should be held against him or her. There is little reason to believe that those voids would be filled after a presidency begins.

MAKE USE OF THE POLLSTERS, BUT DON'T OVERDO IT

Some political scientists warn that it's dangerous for a president to rely too much on polls and pollsters. Political scientists Thomas E. Cronin and Michael A. Genovese write that "'pandering to the polls' can be a highly undesirable practice in the White House. The presidency is not and should not be a popularity contest."[7]

Cronin and Genovese also write, "A democratic republic puts its faith in the people, faith that they will not merely elect presidents who will be responsive to their desires, but also do what is right. Americans want to be heard, yet they also want leaders who will independently exercise their own judgment. We honor courageous leaders who refuse to be intimidated by contrary public opinion data. Although presidents, to be sure, must take care not to be so self-assured that they become insensitive to criticism and counsel, they also need a certain inner sense of what has to be done. In the end, the best of presidents are likely to be those who can accurately interpret or anticipate the sentiments of the nation and rally the people and other political leaders to do what must be done, and what the public will later learn to respect. These presidents will commonly be strong political leaders with a vision, if not a detailed program, of where they think the nation should go."[8]

Elaine Kamarck, a former senior adviser to Vice President Al Gore, once said, "Polls provide an illusion of certainty. Outside of the academy, there are few people who understand social science and research methods. Provide a table, a graph, and a chi-square, and you've got the whole room thinking you're a genius."[9]

But George W. Bush showed the problems that arise when a president goes too far in ignoring public opinion. He had a sense of destiny that encouraged him to overlook public opinion as he waged his "war on terror" and the wars in Iraq and Afghanistan. "I'm here for a reason," Bush told an aide not long after the terrorist attacks of September 11, 2001. "And this is going to be how we're going to be judged." A senior administration official told author Bob Woodward that Bush "really believes he was placed here to do this as part of a divine plan."[10]

The fact is that polling also can be very useful. Peter Hart, one of America's most esteemed pollsters, told me that "in the past, the pollsters have become the gate keepers and the conduit for the public voice, and that's a plus and a minus. The plus is, at least you're getting a sampler of public opinion but it's also a filter, shadows on the cave wall."[11] Hart says that, on balance, using a pollster is "better than a crowd of sycophants" in helping a president to govern.

Bill Clinton made this point after a few months in office. He called in his senior staff and said that people were giving him "an awful lot of what they thought I wanted to hear" and not enough of what they really thought. So he turned to his pollster.[12]

BREAK OUT OF THE BUNKER

Frank Luntz, a veteran pollster for Republican candidates, GOP members of Congress, and corporate clients, says that, with the need to protect a president seemingly growing more intense because of threats from terrorists and others who might want to harm America's leader, it's more difficult than ever for a president to interact with everyday people. This severely limits his ability to understand people's concerns. "The people don't have access to tell the president what they're thinking," Luntz told me. "And the president is not going to get direct feedback and contact."[13]

This was especially true for George H.W. Bush in his 1992 re-election campaign. He couldn't grasp how anxious and angry voters were because of the economy, Luntz says. He adds, "The day [presidents] get elected is the last day they are in touch with people. When they run for re-election, it's all fake. Everything is controlled; everything is staged; everything is a photo op," and it's nearly impossible for a president to be in touch with reality.[14]

There is another problem—presidents often try to create the impression that they are in touch when they really aren't. Sean Spicer, communications director of the Republican National Committee, told me during the presidential campaign of 2012 that many of President Obama's highly visible efforts to connect with everyday people were really hollow public-relations gambits.[15]

Spicer pointed to Obama's going out for burgers at Washington-area fast-food restaurants and his wife Michelle's shopping at Target—with contingents of Secret Service agents in tow—as PR stunts that didn't give them any real opportunity to interact with everyday people and learn their concerns. He was similarly skeptical of President Obama's frequent references to the 10 letters from citizens that he said he reads nearly every day. "A lot of it is for show," Spicer says.

It would be better for Obama, or any president, to go out to dinner as President George H.W. Bush did, mingle with fellow customers, and talk to people at restaurants, than to orchestrate such high-visibility moments that don't allow for such interactions.

And it's almost always valuable to get out of town. Jack Valenti, an adviser to Lyndon Johnson, once suggested that the president set up "regional White Houses" in six or seven communities around the country. "Visit them at least once a year for a three- or four-day stay," Valenti advised in an open letter. "Foray into the adjoining countryside. Do not schedule set speeches in large halls before big audiences. Schedule no speeches. Literally get out among the people. I know it is difficult for a

President to really visit, listen, see with a battalion of aides, Secret Service, press and assorted curious onlookers crowding his every move. But you will, if you choose, be able to sense and touch as well as hear and see what the folks outside Washington are concerned about. It is good medicine for a President to gather in, through his own instincts and tactile senses, a microcosm of the people's views."[16]

Not a bad idea, but the cost of maintaining such regional centers could be prohibitive. Even better is a thought passed on to me by Gary Johnson, the Libertarian Party presidential candidate in 2012. He said that when he was governor of New Mexico for eight years, he held "open-door-after-4" meetings with citizens on the third Thursday of every month. From 4 to 10 p.m., Johnson's door would be open at his office to allow citizens to visit him, one by one, for five minutes each. It was first come, first served, and people would simply get in line and walk in to see the governor when their turns came.

"It was incredibly invaluable," Johnson told me in an interview during his campaign for the presidency as the Libertarian Party nominee in August 2012.[17] He dealt with his share of "kooks," such as the people who quizzed him about whether the government was holding aliens from outer space at a special facility in Roswell, New Mexico. But he also heard some good ideas, such as when a citizen wondered why trucks were being suddenly stopped from driving under a bridge. Johnson called the appropriate officials, learned that a mistake had been made on height restrictions, and ordered the road opened immediately.

Johnson said he would have created a similar system to keep in touch had he won the White House, and he was on to something. Every president should adopt a similar, regularly scheduled session with everyday voters, cleared by security of course, but also chosen by White House staffers for their diversity and range of views.

And a president can rely on his wife and children to keep him grounded. This has been done by some presidents, including Clinton and Obama, who found their families to be valuable sounding boards.

Largely unknown the public, presidents have found intense emotional connections with members of the U.S. military, especially soldiers wounded in war and the families of troops who were killed in combat. "That's a dramatic thing," says former presidential adviser Ed Gillespie, who attended several such meetings with President George W. Bush. Bush insisted, as do most presidents under similar conditions, that reporters and news photographers be kept out to ensure privacy and a candid exchange of views. Often the family members and the wounded soldiers would bravely say things like "don't give up" the fight, but the broader point is to bring the president close to the people he is ordering into harm's way and to show him the cost of war. "It fortified the president in a lot of ways," Gillespie recalls.[18]

This is the kind of interaction that should continue.

LISTEN TO CONGRESS

In recent years, when Congress has been deeply polarized between the Democrats and Republicans, presidents have paid less attention to ascertaining the country's mood from discussions with legislators. That's a shame, because members of the House and Senate do tend to keep their ears to the ground.

"The Congress," Reedy says, "is one of the most sensitive barometers of public opinion available to the chief executive. The barometer may tell him some unpleasant things—but this is the function of a barometer.... Truly philosophical presidents who understand the nature of the problems of the office would welcome the midterm election regardless of its outcome. This is one of the few opportunities they have during the course of their administration of taking a sounding of the American people that is far superior to any readings that may be obtained by [pollsters] Dr. Gallup or Mr. Harris."[19]

This is something that President Obama has neglected. He is widely criticized on Capitol Hill for being aloof and showing little interest in developing personal relationships with legislators, even though he is a former senator from Illinois. But Obama says he is a husband and father first, and prefers to spend his private time with his wife Michelle and his young daughters Malia and Sasha. Those are admirable sentiments, but it's also true that he could probably have more influence—and occasionally get the benefit of the doubt—if he spent more time socializing with his allies and adversaries on Capitol Hill.

CONSULT THE EXES

Former presidents represent a resource that is relatively little-used. Each president has his own area of expertise, and it would behoove an incumbent to stay in contact with his predecessors, benefit from their knowledge, and learn from their successes and their mistakes. Most of the time, a former president is eager to be useful.

Consider the case of Richard Nixon. He had resigned the presidency amid the Watergate scandal in 1974, and he was eager for the rest of his life to rehabilitate himself and help to shape U.S. policies. After Ronald Reagan won the White House in 1980, Nixon took it upon himself to write a private, single-spaced memo to the new Republican president. It was dated November 17, 1980, not long after Election Day, and signed with the initials RN. Nixon's advice was sage. "As you know," he wrote, "I believed before the election that, while foreign policy was to me the most important issue of the campaign, the economic issue was the one which would have the greatest voter impact. Now I am convinced that decisive action on the home front is by far the number one priority. Unless you are able to shape up our home base it will be almost impossible to conduct an effective foreign policy. Consequently, I would suggest that for at least six months you not travel abroad and that you focus the attention of your appointees, the Congress and the people on your battle against inflation.... The time to take the heat for possibly unpopular budget cuts is in 1981, not 1982 or 1984."[20] This is what Reagan was inclined to do anyway, but Nixon's letter reinforced his views. [21]

Nixon also sent lengthy memos to Bill Clinton, which the young Democratic president described as brilliant and very helpful, especially on foreign policy. The two also talked on the phone late at night to discuss Russia and China and how a president should allocate his time.[22]

And sometimes a former president can give helpful hints on day-to-day life. At a postelection meeting in his Los Angeles office in 1992, Reagan taught Clinton, who had never served in uniform, how to give a military salute, which came in handy for the newly elected commander in chief during the many occasions when he was dealing with the armed forces. Dwight Eisenhower told John F. Kennedy how to summon an evacuation helicopter to the White House lawn on a moment's notice.[23]

Obama has tried to stay in contact with his predecessors. Just before he took office, he hosted all of the living presidents at the White House— George W. Bush, Bill Clinton, George H.W. Bush, and Jimmy Carter—and they posed for a group photograph as a gesture of solidarity. He has sent them individually or in tandem on charitable and other missions, such as trips to raise money for tsunami relief in Asia. And he used Clinton to court centrist voters and make his case to independents in the 2012 campaign.

But Obama would be wise to reach out to his predecessors a lot more. They are a valuable resource, and can connect him to a host of ideas, policies, and people, including foreign leaders, that will help him do his job.

DON'T IGNORE THE MEDIA

Harry Truman's experience is worth examining because he showed the importance of presidential intuition and instincts in staying in touch.

Truman did read the newspapers and magazines and listened to the radio to find out what was happening around the country. (The fledgling medium of television news was so new that he barely watched.) But in Truman's time, unlike today, politicians commonly believed that the media played an essential role in keeping them, and the country, informed. As the influential columnist Walter Lippmann said, "If the country is to be governed with the consent of the governed, then the governed must arrive at opinions about what their governments want them to consent to. How do they do this? They do it by hearing on the radio and reading in the newspapers what the corps of correspondents tell them is going on in Washington, and in the country at large, and in the world. Here, we correspondents perform an essential service. In some field of interest, we make it our business to find out what is going on under the surface and beyond the horizon, to infer, to deduce, to imagine, and to guess what is going on inside, what this meant yesterday and what it could mean tomorrow. In this we do what every sovereign citizen is supposed to do but has not the time or the interest to do for himself. This is our job. It is no mean calling."[24]

Today such an exalted statement of the media's mission seems quaint and totally out of date. The media are no longer trusted by wide swaths of a deeply polarized electorate that considers mainstream journalists inaccurate, biased, and often focused on real or imagined conflicts that are irrelevant to everyday American life.

Members of the news media clamor regularly for more news conferences with the president. They argue that such encounters enable the country to see a president operate under pressure and respond in a relatively uncontrolled environment. But the value of news conferences as a communications tool is overrated. Presidents and their staffs can predict the questions with precision since the reporters almost always ask about what's in the news that day. As George Reedy has written, "Any president who has done his homework will emerge unscathed, with a generality for the 'tough' questions and a rebuff for the 'impertinent' questions. It is a breeze."[25] This has been the common assessment of the press secretaries, communications directors, and other public-relations officials at the White House since LBJ.

Yet news conferences should be a part of the mix of presidential accesses. They may try the patience of the chief executive and be too subject to stagecraft, but they do subject a president to at least a small degree of give and take that he would not ordinarily receive, and this is healthy.

*   *   *

HARRY TRUMAN HAD an interesting idea. He said the best polling he ever got as president was when Secretary of the Senate Lester Biffle, a friend from Truman's years as a senator from Missouri, traveled around during the 1948 campaign disguised as a chicken peddler. He talked to many people, got an idea of their concerns and their needs, and concluded that Truman would win. This was at a time when the professional pollsters, the political strategists, and the journalists said Republican nominee Thomas Dewey had a lock on victory.

Truman, a former farmer, explained, "Well, in every neighborhood in the country where they raise chickens there was always a fella who drove around either in a truck or an old spring wagon with a team of mules who bought the surplus chickens and eggs." He recounted that Biffle "went around in a spring wagon and dressed in overalls, and he got more information for me than anybody else in the business. He said, 'Now listen, Harry, you don't have to worry. The common people are for ya.' And they were."[26]

Perhaps we need more officials posing as chicken peddlers today.

NOTES

Introduction

1. Author's interview with Mack McLarty, Clinton's first White House chief of staff, June 12, 2012.
2. Chandrasekaran, Rajiv and Greg Jeffe. 2012. "The Four-Star Lifestyle." The *Washington Post* (Nov. 18), p. A1.
3. Reedy, George E. 1970. *The Twilight of the Presidency*. New York: New American Library, Inc., p. 3.
4. Ibid.
5. Saslow, Eli. 2012. *Ten Letters: The Stories Americans Tell Their President*. New York: Anchor Books, p. 16.
6. Donald, David Herbert. 1999. *Lincoln at Home: Two Glimpses of Abraham Lincoln's Family Life*. New York: Simon & Schuster, pp. 24, 230.
7. Donald. *Lincoln at Home: Two Glimpses of Abraham Lincoln's Family Life*, p. 25.
8. Saslow. *Ten Letters: The Stories Americans Tell Their President*, p. 17.
9. Reedy. *The Twilight of the Presidency*, p. 15.
10. Tumulty, Karen. 2012. The *Washington Post* (Nov. 8), p. A39.
11. Martin, Jonathan. 2012. "The GOP's media cocoon." www.politico.com (Nov. 12).
12. Ibid.
13. Author's interview with Frank Donatelli, Sept. 27, 2011.
14. Smith, Hedrick. 2008. *The Power Game: How Washington Works*. New York: Ballantine Books, p. 113.
15. Sloan and the other Nixon aides in this paragraph were quoted in Schlesinger, Arthur M. Jr. 1973. "The Runaway Presidency." *The Atlantic Monthly*, www.theatlantic.com (Nov.), p. 2.
16. Cronin, Thomas E. 2009. *On the Presidency: Teacher, Soldier, Shaman, Pol*. Boulder, Colo.: Paradigm Publishers, p. 24.
17. Reedy. *The Twilight of the Presidency*, p. 9.
18. Author's interview with Jay Carney, Oct. 29, 2011.

19. Author's interview with Julian Zelizer, Dec. 16, 2011.
20. Author's interview with Doug Brinkley, Dec. 18, 2011.
21. Author's interview with Ross Baker, Feb. 8, 2012.
22. Author's interview with George and Barbara Bush, May 3, 2012.
23. Eisinger, Robert M. 2003. *The Evolution of Presidential Polling.* New York: Cambridge University Press, pp. 21–22.
24. Eisinger. *The Evolution of Presidential Polling,* p. 22.
25. Ibid., p. 40.
26. Ibid., pp. 105, 110.
27. Author's interview with Bill Galston, Sept. 2, 2011.
28. Obama speech on healthcare, Strongsville, Ohio, March 15, 2010.
29. Reedy. *The Twilight of the Presidency,* pp. 99–100.
30. Author's interview with Julian Zelizer, Dec. 16, 2011.
31. Miller, Merle. 1973, 1974. *Plain Speaking: An Oral Biography of Harry Truman.* New York: Berkley Publishing Corp., p. 431.

Chapter One

1. Updegrove, Mark K. 2012. *Indomitable Will: LBJ in the Presidency.* New York, Crown Publishers, pp. 253–254.
2. Ibid.
3. Dallek, Robert. 1998. *Flawed Giant: Lyndon Johnson and His Times 1961–1973.* New York: Oxford University Press, p. 522.
4. Ibid., pp. 503–504.
5. Ibid., p. 506.
6. Ibid., pp. 506–507.
7. Ibid., pp. 529–530.
8. Reedy, George E. 1970. *The Twilight of the Presidency.* New York: New American Library, Inc., p. 95.
9. Troy, Gil. 2008. *Leading from the Center: Why Moderates Make the Best Presidents.* New York: Basic Books, p. 177.
10. Ibid.
11. Ibid.
12. Naughton, James M. 1973. "How the President Feels the Nation's Pulse." *New York Times* (Dec. 12), p. 3.
13. Rosenthal, Jack. 1973. "Johnson's Washington Recalled as Time of Restless Volubility." *New York Times* (Jan. 25), p. 34.
14. Updegrove. *Indomitable Will: LBJ in the Presidency,* pp. 178–179.
15. Troy. *Leading from the Center: Why Moderates Make the Best Presidents,* p. 166.
16. Dallek. *Flawed Giant: Lyndon Johnson and His Times, 1961–1973,* p. 6.
17. Updegrove. *Indomitable Will: LBJ in the Presidency,* p. 237.
18. Troy. *Leading from the Center: Why Moderates Make the Best Presidents,* p. 17.
19. Ibid.
20. Ibid.
21. Updegrove. *Indomitable Will: LBJ in the Presidency,* pp. 237–238.
22. Dallek, *Flawed Giant: Lyndon Johnson and His Times, 1961–1973,* p. 265.
23. Ibid., p. 267.
24. Ibid., p. 244.

25. Ibid., p. 245.
26. Ibid., p. 245.
27. Beschloss, Michael R., ed. 1997. *Taking Charge: The Johnson White House Tapes, 1963–1964*. New York: Simon & Schuster, p. 288.
28. Ibid., pp. 289–290.
29. Ibid., pp. 127–128.
30. Ibid., p. 13.
31. Ibid., p. 13 (footnote).
32. Updegrove. *Indomitable Will: LBJ in the Presidency*, p. 219.
33. Beschloss. *Taking Charge: The Johnson White House Tapes, 1963–1964*, p. 184.
34. Ibid., pp. 184–185.
35. Troy *Leading from the Center: Why Moderates Make the Best Presidents*, p. 175.
36. Dallek. *Flawed Giant*, p. 49.
37. Updegrove. *Indomitable Will: LBJ in the Presidency*, p. 216.
38. Ibid., p. 220.
39. Ibid., p. 22.
40. Eisinger. *The Evolution of Presidential Polling*, pp. 4, 126.
41. Ibid., p. 58.
42. Ibid.
43. Ibid., p. 59.
44. Ibid., p. 4.
45. Ibid., p. 5.
46. Ibid., p. 97.
47. Troy. *Leading from the Center: Why Moderates Make the Best Presidents*, p. 180.
48. Ibid.
49. Eisinger. *The Evolution of Presidential Polling*, p. 125.
50. Dallek, *Flawed Giant: Lyndon Johnson and His Times, 1961–1973*, pp. 129–130.
51. Ibid., p. 205.
52. Updegrove. *Indomitable Will: LBJ in the Presidency*, p. 24
53. Astor, Gerald. 2006. *Presidents at War: From Truman to Bush, the Gathering of Military Power to Our Commanders in Chief*. Hoboken, New Jersey: John Wiley & Sons, p. 14
54. Ibid.

Chapter Two

1. Troy, Gil. 2008. *Leading from the Center: Why Moderates Make the Best Presidents*. New York: Basic Books, p. 187.
2. Ibid.
3. Ibid., p. 188.
4. Ibid., p. 189.
5. Pierson, John. 1970. "Presidential Isolation Is Part of the Job." The *Wall Street Journal* (June 5), p. 8.
6. McGinniss, Joe. 1969. *The Selling of the President 1968*. New York: Trident Press, pp. 80–88.
7. Ibid., pp. 123–124.
8. Ibid., p. 125.
9. Ibid., pp. 204–205.

10. Ibid., p. 22.
11. Ibid.
12. Heith, Diane J. 2004. *Polling to Govern: Public Opinion and Presidential Leadership*. Stanford, California: Stanford University Press, p. 138.
13. White, Theodore H. 1975. *Breach of Faith: The Fall of Richard Nixon*. New York: Atheneum Publishers, p. 117.
14. Ibid., p. 119.
15. Eisinger, Robert M. 2003. *The Evolution of Presidential Polling*. New York: Cambridge University Press, p. 5.
16. Updegrove, Mark K. 2008. *Baptism by Fire: Eight Presidents Inaugurated in a Time of Crisis*. New York: Thomas Dunne Books, p. 129.
17. Eisinger. *The Evolution of Presidential Polling*, pp. 4–5.
18. Ibid., p. 5.
19. Heith. *Polling to Govern: Public Opinion and Presidential Leadership*, p. 3
20. Ibid., p. 6.
21. Ibid., pp. 61–66.
22. Ibid., p. 8.
23. Ibid.
24. Eisinger. *The Evolution of Presidential Polling*, p. 3.
25. Ibid., p. 67.
26. Ibid., pp. 67–68.
27. Ibid., p. 127.
28. Ibid.
29. Ibid., p. 129.
30. Ibid.
31. Ibid., p. 130.
32. Ibid., p. 13.
33. Ibid.
34. Ibid.
35. Ibid.
36. Ibid.
37. Ibid., p. 68 (footnote).
38. Ibid.
39. Heith. *Polling to Govern: Public Opinion and Presidential Leadership*, p. 9.
40. Ibid., p. 94.
41. Eisinger, *The Evolution of Presidential Polling*, p. 64.
42. Ibid.
43. Heith. *Polling to Govern: Public Opinion and Presidential Leadership*, p. 125.
44. Ibid.
45. Ibid.
46. Ibid., p. 127.

Chapter Three

1. Heith, Diane J. 2004. *Polling to Govern: Public Opinion and Presidential Leadership*. Stanford, California: Stanford University Press, p. 106.
2. Glad, Betty. 1980. *Jimmy Carter: In Search of the Great White House*. New York: W.W. Norton & Company, p. 413.

3. Heith. *Polling to Govern: Public Opinion and Presidential Leadership*, pp. 107–108.

4. Troy, Gil. 2008. *Leading from the Center: Why Moderates Make the Best Presidents*. New York: Basic Books, p. 184.

5. Ibid., p. 410.

6. Ibid., p. 412.

7. Ibid., pp. 410–411.

8. Ibid., p. 410.

9. Ibid., p. 464.

10. Carter, Jimmy. 2010. *White House Diary*. New York: Farrar, Straus and Giroux, p. 323.

11. Ibid.

12. Troy. *Leading from the Center: Why Moderates Make the Best Presidents*, p. 199.

13. Morris, Kenneth E. 1996. *Jimmy Carter: American Moralist*. Athens, Georgia: University of Georgia Press, p. 2.

14. Troy. *Leading from the Center: Why Moderates Make the Best Presidents*, p. 199.

15. Morris. *Jimmy Carter: American Moralist*, p 5.

16. Carter. *White House Diary*, p. 367.

17. Troy. *Leading from the Center: Why Moderates Make the Best Presidents*, p. 199.

18. Carter. *White House Diary*, p. 367.

19. Ibid., p. 458.

20. Ibid., p. 340.

21. Carter, Jimmy. 1979. "Energy and National Goals: Address to the Nation." Jimmy Carter Library and Museum, Atlanta, Georgia, jimmycarterlibrary.gov/documents/speeches (July 15).

22. Carter. *White House Diary*, p. 387.

23. Ibid., p. 388.

24. Ibid., p. 390.

25. Morris. *Jimmy Carter: American Moralist*, p. 294.

26. Carter. *White House Diary*, p. 459–460.

27. Ibid., p. 476.

28. Ibid., p. 479.

Chapter Four

1. Author's interview with Roman Popadiuk, Nov. 15, 2011.

2. Author's interview with Barbara Bush, May 3, 2012.

3. Author's interview with Roman Popadiuk, Nov. 15, 2011.

4. Schweizer, Peter and Rochelle Schweizer. 2004. *The Bushes: Portrait of a Dynasty*. New York: Doubleday, p. 399.

5. Ibid., pp. 402–403.

6. Ibid., p. 404.

7. This story of Bush and the scanner was recounted in Schweizer and Schweizer, *The Bushes: Portrait of a Dynasty*, pp. 402–403. I also covered it as a White House correspondent for *U.S. News & World Report*.

8. Memo from Tony Snow to Samuel K. Skinner, Clayton Yeutter, Marlin Fitzwater, David Demarest, Dorrance Smith, Robert Teeter, April 5, 1992, Document 6523, p. 2, George Bush Library.

9. Memo from Tony Snow to the president, "Los Angeles," June 1, 1992, Document 6530, George Bush Library.
10. Memo from Tony Snow to Ray Price, Robert Teeter, Samuel K. Skinner, and Clayton Yeutter, "Convention Speech," Aug. 12, 1992, Document 6534, p. 2–3, George Bush Library.
11. Ibid., p. 2.
12. Memo from Fred Steeper to Ed Rogers, "Highlights of RNC and Public Poll Results," Feb. 20, 1991, Document 10 18 74, John Sununu Files at George Bush Presidential Library.
13. Ibid.
14. Heith, Diane J. 2004. *Polling to Govern: Public Opinion and Presidential Leadership.* Stanford, California: Stanford University Press, pp. 69–70.
15. Ibid., p. 81.
16. Ibid., p. 91.
17. Memo from Fred Steeper to Robert Teeter, Item 13237, George Bush Presidential Library.
18. Letter from Bill Kristol to Sam Skinner, Robert Teeter et al., July 22 1992, George Bush Presidential Library.
19. Author's interview with Frank Luntz, April 16, 2012.

Chapter Five

1. Cronin, Thomas E. 2009. *On the Presidency: Teacher, Soldier, Shaman, Pol.* Boulder, Colo.: Paradigm Publishers, p. 86–87.
2. Kennedy, John F. 1964, 1956. *Profiles in Courage, Commemorative Edition.* New York: Harper & Row Publishers, pp. 17–18.
3. Ibid., pp. 251–252.
4. Coleman, David G. 2012. *The Fourteenth Day: JFK and the Aftermath of the Cuban Missile Crisis.* New York: W.W. Norton & Company, p. 9.
5. Ibid., p. 10.
6. Troy, Gil. 2008. *Leading from the Center: Why Moderates Make the Best Presidents.* New York: Basic Books, p. 152.
7. Author's interview with Peter Hart, June 18, 2012.
8. Stein, M.L. 1969. *When Presidents Meet the Press.* New York: Julian Messner, pp. 148–149.
9. Eisinger, Robert M. 2003. *The Evolution of Presidential Polling.* New York: Cambridge University Press, p. 121 (footnote).
10. Cronin. *On the Presidency: Teacher, Soldier, Shaman, Pol,* p. 108.
11. White, Theodore H. 1961. *The Making of the President 1960.* New York: Atheneum House, Inc., p. 106.
12. Sorensen, Theodore C. 1965. *Kennedy.* New York: Harper & Row, p. 106.
13. Ibid.
14. Ibid., pp. 106–107.
15. White. *The Making of the President 1960,* p. 51.
16. Ibid., p. 353.
17. Ibid., p. 15.
18. Ibid., pp. 16, 21.

19. Troy. *Leading from the Center: Why Moderates Make the Best Presidents*, p. 149.
20. Bryant, Nick. 2006. *The Bystander: John F. Kennedy and the Struggle for Black Equality*. New York: Basic Books, p. 223.
21. Ibid., p. 463.
22. Eisinger. *The Evolution of Presidential Polling*, p. 4.
23. Sorensen. *Kennedy*, p. 107.
24. Ibid., p. 139.
25. Sorensen. *Kennedy*, p. 146.
26. Author's interview with Democratic pollster Peter Hart (who worked with Harris), June 18, 2012.
27. Ibid., p. 132.
28. Ibid., p. 162.
29. Eisinger. *The Evolution of Presidential Polling*, p. 87.
30. Ibid., p. 87.
31. Sorensen. *Kennedy*, p. 411.
32. Ibid., pp. 411–412.
33. Eisinger. *The Evolution of Presidential Polling*, p. 55.
34. Ibid., pp. 55–56.
35. Troy. *Leading from the Center: Why Moderates Make the Best Presidents*, p. 248.
36. Branch, Taylor. 1988. *Parting the Waters: America in the King Years 1954–63*. New York: Simon & Schuster, p. 764.
37. Schlesinger, Robert. 2008. *White House Ghosts: Presidents and Their Speechwriters*. New York: Simon & Schuster, p. 136.
38. Troy. *Leading from the Center: Why Moderates Make the Best Presidents*, p. 162.
39. Walsh, Kenneth T. 2005. *From Mount Vernon to Crawford: A History of the Presidents and their Retreats*. New York: Hyperion, p. 3.
40. Author's interview with Matthew Dowd, Jan. 18, 2012.
41. Troy. *Leading from the Center: Why Moderates Make the Best Presidents*, p. 255.
42. Fleischer, Ari. 2005. *Taking Heat: The President, the Press, and My Years in the White House*. New York: William Morrow, p. 307.
43. Troy. *Leading from the Center: Why Moderates Make the Best Presidents*, p. 259.
44. Schlesinger, *White House Ghosts*, p. 468.
45. Ibid., p. 471.
46. Green, Joshua. 2002. "The Other War Room." *Washington Monthly* (April), pp. 2, 3.
47. Author's interview with Ed Gillespie, Jan. 11, 2012.
48. Troy. *Leading from the Center: Why Moderates Make the Best Presidents*, p. 266.

Chapter Six

1. Goodwin, Doris Kearns. 1994. *No Ordinary Time: Franklin and Eleanor Roosevelt: The Home Front in World War II*. New York: Simon & Schuster, p. 27.
2. Black, Conrad. 2003. *Franklin Delano Roosevelt: Champion of Freedom*. New York: Public Affairs, p. 1128.
3. Ibid., p. 1129.
4. Ibid., p. 387.
5. Ibid., p. 384.

6. Updegrove, Mark K. 2008. *Baptism by Fire: Eight Presidents Inaugurated in a Time of Crisis.* New York: Thomas Dunne Books, p. 148. Also see Goodwin. *No Ordinary Time: Franklin and Eleanor Roosevelt: The Home Front in World War II,* p. 27.

7. Updegrove, *Baptism by Fire: Eight Presidents Inaugurated in a Time of Crisis,* p. 148.

8. Goodwin, *No Ordinary Time: Franklin and Eleanor Roosevelt: The Home Front in World War II,* p. 27.

9. Ibid., p. 28.

10. Ibid.

11. Ibid.

12. Ibid., p. 29.

13. Ibid.

14. Ibid.

15. Ibid., pp. 38–39.

16. Ibid., p. 86.

17. Seeber, Frances M. 1987. "'I Want You to Write to Me': The Papers of Anna Eleanor Roosevelt." *Prologue* (Summer), p. 1. Available at Franklin D. Roosevelt Presidential Library and Museum.

18. Ibid., p. 2.

19. Ibid.

20. Ibid.

21. Ibid., p. 3.

22. Ibid.

23. Ibid., p. 4.

24. Ibid., p. 3.

25. Hand-written letter available online from Franklin Roosevelt Library and Museum.

26. Ibid.

27. Ibid.

28. Goodwin. *No Ordinary Time: Franklin and Eleanor Roosevelt: The Home Front in World War II,* p. 86.

29. Ibid., p. 87.

30. Ibid., p 627.

31. Ibid., p. 447.

32. Heith, Diane J. 2004. *Polling to Govern: Public Opinion and Presidential Leadership.* Stanford, California: Stanford University Press, p. 2.

33. Goodwin. *No Ordinary Time: Franklin and Eleanor Roosevelt: The Home Front in World War II,* p. 236.

34. Ibid., p 236.

35. Heith. *Polling to Govern: Public Opinion and Presidential Leadership,* p. 3.

36. Eisinger. *The Evolution of Presidential Polling,* p. 3.

37. Ibid., p. 3.

38. Ibid., pp. 43, 44–45.

39. Reedy, George E. 1970. *The Twilight of the Presidency.* Cleveland, Ohio and New York: New American Library/World Publishing Company, pp. 95–96.

40. Ibid., p. 96.

41. Stein, M.L. 1969. *When Presidents Meet the Press*. New York: Julian Messner, p. 90.
42. Stein. *When Presidents Meet the Press*, p. 90.
43. Black. *Franklin Delano Roosevelt: Champion of Freedom*, p. 382.
44. Ibid., p. 388.
45. Ibid., p. 427.
46. Ibid.
47. Ibid.
48. Ibid., p. 491.
49. Goodwin. *No Ordinary Time: Franklin and Eleanor Roosevelt: The Home Front in World War II*, p 236.

Chapter Seven

1. Truman, Margaret. 1973. *Harry S. Truman*. New York: William Morrow & Company, p. 327.
2. Miller, Merle. 1973, 1974. *Plain Speaking: An Oral Biography of Harry Truman*. New York: Berkley Publishing Corp., p. 211.
3. Ibid., pp. 211–212.
4. Ibid., p. 212.
5. Truman. *Harry S. Truman*, p. 3.
6. Troy, Gil. 2008. *Leading from the Center: Why Moderates Make the Best Presidents*. New York: Basic Books, p. 132.
7. Ibid., p. 131.
8. Ibid., p. 128.
9. Remark by Truman to Arthur Krock of the *New York Times*, quoted in Karabell, Zachary. 2000. *The Last Campaign: How Harry Truman Won the 1948 Election*. New York: Alfred A. Knopf, p. 94.
10. Karabell. *The Last Campaign: How Harry Truman Won the 1948 Election*, p. 258.
11. Miller. *Plain Speaking: An Oral Biography of Harry Truman*, p. 250.
12. Ibid., pp. 250, 260–261.
13. Ibid., p. 253.
14. Truman. *Harry S. Truman*, p. 28.
15. Ibid., p. 39.
16. Ibid., pp. 24–25.
17. Miller. *Plain Speaking: An Oral Biography of Harry Truman*, pp. 262–263.
18. Karabell. *The Last Campaign: How Harry Truman Won the 1948 Election*, p. 93.
19. Troy. *Leading from the Center: Why Moderates Make the Best Presidents*, p. 133.
20. Truman. *Harry S. Truman*, p. 392.
21. Dallek, Robert. 2010. *The Lost Peace: Leadership in a Time of Horror and Hope, 1945–1953*. New York: HarperCollins Publishers, p. 217.
22. Ibid., p. 217.
23. Ibid., pp. 217–218.
24. Ibid., p. 221.
25. Miller. *Plain Speaking: An Oral Biography of Harry Truman*, p. 431.

Chapter Eight

1. Walsh, Kenneth T. 1997. *Ronald Reagan*. New York: Park Lane Press, p. 87.
2. Cannon, Lou. 1991, 2000. *President Reagan: The Role of a Lifetime*. New York: Public Affairs, p. 711.
3. Ibid., pp. 748, 751.
4. Author's interview with Frank Donatelli, Nov. 20, 2012.
5. Shirley, Craig. 2009. *Rendezvous with Destiny: Ronald Reagan and the Campaign That Changed America,* Wilmington, Delaware: ISI Books, pp. 399–400.
6. Reagan, Nancy with William Novak. 1989. *My Turn: The Memoirs of Nancy Reagan*. New York: Random House, p. 112.
7. Cannon. *President Reagan: The Role of a Lifetime,* p 711.
8. Troy, Gil. 2008. *Leading from the Center: Why Moderates Make the Best Presidents*. New York: Basic Books, p. 215, and my own reporting as White House correspondent at the time for *U.S. News & World Report*.
9. Troy. *Leading from the Center: Why Moderates Make the Best Presidents,* p. 212.
10. Ibid., pp. 217–218.
11. Skinner, Kiron K., Annelise Anderson, and Martin Anderson. 2001. *Reagan: In His Own Hand*. New York: Free Press, pp. 403–404.
12. Smith, Hedrick. 1988. *The Power Game: How Washington Works*. New York: Ballantine Books, p 343.
13. Ibid.
14. Heith, Diane J. 2004. *Polling to Govern: Public Opinion and Presidential Leadership*. Stanford, California: Stanford University Press, p. 33.
15. Ibid., p. 65.
16. These groups are described in Heith. *Polling to Govern: Public Opinion and Presidential Leadership,* p. 65, chart.
17. Ibid., p. 66.
18. Ibid.
19. Smith. *The Power Game: How Washington Works,* p. 700.
20. Author's interview with Ken Duberstein, Jan. 17, 2013.
21. Heith. *Polling to Govern: Public Opinion and Presidential Leadership,* pp. 67–68.
22. Author's interview with Ken Duberstein, Oct. 18, 2012.
23. Kuhn, Jim. 2004. *Ronald Reagan in Private: A Memoir of My Years in the White House*. New York: Sentinel, pp. 82–83.
24. Cannon. *President Reagan: The Role of a Lifetime,* p. 107.
25. Ibid., p. 107.
26. Ibid., p. 112.
27. Stockman, David. 1987. *The Triumph of Politics: The Inside Story of the Reagan Revolution*. New York: Avon Books, p. 15.
28. Ibid., p. 12.
29. Cannon. *President Reagan: The Role of a Lifetime,* pp. 117–118.
30. Skinner, Kiron K., Annelise Anderson, and Martin Anderson, eds. 2003. *Reagan: A Life in Letters*. New York: Free Press, p. 609.
31. Cannon. *President Reagan: The Role of a Lifetime,* p. 118.
32. Skinner et al., *Reagan: A Life in Letters,* p. 622.
33. Ibid., pp. 625–626.

34. Vongs, Pueng. 2012. "Funny Letter from Ronald Reagan to Seventh-Grader Resurfaces." *Yahoo News,* www.news.yahoo.com/blogs (May 18). Also quoted in Skinner et al., *Reagan: A Life in Letters,* pp. 664–665.

35. Skinner et al., *Reagan: A Life in Letters,* p. 664.

36. Ibid., p. 260.

37. Kuhn. *Ronald Reagan in Private: A Memoir of My Years in the White House,* pp. 121–122.

38. Wallison, Peter J. 2003. *Ronald Reagan: The Power of Conviction and the Success of His Presidency.* Boulder. Colo.: Westview Press, pp. 89–90.

39. Smith. *The Power Game: How Washington Works,* p. 421.

40. Kuhn. *Ronald Reagan in Private: A Memoir of My Years in the White House,* p. 126.

41. Ibid., p. 157.

42. Skinner et al., *Reagan: A Life in Letters,* p. 748.

43. Ibid., p. 748.

44. Kuhn. *Ronald Reagan in Private: A Memoir of My Years in the White House,* p. 157.

45. Ibid., pp. 157–158.

46. Author's interview with Ken Duberstein, Oct 18, 2012.

47. Herbert, Bob. 2012. "In America; It Hasn't Gone Away," www.nytimes.com (May 31).

48. Cannon. *President Reagan: The Role of a Lifetime,* pp. 731–736.

49. Reagan with Novak. *My Turn: The Memoirs of Nancy Reagan,* pp. 64–65.

Chapter Nine

1. Author's interview with Stan Greenberg, March 26, 2012.

2. Author's interview with Mack McLarty (Clinton's first White House chief of staff), June 12, 2012.

3. Ornstein, Norman J. 2012. "Why Obama Doesn't Need to Be Bill Clinton." The *Miami Herald* (Sept. 14), p. A17.

4. Troy, Gil. 2008. *Leading from the Center: Why Moderates Make the Best Presidents.* New York: Basic Books, p. 224.

5. Author's interview with Peter Hart (Democratic pollster), June 18, 2012.

6. Morris, Dick. 1997. *Behind the Oval Office: Winning the Presidency in the Nineties.* New York: Random House, p. 247.

7. Memo from Stan Greenberg to President Bill Clinton, First Lady Hillary Clinton, Vice President Al Gore, and four other senior White House advisers, "The First 1994 Survey," Jan. 6, 1994, p. 1.

8. Ibid., pp. 2, 5–6.

9. Memo from Stan Greenberg to the 1993 Political Team. "1994: Strategic Concepts." Undated. p. 1.

10. Memo from Stan Greenberg to the Political/Communications Team, "The 1994 Race Defined," Oct. 6, 1994, pp. 1–2.

11. Memo from Stan Greenberg to President Clinton and seven other senior advisers, "Strategic Issues: Final 3 Weeks," Oct. 20, 1994, pp. 1–2.

12. Ibid., pp. 3, 6.
13. Memo from Stan Greenberg to President Clinton and seven top advisers, "President Bill Clinton in the Public Mind: A Post–Election Analysis: Report One," Nov. 22, 1994, p. 1.
14. Ibid., p. 6.
15. Woodward, Bob. 1996. *The Choice.* New York: Simon & Schuster, p. 56.
16. Schoen, Douglas E. 2007. *The Power of the Vote: Electing Presidents, Overthrowing Dictators, and Promoting Democracy Around the World.* New York: HarperCollins Publishers, p. 214.
17. Ibid., p. 215.
18. Ibid., p. 216.
19. Ibid.
20. Heith, Diane J. 2004. *Polling to Govern: Public Opinion and Presidential Leadership.* Stanford, California: Stanford University Press, p. 34.
21. Schoen. *The Power of the Vote: Electing Presidents, Overthrowing Dictators, and Promoting Democracy Around the World,* pp. 216–217.
22. Morris. *Behind the Oval Office,* pp. 202–203.
23. Ibid., pp. 13, 40, 80, 83.
24. Troy. *Leading from the Center: Why Moderates Make the Best Presidents,* p. 237.
25. Schoen. *The Power of the Vote: Electing Presidents, Overthrowing Dictators, and Promoting Democracy Around the World,* p. 217–218.
26. Ibid., pp. 222–223.
27. Ibid., p. 225.
28. Ibid., p. 227.
29. Ibid., p. 228.
30. Heith. *Polling to Govern: Public Opinion and Presidential Leadership,* p. 118.
31. Author's interview with Stan Greenberg, March 26, 2012.
32. Author's interview with Mike McCurry, March 23, 2011.
33. Woodward. *The Choice,* p. 417.
34. Morris. *Behind the Oval Office,* p. 238.
35. Ibid., pp. 237–238.
36. Ibid., p. 239.
37. Heith. *Polling to Govern: Public Opinion and Presidential Leadership,* p. 129.
38. Ibid., p. 130.

Chapter Ten

1. Saslow, Eli. 2012. *Ten Letters: The Stories Americans Tell Their President.* New York: Anchor Books, p. 16.
2. Woodyard, Chris. "Obama's 'Secret': He Drove a Chevrolet Volt." 2012. www.usatoday.com (Oct. 25).
3. Dowd, Maureen. 2012. "Showtime At the Apollo," *New York Times* (Jan. 22, Sunday Review), p. 13.
4. Author's interview with Peter Hart, June 18, 2012.
5. Dowd, Maureen. 2012. "Showtime at the Apollo." *New York Times* (Jan. 22, Sunday Review), p. 13.
6. Author's interview with Cornell Belcher, May 16, 2012.

7. Saslow. *Ten Letters: The Stories Americans Tell Their President,* p. 4.

8. Bedard, Paul. 2012. "Privately, Obama Sees Recovery 1-2 Years Off." www .washingtonexaminer.com/blogs/beltway–confidential (Feb. 13).

9. Quote from Obama fund-raising letter sent by the Democratic National Committee in July 2012.

10. Saslow. *Ten Letters: The Stories Americans Tell Their President,* p. 3.

11. Poulton, Diane. 2012. "Merrillville Businessman Captures National Spotlight with Letter to Obama." www.nwitimes.com/news/local (Nov. 15).

12. Associated Press. 2010. "Woman 'Exhausted' Defending Obama Loses Job." www.foxnews.com (Nov. 23).

13. Maraniss, David. 2012. "President Obama's Love for Basketball Can Be Traced Back to His High School Team." The *Washington Post* (June 10), p. D1.

14. Allen, Mike. 2011. "First Look—Fortune's 2001 'Business Person of the Year.'" Politico Playbook, www.politico.com (Nov. 17), p. 2.

15. Author's interview with Robert Dallek, Feb. 3, 2012.

16. Goldfarb, Zachary A. 2012. "Why Has the U.S. Recovery Sputtered?" The *Washington Post* (Nov. 23), p. A1.

17. Author's interview with Matthew Dowd, Jan. 18, 2012.

18. Wenner, Jann S. 2012. "Ready for the Fight: *Rolling Stone* Interview with Barack Obama." www.rollingstone.com (May 10).

19. Chozick, Amy. 2012. "Obama Is an Avid Reader, and Critic, of the News." *New York Times,* www.nytimes.com (Aug. 7).

20. Ibid.

21. Ibid.

22. Heilemann, John and Mark Halperin. 2010. *Game Change: Obama and the Clintons, McCain and Palin, and the Race of a Lifetime.* New York: HarperCollins, p. 65.

23. Ibid.

24. Ibid., pp. 65–66.

25. Ibid., pp. 104–105.

26. Ibid., p. 105.

27. Ibid., pp. 104–105.

28. Allen, Mike. 2012. "Politico Playbook Veterans Day Edition—Axelrod." Politico Playbook, www.politico.com (Nov. 11), p. 3.

29. Author's interview with Joel Benenson, Nov. 24, 2012.

30. Ibid.

31. Allen. "Political Playbook Veterans Day Edition—Axelrod," p. 3.

32. Ibid.

33. Ibid.

34. Klein, Edward. 2012. *The Amateur: Barack Obama in the White House,* Washington, D.C.: Regnery Publishing, Inc., p. 86.

35. Ibid., p. 87.

36. Ibid., pp. 102–103.

37. Author's interview with Frank Luntz, April 16, 2012.

38. Hunt, Kasie. 2012. "Romney: Regular People Teach Him about Struggles." Associated Press (May 4).

39. Ibid.

40. Ibid.

41. Dickerson, John. 2012. "The Bubble Wars: Obama and Romney Battle Over Who Is 'Out of Touch.'" *Slate* (April 17).
42. Ibid.
43. Ibid.
44. Ibid.
45. Carville, James and Stan Greenberg. 2012. "How Unmarried Women, Youth and People of Color Defined This Election." www.democracycorps.com/In-the -News/how-unmarried-women-youth-and-people-of-color-defined-this election" (Nov. 8).
46. "Full Transcript of President Obama's Press Conference," www.nytimes.com, January 14, 2013, p. 13.
47. Ibid, p. 14.
48. Ibid.

Chapter Eleven

1. Heith, Diane J. 2004. *Polling to Govern: Public Opinion and Presidential Leadership*. Stanford, California: Stanford University Press, p. 2.
2. Ibid., p. 3.
3. Ibid., p. 3.
4. Ibid., p. xiii.
5. Ibid., p. 15.
6. Eisinger, Robert M. 2003. *The Evolution of Presidential Polling*. New York: Cambridge University Press, p. 45.
7. Ibid., p. 7.
8. Ibid., pp. 48–49.
9. Ibid., p. 51.
10. Ibid., p. 12.
11. Ibid., p. 21.
12. Heith. *Polling to Govern: Public Opinion and Presidential Leadership*, p. 120.
13. Sorensen, Theodore C. 1965. *Kennedy*. New York: Harper & Row, p. 106.
14. Eisinger. *The Evolution of Presidential Polling*, p. 81–83.
15. Ibid., p. 42.
16. Ibid., p. 43.
17. Ibid., p. 43.
18. Ibid., p. 48.
19. Ibid., p. 43.
20. Ibid., p. 43.
21. Ibid., p. 45.
22. Ibid., p. 111.
23. Ibid.
24. Ibid., pp. 111–112.
25. Eisinger. *The Evolution of Presidential Polling*, p. 111 (footnote).
26. Morris, Kenneth E. 1996. *Jimmy Carter: American Moralist*. Athens, Georgia: University of Georgia Press, p. 3.
27. Eisinger. *The Evolution of Presidential Polling*, p. 156.
28. Heith. *Polling to Govern: Public Opinion and Presidential Leadership*, p. 28.

29. Ibid., pp. 27–28.
30. Ibid., p. 35.
31. Ibid., pp. 35–36.
32. Eisinger. *The Evolution of Presidential Polling,* pp. 158–159.
33. Carter, Jimmy. 2010. *White House Diary.* New York: Farrar, Straus and Giroux, pp. 316–317.
34. Heith. *Polling to Govern: Public Opinion and Presidential Leadership,* p. 36.
35. Ibid., p. 37.
36. Ibid., p. 65.
37. Eisinger. *The Evolution of Presidential Polling,* p. 162.
38. Wirthlin, Dick with Wynton C. Hall. 2004. *The Greatest Communicator: What Ronald Reagan Taught Me about Politics, Leadership, and Life.* Hoboken. New Jersey: John Wiley & Sons, pp. 91–92.
39. Ibid., p. 92.
40. Ibid. See also Bush, George W. with Victor Gold. 1987. *Looking Forward.* New York: Doubleday, pp. 7–8.
41. Smith, Hedrick. 1988. *The Power Game: How Washington Works.* New York: Ballantine Books, p. 355.
42. Ibid., p. 355.
43. Ibid., p. 356.
44. Eisinger. *The Evolution of Presidential Polling,* pp. 164–165.
45. Wirthlin with Hall. *The Greatest Communicator: What Ronald Reagan Taught Me about Politics, Leadership, and Life,* pp. 104–105.
46. Ibid., p. 105.
47. Ibid., p. 143.
48. Ibid., p. 144.
49. Eisinger. *The Evolution of Presidential Polling,* p. 166.
50. Ibid., p. 166.
51. Ibid., p. 168.
52. Wirthlin with Hall, p. 142.
53. Ibid., pp. 142–143.
54. Ibid., pp. 176–177.
55. Ibid., p 177.
56. Ibid., pp. 178–179.
57. Ibid., pp.191–2, 194.
58. Ibid., p. 194.
59. Eisinger. *The Evolution of Presidential Polling,* p. 100.
60. Ibid., p. 101.
61. Ibid., pp 101–102.
62. Ibid., pp. 103–104.
63. Ibid., p. 149.
64. Ibid., p. 155.
65. Ibid., p. 150. Also see Glassman, Mark. 2004. "Robert M. Teeter, G.O.P. Pollster, Dies at 65." *New York Times,* www.nytimes.com (June 17).
66. Glassman, "Robert M. Teeter, G.O.P. Pollster, Dies at 65."
67. Ibid.
68. Eisinger. *The Evolution of Presidential Polling,* pp. 155–156.
69. Ibid., p. 176.

70. Ibid., p. 177.
71. Ibid., p. 177.
72. Author's interviews with Stan Greenberg, March 25–26, 2012.
73. Ibid.
74. Eisinger. *The Evolution of Presidential Polling*, p. 180.
75. Memo from Stan Greenberg to President Bill Clinton and Hillary Rodham Clinton, "May 1994: Turning Point," May 17, 1994, p. 1.
76. Ibid., p. 9.
77. Memo from Stan Greenberg to President Clinton and seven others, "Strategic Definition of the Clinton Presidency," Dec. 2, 1994, pp. 1–2.
78. Morris, Dick. 1997. *Behind the Oval Office: Winning the Presidency in the Nineties.* New York: Random House, back-cover blurb.
79. Woodward, Bob. 1996. *The Choice.* New York: Simon & Schuster, p. 17.
80. Morris. *Behind the Oval Office: Winning the Presidency in the Nineties,* p. 9.
81. Ibid., p. 11.
82. Ibid., p. 10.
83. Ibid., p. 8.
84. Ibid., p. 11.
85. Woodward. *The Choice,* p. 18.
86. Ibid., p. 25.
87. Morris. *Behind the Oval Office: Winning the Presidency in the Nineties,* p. 25.
88. Ibid., p. 26.
89. Woodward. *The Choice,* p. 25.
90. Morris. *Behind the Oval Office: Winning the Presidency in the Nineties,* p. 28.
91. Woodward. *The Choice,* pp. 140–141.
92. Ibid., p. 45.
93. Ibid., p. 46.
94. Ibid., p. 202.
95. Ibid., p. 143.
96. Ibid., p. 204.
97. Ibid., p. 416.
98. Schoen, Douglas E. 2008. *The Power of the Vote: Electing Presidents, Overthrowing Dictators, and Promoting Democracy Around the World.* New York: Harper, p. 230.
99. Ibid., p. 231.
100. Ibid.
101. Ibid., pp. 231–232.
102. Ibid., pp. 232–233.
103. Ibid., p. 233.
104. Ibid., p. 235.
105. Ibid., p. 236.
106. Ibid., p. 236.
107. Ibid., p. 241.
108. Author's interview with Joel Benenson, Nov. 24, 2012.
109. Author's interviews with Joel Benenson, June 7, 2012 and Nov. 24, 2012.
110. Author's interview with Joel Benenson, Nov. 24, 2012.
111. Author's interview with Joel Benenson, June 7, 2012.
112. Author's interview with Joel Benenson, Nov. 24, 2012.

113. Author's interview with Joel Benenson, June 7, 2012.
114. Allen, Michael. 2012. Politico Playbook, www.politico.com (June 11).
115. Ibid.
116. Sargent, Greg. 2012. "Obama Pollster: GOP Is Trapped in the 1980s, 'Out of Gas,'" www.washingtonpost.com (Nov. 8).
117. Ibid.
118. Ibid.
119. Simon, Roger. 2012. "Obama Pollster: Mitt Wasn't Trusted." www.politico.com (Nov. 7).
120. Author's interviews with Joel Benenson, Nov. 24, 2012 and Nov. 13, 2012.
121. Simon. "Obama Pollster: Mitt Wasn't Trusted."

Chapter Twelve

1. Reedy, George E. 1970. *The Twilight of the Presidency*. New York: New American Library, Inc., p. 15.
2. Ibid., p. 144.
3. Schlesinger, Arthur M. Jr. 1973. "The Runaway Presidency." The *Atlantic Monthly*, www.theatlantic.com (Nov.), p. 7.
4. White, Theodore H. 1975. *Breach of Faith: The Fall of Richard Nixon*. New York: Atheneum Publishers, pp. 338–339.
5. Ibid., p. 339.
6. Granholm, Jennifer. 2012. "The Bubble Candidate." www.politico.com (Sept. 24).
7. Cronin, Thomas E. and Michael A. Genovese. 1998. *The Paradoxes of the American Presidency*. New York: Oxford University Press, p. 95.
8. Ibid., p. 96.
9. Eisinger, Robert M. 2003. *The Evolution of Presidential Polling*. New York: Cambridge University Press, p. 190.
10. "I'm here" and the quote from the senior administration official related in Alterman, Eric and Mark Green. 1994. *The Book on Bush: How George W. (Mis)leads America*. New York: Viking, pp. 231–232.
11. Author's interview with Peter Hart, June 18, 2012.
12. Ibid.
13. Author's interview with Frank Luntz, April 16, 2012.
14. Ibid.
15. Author's interview with Sean Spicer, April 13, 2012.
16. Valenti, Jack. 1972. "Presidential Adviser." *New York Times* (July 19), p. 37.
17. Author's interview with Gary Johnson, Aug. 26, 2012.
18. Author's interview with Ed Gillespie, Jan. 11, 2012.
19. Reedy. *The Twilight of the Presidency*, pp. 145–146.
20. Cannon, Lou. 1991, 2000. *President Reagan: The Role of a Lifetime*. New York: Public Affairs, p. 56.
21. Ibid., pp. 56–57.
22. Gibbs, Nancy and Michael Duffy. 2012. "Inside the Presidents Club." *Time*, www.time.com (April 23), p. 2.
23. Ibid., p. 3.

24. Karabell, Zachary. 2000. *The Last Campaign: How Harry Truman Won the 1948 Election*. New York: Alfred A. Knopf, p. 93.
25. Reedy. *The Twilight of the Presidency*, p. 163.
26. Miller, Merle. 1973, 1974. *Plain Speaking: An Oral Biography of Harry S. Truman*. New York: Berkley Publishing Corp., p. 262.

BIBLIOGRAPHY

Alterman, Eric and Mark Green. 1994. *The Book on Bush: How George W. (Mis)leads America*. New York: Viking.

Astor, Gerald. 2006. *Presidents at War: From Truman to Bush, the Gathering of Military Power to Our Commanders in Chief*. Hoboken, New Jersey: John Wiley & Sons.

Beschloss, Michael R., ed. 1997. *Taking Charge: The Johnson White House Tapes, 1963–1964*. New York: Simon & Schuster.

Black, Conrad. 2003. *Franklin Delano Roosevelt: Champion of Freedom*. New York: Public Affairs.

Bryant, Nick. 2006. *The Bystander: John F. Kennedy and the Struggle for Black Equality*. New York: Basic Books.

Bush, George with Victor Gold. 1987. *Looking Forward*. New York: Doubleday.

Cannon, Lou. 1991, 2000. *President Reagan: The Role of a Lifetime*. New York: Public Affairs.

Carter, Jimmy. 1982. *Keeping Faith: Memoirs of a President*. New York: Bantam Books.

Carter, Jimmy. 2010. *White House Diary*. New York: Farrar, Straus and Giroux.

Coleman, David G. 2012. *The Fourteenth Day: JFK and the Aftermath of the Cuban Missile Crisis*. New York: W.W. Norton & Company.

Cronin, Thomas E. 2000. *On the Presidency: Teacher, Soldier, Shaman, Pol*. Boulder, Colo.: Paradigm Publishers.

Cronin, Thomas E. and Michael A. Genovese. 1998. *The Paradoxes of the American Presidency*. New York: Oxford University Press.

Dallek, Robert. 1998. *Flawed Giant: Lyndon Johnson and His Times 1961–1973*. New York: Oxford University Press.

Dallek, Robert. 2010. *The Lost Peace: Leadership in a Time of Horror and Hope, 1945–1953*. New York: HarperCollins.

D'Souza, Dinesh. 2012. *Obama's America: Unmaking the American Dream*. Washington, D.C.: Regnery Publishing.

Eisinger, Robert M. 2003. *The Evolution of Presidential Polling*. New York: Cambridge University Press.

Fleischer, Ari. 2005. *Taking Heat: The President, the Press, and My Years in the White House.* New York: William Morrow.

Glad, Betty. 1980. *Jimmy Carter: In Search of the Great White House.* New York: W.W. Norton & Company.

Goodwin, Doris Kearns. 1994. *No Ordinary Time: Franklin and Eleanor Roosevelt: The Home Front in World War II.* New York: Simon & Schuster.

Heilemann, John and Mark Halperin. 2010. *Game Change: Obama and the Clintons, McCain and Palin, and the Race of a Lifetime.* New York: HarperCollins.

Heith, Diane J. 2004. *Polling to Govern: Public Opinion and Presidential Leadership.* Stanford, California: Stanford University Press.

Karabell, Zachary. 2000. *The Last Campaign: How Harry Truman Won the 1948 Election.* New York: Alfred A. Knopf.

Kennedy, John F. 1964, 1956. *Profiles in Courage, Commemorative Edition.* New York: Harper & Row.

Klein, Edward. 2012. *The Amateur: Barack Obama in the White House.* Washington, D.C.: Regnery Publishing, Inc.

Kuhn, Jim. 2004. *Ronald Reagan in Private: A Memoir of My Years in the White House.* New York: Sentinel.

Kurtz, Stanley. 2012. *Spreading the Wealth: How Obama Is Robbing the Suburbs to Pay for the Cities.* New York: Sentinel.

Lichtblau, Eric. 2008. *Bush's Law: The Remaking of American Justice.* New York: Pantheon Books.

Lippmann, Walter. *Public Opinion.* 1922. New York: Harcourt Brace and Co.

McGinniss, Joe. 1969. *The Selling of the President 1968.* New York: Trident Press.

Miller, Merle. 1973, 1974. *Plain Speaking: An Oral Biography of Harry Truman.* New York: Berkley Publishing Corp.

Morris, Dick. 1997. *Behind the Oval Office: Winning the Presidency in the Nineties.* New York: Random House.

Morris, Kenneth E. 1996. *Jimmy Carter: American Moralist.* Athens, Georgia: University of Georgia Press.

Patterson, Bradley H., Jr. 2000. *The White House Staff: Inside the West Wing and Beyond.* Washington, D.C.: Brookings Institution Press.

Popadiuk, Roman. 2009. *The Leadership of George Bush: An Insider's View of the Forty-First President.* College Station, Texas: Texas A&M University Press.

Reagan, Nancy with William Novak. 1989. *My Turn: The Memoirs of Nancy Reagan.* New York: Random House.

Reedy, George E. 1970. *The Twilight of the Presidency.* Cleveland, Ohio and New York: New American Library/World Publishing Company.

Sabato, Larry. 1991. *Feeding Frenzy: How Attack Journalism Has Transformed American Politics.* New York: Free Press.

Saslow, Eli. 2011. *Ten Letters: The Stories Americans Tell Their President.* New York: Anchor Books.

Schlesinger, Robert. 2008. *White House Ghosts: Presidents and Their Speechwriters.* New York: Simon & Schuster.

Schoen, Douglas E. 2008. *The Power of the Vote: Electing Presidents, Overthrowing Dictators, and Promoting Democracy Around the World.* New York: Harper.

Schweizer, Peter and Rochelle Schweizer. 2004. The Bushes: Portrait of a Dynasty. New York: Doubleday.

Skinner, Kiron K., Annelise Anderson, and Martin Anderson. 2001. *Reagan: In His Own Hand*. New York: Free Press.

Smith, Hedrick. 1988. *The Power Game: How Washington Works*. New York: Ballantine Books.

Sorensen, Theodore C. 1965. *Kennedy*. New York: Harper & Row.

Stein, M.L. 1969. *When Presidents Meet the Press*. New York: Julian Messner.

Stephanopoulos, George. 1999. *All Too Human: A Political Education*. Boston: Little, Brown.

Stockman, David A. 1987. *The Triumph of Politics: The Inside Story of the Reagan Revolution*. New York: Avon Books.

Tourtellot, Arthur Bernon. 1964. *The Presidents on the Presidency*. Garden City, New York: Doubleday & Company.

Truman, Margaret. 1973. *Harry S. Truman*. New York: William Morrow & Company.

Updegrove, Mark K. 2008. *Baptism by Fire: Eight Presidents Inaugurated in a Time of Crisis*. New York: Thomas Dunne Books.

Updegrove, Mark K. 2012. *Indomitable Will: LBJ in the Presidency*. New York: Crown Publishers.

Van Natta, Don Jr. 2003. *First Off the Tee: Presidential Hackers, Duffers, and Cheaters from Taft to Bush*. New York: Public Affairs.

Wallison, Peter J. 2003. *Ronald Reagan: The Power of Conviction and the Success of His Presidency*. Boulder, Colo.: Westview Press.

Walsh, Kenneth T. 1997. *Ronald Reagan*. New York: Park Lane Press.

Walsh, Kenneth T. 2005. *From Mount Vernon to Crawford: A History of the Presidents and Their Retreats*. New York: Hyperion.

Walton, Hanes, Jr., Josephine A.V. Allen, Sherman C. Puckett, and Donald R. Deskins, Jr. 2009. *Letters to President Obama: Americans Share Their Hopes and Dreams with the First African-American President*. New York: Skyhorse Publishing.

White, Theodore H. 1961. *The Making of the President 1960*. New York: Atheneum House, Inc.

White, Theodore H. 1975. *Breach of Faith: The Fall of Richard Nixon*. New York: Atheneum Publishers.

Wirthlin, Dick with Wynton C. Hall. 2004. *The Greatest Communicator: What Ronald Reagan Taught Me about Politics, Leadership, and Life*. Hoboken, New Jersey: John Wiley & Sons, Inc.

Woodward, Bob. 1995. *The Agenda: Inside the Clinton White House*. New York: Simon and Schuster.

Woodward, Bob. 1996. *The Choice*. New York: Simon & Schuster.

INDEX

ABOUT THE AUTHOR

Kenneth T. Walsh has been White House correspondent for *U.S. News & World Report* since 1986. He writes a weekly column, "The Presidency," for the *U.S. News Weekly,* an online publication; presents a weekly video report for *U.S. News*'s digital edition; and is the author of a daily blog for usnews.com, "Ken Walsh's Washington." He is one of the longest-serving White House correspondents in history. This is his sixth book. Walsh is the former president of the White House Correspondents' Association, and he has won the most prestigious awards for White House coverage. Walsh is also an adjunct professorial lecturer at American University's School of Communication in Washington, D.C. He appears frequently on TV and radio, and gives many speeches around the country and abroad. He and his wife Barclay live in Bethesda, Maryland, and Shady Side, Maryland. They have two children, Jean and Chris.